Tried and tested

Develop your legal skills

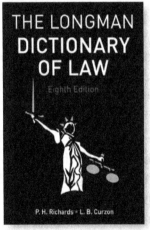

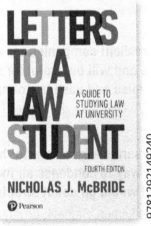

Written to help you develop the essential skills needed to succeed on your course and prepare for practice.

Available from all good bookshops or order online at: **www.pearsoned.co.uk/law**

Question&Answer

TORT LAW

5th edition

Rebecca Gladwin-Geoghegan
Lecturer in Law and Academic Course Director, Undergraduate
LLB Programmes, Coventry University

Pearson

Harlow, England • London • New York • Boston • San Francisco • Toronto • Sydney • Dubai • Singapore • Hong Kong
Tokyo • Seoul • Taipei • New Delhi • Cape Town • São Paulo • Mexico City • Madrid • Amsterdam • Munich • Paris • Milan

PEARSON EDUCATION LIMITED
KAO Two
KAO Park
Harlow
CM17 9SR
United Kingdom
Tel: +44 (0)1279 623623
Web: www.pearson.com/uk

———————————————

First published 2012 (print and electronic)
Second edition published 2014 (print and electronic)
Third edition published 2016 (print and electronic)
Fourth edition published 2018 (print and electronic)
Fifth edition published 2019 (print and electronic)

Contains public sector information licensed under the Open Government Licence (OGL) v3.0.
http://www.nationalarchives.gov.uk/doc/open-government-licence/version/3/

Contains Parliamentary information licensed under the Open Parliament Licence (OPL) v3.0.
http://www.parliament.uk/site-information/copyright/open-parliament-licence/

Pearson Education is not responsible for the content of third-party internet sites.

ISBN: 978-1-292-25384-8 (print)
      978-1-292-25385-5 (PDF)
      978-1-292-25386-2 (ePub)

British Library Cataloguing-in-Publication Data
A catalogue record for the print edition is available from the British Library

10 9 8 7 6 5 4 3 2 1
23 22 21 20 19

Print edition typeset in 10/13 Helvetica Neue LT W1G by Pearson CSC

NOTE THAT ANY PAGE CROSS REFERENCES REFER TO THE PRINT EDITION

Contents

Acknowledgements

This book is dedicated to Harry, Harrison and Zachary - my boys.

Rebecca Gladwin-Geoghegan

Publisher's acknowledgements

Text Credit(s):

1 Middlesex University: Witting, C. (2015) Street on Torts. Oxford: Oxford University Press, p.27 **3 Oxford University Press:** Per Lord Keith in *Hill* v *Chief Constable of West Yorkshire* [1989] AC 53 at 59. **7 Parliamentary Copyright:** *Smith* v *Littlewoods Organisation Ltd* [1987] 1 AC 241 at 279. **11 Parliamentary Copyright:** *Customs and Excise Commissioners* v *Barclays Bank* [2007] 1 A.C. 181 at 190. **15 Parliamentary Copyright:** *Williams* v *Natural Life Health Foods Ltd* [1998] **17 Parliamentary Copyright:** *Customs & Excise Commissioners* v *Barclays Bank plc* [2007] 1 AC 181, [32]–[34] **20 Parliamentary Copyright:** *Hedley Byrne & Co. Ltd* v *Heller & Partners Ltd* [1964] AC 465 at 482. **25 Parliamentary Copyright:** Teff, H. (1998) Liability for Negligently Inflicted Psychiatric Harm: Justifications and Boundaries. *The Cambridge Law Journal*, 57. 91–122 at 93 **29 Cambridge University Press:** *White* v *Chief Constable of South Yorkshire Police* [1999] 2 AC 455 at 509 **34 Parliamentary Copyright:** Stapleton (1994a) 'In restraint of tort', in P. Birks (ed.), The Frontiers of Liability. Oxford: Oxford University Press. **39 Oxford University Press:** *Montgomery* v *Lanarkshire Health Board* [2015] A.C. 1430 at [1462–1463] **43 Crown Copyright:** *Montgomery* v *Lanarkshire Health Board* [2015] A.C. 1430 at [1462–1463] **46 Crown Copyright:** *Bailey* v *Ministry of Defence* [2009] 1 WLR 1052 at [46]) **48 Crown Copyright:** *Gregg* v *Scott* [2005] 2 AC 176 at 185E **53 Parliamentary Copyright:** *Overseas Tankship (UK) Ltd* v *Morts Dock & Engineering Co. Ltd (The Wagon Mound (No. 1))* [1961] AC 388 at 424) **57 Crown Copyright:** *Hall* v *Hebert* (1993) 101 DLR (4th) 129, 179) **61 Supreme Court of Canada:** *Rahman* v *Arearose Ltd* [2001] QB 351 at [29]. **66 Crown Copyright:** (2014) Clerk & Lindsell on Torts, 21st edition. London: Sweet & Maxwell. 11–45 **111 Thomson Reuters Corporation:** Consumer Protection Act 1987, Section 3 **114 Crown Copyright:** *Various Claimants* v *Catholic Welfare Society* [2012] UKSC 56 at [19] **131 Crown Copyright:** *Dubai Aluminium Co. Ltd* v *Salaam & Others* [2003] 1 AC 366 at [22]) **136 Parliamentary Copyright:** *Cox* v *Minsistry of Justice* [2016] UKSC 10; [2016] A.C. 660, [2]. **145 Crown Copyright:** *Lord Upjohn in London Passenger Transport Board* v *Upson* [1949] AC 155, 168 **159 Parliamentary Copyright:** Law Commission, Liability for Damage or Injury to Trespassers and Related Questions of Occupiers' Liability (Law Com No. 75, 1976) **175 Crown Copyright:** *Home Brewery Co.* v *William Davis & Co. (Loughborough) Ltd* [1987] QB 339, 354E **190 Crown Copyright:** *McKenna v British Aluminum Ltd* [2002] En LR 30, [53] **205 Crown Copyright:** Murphy, J.

(2004) *The Merits of Rylands* v *Fletcher. Oxford Journal of Legal Studies,* 24(4): 643 at 643–644 **223 Oxford University Press:** *Cole* v *Turner* (1704) **235 Crown Copyright:** P. Cane (1999) Fault and strict liability for harm in tort law, in The Search for Principle: Essays in Honour of Lord Goff of Chieveley, ed. W. Swaddling and G. Jones, Oxford: OUP **248 Oxford University Press:** Mullis, A. and Scott, A. (2012) The swing of the pendulum: reputation, expression and the re-centring of English libel law, in D. Capper (ed.), Modern Defamation Law: Balancing Reputation and Free Expression. Belfast: Queens University Belfast Press **273 Queens University Belfast Press:** Google Inc. and Vidal-Hall & Others [2015] EWCA Civ 311; [2015] 3 WLR 409, [43] **278 Crown Copyright:** *Jameel* v *Wall Street Journal Europe Sprl* [2006] UKHL 44 at [26] **282 Parliamentary Copyright:** per Romer LJ in *Attorney General* v *PYA Quarries Ltd* [1957] 2 QB 169 **211 Crown Copyright:** Michael Paxman, The Westminster Echo **257 The Westminster Echo:** Peter Seldon **257 Peter Seldon:** Louis Barlow **267 Louis Barlow:** Singing Simon **268 Singing Simon:** A. Mullis and A. Scott, 'Tilting at Windmills: the Defamation Act 2013', (2014), *Modern Law Review,* 77(1) 87–109, at p108.

Guided tour

How to use features in the book 📖 and on the companion website 🖱

What to do for every question – Identify the key things you should look for and do in any question and answer on the subject, ensuring you give every one of your answers a great chance from the start.

How this topic might come up in exams – Understand how to tackle any question on this topic by using the handy tips and advice relevant to both essay and problem questions. In text, symbols clearly identify each question type as they occur.

Before you begin – Visual guides to help you confidently identify the main points covered in any question asked. You can also download them from the companion website to pin on your wall or add to your revision notes.

Answer plans and Diagram plans – A clear and concise plan is the key to a good answer and these answer plans and diagram plans support the structuring of your answers.

Answer with accompanying guidance – Make the most out of every question by using the guidance; recognise what makes a good answer and why. The length of the answers reflect what you could realistically achieve in an exam and show you how to gain marks quickly when under pressure.

Make Your Answer Stand Out – Impress your examiners with these sources of further thinking and debate.

Don't be Tempted to – Spot common pitfalls and avoid losing marks.

Try it yourself – Compare your responses with that of the answer guidance on the companion website.

Visit **www.pearsoned.co.uk/lawexpressqa** for a wealth of additional resources to support your revision, including:

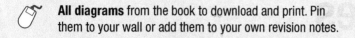

All diagrams from the book to download and print. Pin them to your wall or add them to your own revision notes.

Additional Essay and Problem questions with **Diagram plans** give you more opportunity to help you to practise and hone your exam skills.

You be the marker – Evaluate sample exam answers and understand how and why an examiner awards marks.

Table of cases and statutes

■ Table of cases

Statutes

■ European and International Legislation

What you need to do for every question in Tort Law

Books in the *Question and Answer* series focus on the *why* of a good answer alongside the *what,* thereby helping you to build your question answering skills and technique.

This guide should not be used as a substitute for learning the material thoroughly, your textbook and your lecture notes. It is not a silver bullet. It *will* help you though to make the most out of what you have already learned when answering an exam or coursework question. Remember that the answers given here are not the *only* correct way of answering the question but serve to show you some good examples of how you *could* approach the question set.

Make sure that you refer regularly to your course syllabus, check which issues are covered (as well as to what extent they are covered) and whether they are usually examined with other topics. Remember that what is required in a good answer could change significantly with only a slight change in the wording of a question. Therefore, do not try to memorise the answers given here; instead use the answers and the other features to understand what goes into a good answer and why.

It is also important not to worry about trying to learn all of the case citations. These are listed in the answers for information purposes only. You are unlikely to be expected to include these in an exam. Tort is predominantly a case-based subject and so you would be using a lot of your time if you listed the citations every time. However, you should obviously just confirm this with your tutors. Citations for journal articles are slightly different. While, again, it is very unlikely that you will be expected to write the full details of articles, you should give some indication as to where they are from, such as the journal abbreviation and year.

All torts have an inherent structure because of the elements which make up each tort. Use these elements to form the basis of your structure, particularly for problem questions. Deal with the first element and then move on to the next. The key is to spot how much weight you need to give each element, as questions are likely to focus on particular elements of the tort.

Tort also has a large amount of theory underpinning it and is influenced by certain principles. Make sure you learn these and always try to incorporate these into your answer. This is particularly beneficial when the question is an essay assessing the merits of an overall tort, or the component elements required by the courts for a particular tort, but even in problem questions it strengthens the advice you are giving someone and demonstrates the level of knowledge and understanding that you possess.

Negligence: Duty of care

1

How this topic may come up in exams

While negligence is examinable as a whole (see Chapter 5), the various individual components can be, and often are, examined separately as essays. Duty of care is particularly ripe for essay questions because of its complexity and differing components. There is also a large amount of policy considerations in the decisions, and within the law's development, of which you should also be aware. The more restrictive duty situations of psychiatric injury and economic loss may form part of an overall examination of the duty concept, or they may be treated distinctly, so do check your particular module guides for that.

Before you begin

Acquaint yourself with the following components and key issues of this topic; and familiarise yourself with how you would structurally progress through them all, if necessary, when attempting to answer a question on this topic.

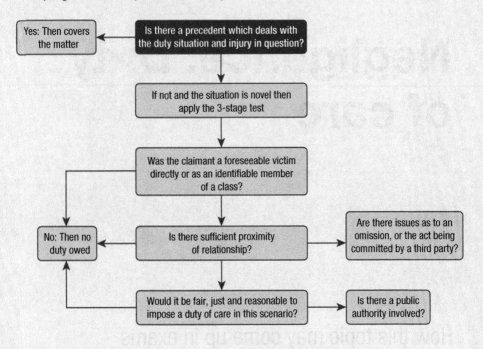

A printable version of this diagram is available from **www.pearsoned.co.uk/lawexpressqa**

🖎 Question 1

'The concept of duty of care in negligence emerged towards the end of the eighteenth century, and is now so firmly rooted that there can be no doubt that actions in negligence must fail where a duty is not established.' Witting, C. (2015) *Street on Torts.* Oxford: Oxford University Press, p. 27.

In light of this statement critically evaluate the role of the duty concept and the need for it to be so firmly rooted in the tort.

Answer plan

→ Provide the historical context and background to the role of the duty concept, discussing whether it needs to be firmly rooted in the tort.

→ Evaluate the role played by the duty concept, including how and why it was developed in the way it has been.

→ Assess the impact of the concept in the modern law and the extent to which it meets the needs of the tort.

→ Conclude whether the concept is needed or could have a less prominent application.

Diagram plan

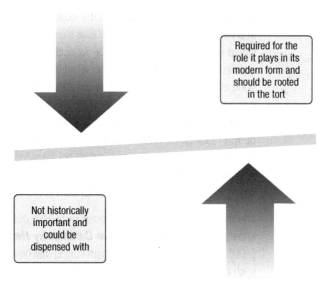

Required for the role it plays in its modern form and should be rooted in the tort

Not historically important and could be dispensed with

A printable version of this diagram plan is available from **www.pearsoned.co.uk/lawexpressqa**

Answer

The issue to be determined is whether it is right that the duty concept is so firmly rooted in negligence or whether it could operate without reliance on the concept, relying instead on the other aspects of negligence to perform the current duty function. This is important, as establishing a duty is the first hurdle which a claimant must overcome; a failure to do so means that, notwithstanding their injury and principles of corrective justice,[1] they will have no redress. It will be argued that while not always valued, the duty concept plays a useful function in seeking to achieve justice for those injured, while preventing punitive liability for those who are negligent.

[1] By including reference to this here you are showing your marker early on that you have an understanding of the underlying fundamental principles of tort and how they relate to the question.

While firmly rooted in the tort today, this has not always been the case and its importance has previously been questioned.[2] Winfield (1934) argued that historically no case was in fact ever lost through the absence of a duty. He noted that the concept of duty was never raised in the cases from which the independent tort of negligence grew, and in those cases arising during its early development. Similarly Buckland (1935) saw the duty concept as merely a fifth wheel: he argued that the more rational explanation for cases is that, as in Roman law, there is a duty to everyone, which is then limited on the basis of other aspects of the tort. By insisting on the existence of a duty to succeed in an action, claimants today now lose claims on a basis which they would not have lost on historically. As such, in Buckland's view the insistence on the need for a duty in all situations creates injustice. A good example of this can be seen in relation to negligently inflicted psychiatric injury where, even if all of the other elements of negligence are present, the duty concept has long been used as the basis for denying liability. However, if liability can be justifiably limited by other factors and the duty's presence would not have mattered, then it is perhaps questionable how much injustice is caused. Arguably, using, say, remoteness to limit liability rather than duty was not any fairer.[3]

[2] Due to the view I have of this issue, I am starting by dealing with the idea it should not be so rooted and we could do without the concept.

[3] While you have advanced Buckland's view, you still need to subject it to some critical evaluation – is there a link between the concept and injustice or would it exist anyway?

The debate around shifting the focus away from duty received fresh impetus in **JD v East Berkshire Community Health NHS Trust** [2005] 2 AC 373 with Lord Bingham stating that he would 'welcome' such a shift in focus so that breach of duty becomes the dividing line between success and failure.[4] Lord Nicholls in the same case noted the argument is 'not without attraction'. However, he noted that while

[4] The point here is for you to say that, notwithstanding the time lapse and the changes to the law since the above views were first aired, there is prominent, recent support. This will then strengthen any argument you may want to advance that the concept need not be so rooted in the law.

such a move would work in the field of human rights, in other cases it would cause lengthy uncertainty until a new control mechanism is devised which recognises that liability is not dependent on foreseeability. Therefore, if remoteness would also potentially cause unfairness and breach is not yet set up to act as an adequate control mechanism to contain claims, the duty concept needs to remain rooted in the law.

Therefore, need to firmly root the duty concept in the law as a control mechanism grew in importance following *Anns v Merton LBC* [1978] AC 728. The test proposed there for establishing a duty was seen as expanding negligence into areas that the law had been reluctant for it to explore, particularly economic loss. Generally, claims have to fit within an existing precedent which has recognised a duty in that situation. This rejects arguments of corrective justice whereby a person should have redress for any injury suffered through a want of care. Although it could be argued that by performing this role it reflects the fact that the law should also be just towards defendants.

[5] This part of your answer is quite important. Naturally, if you are discussing duty of care, you need to discuss how it arises. You need to link, though, how it arises to the wider discussion about what the role is and how well the test for establishment performs the role given to the concept.

However, negligence cannot be completely rigid and it needs to expand into new situations, but the duty concept firmly dictates when, so as to keep the law within acceptable bounds.[5] This role is reflected in the test for establishing a new duty situation. In *Caparo v Dickman* [1990] 2 AC 605 it was determined that the following factors would need to be present on the facts. First, it must be reasonably foreseeable that the particular claimant would suffer the particular type of loss which did in fact occur. The issue of the foreseeable claimant leads to the second factor, which is proximity. There must be a sufficient closeness between the parties in view of the type of loss which justifies imposing a duty. This, in turn, leads to the third element, which is that it is 'fair, just and reasonable' to impose the duty. The presence of the first two factors means it generally will be, but this element is also where public policy comes in. Even today this still leads to injustice being caused, as with psychiatric injury, although the judges, rather than talking specifically about policy, can use the policy to find that there was insufficient proximity or foreseeability.

The converse can also be said to be true though. The third element and the presence of policy can lead to justice for the defendants and thus it reinforces the modern role of the concept. A good example of

[6] As the reasoning is from a specific judge, name him/her as this shows a greater level of knowledge and understanding of the case, and that you have read, learnt and understood the judge's views.

[7] Whereas normally you would not need the journal's full name, where it is one from another jurisdiction it is worth stating it in full, because the marker may not be familiar with the abbreviated initials, unlike, say, *LQR.*

[8] This is where you could still expand on a comparative evaluation if you have not chosen to include a paragraph in the main body on other jurisdictions. The benefit of doing this is that the quote suggests the concept is indispensable. Show how other jurisdictions get by without it. This will then tie in to your discussion of the history of English law from Buckland (1935) and Winfield (1934).

this would be *Caparo,* where the auditor's negligence was argued to have caused the claimant to buy, first, a significant shareholding, and then the entire third-party company. The claim was rejected by Lord Bridge[6] because to hold otherwise would result in an indeterminate amount of liability, owed to an indeterminate class of people for an indeterminate length of time. If a duty was owed to potential shareholders, or even shareholders in relation to publicly released information, there was nothing to stop banks and merchants supplying credit to the company in reliance on the accounts having a claim. Therefore, for these reasons it was determined that it would not be fair, just and reasonable to impose what would have been a potentially crushing duty of care on the auditors.

In conclusion, notwithstanding the arguments that the duty concept serves no function, or simply duplicates a role which could be performed by another aspect of negligence, as Winfield (1934) noted,[7] it is so deeply entrenched in the law now that only legislation can eradicate it. This is even more the case today, and therefore the debate now really is purely academic in nature even though different jurisdictions also provide a model as to how the law could operate without it.[8] The modern approach utilises the concept as a way of balancing when liability can justifiably be imposed on the one hand with the need to ensure the potential liability is not too excessive on the other. Although, as the cases show, this may not always be satisfactorily achieved, depending on how strictly one adheres to corrective justice.

 Make your answer stand out

- Read in full the following articles: Buckland, W.W. (1935) The duty to take care. *Law Quarterly Review,* 51: 637; Winfield, P.M. (1934) Duty in tortious negligence. *Columbia Law Review,* 34(1): 41–66; and Howarth, D. (2006) Many duties of care: or a duty of care? Notes from the underground. *Oxford Journal of Legal Studies,* 26: 449.

- Read the debate on the role of the duty concept in *JD* v *East Berkshire Community Health NHS Trust* [2005] 2 AC 373.

- Draw on human rights arguments and the application of Article 6 as to whether there are further arguments against placing such importance on the duty concept.

- Consider how other jurisdictions deal with the issue and undertake a comparative evaluation to see if they have a better system.

! Don't be tempted to . . .

- Get bogged down describing the historical development of the duty concept.
- Discuss in great detail the different specialist duty situations and their merits; just draw on specific examples where relevant to your argument.
- Discuss all the different components of the whole tort of negligence as the question is specifically on duty.

🖎 Question 2

'There is no question that a police officer, like anyone else, may be liable in tort to a person who is injured as a direct result of his acts or omissions. So he may be liable in damages for assault, unlawful arrest, wrongful imprisonment and malicious prosecution, and also for negligence'. *Per* Lord Keith in *Hill* v *Chief Constable of West Yorkshire* [1989] AC 53 at 59.

Evaluate how the courts determine whether the police owe a duty of care in negligence to a member of the public in respect of the prevention and investigation of crime and the impact that policy considerations have in establishing the existence of a duty of care in this context.

Answer plan

→ Highlight that the police are treated no differently to any other party in respect of establishing a duty of care and should utilise the approach endorsed in *Caparo*.

→ Identify the particular issues that arise in relation to establishing a duty of care in the context of the prevention and investigation of crime, namely liability for omissions and liability for the acts of a third party.

→ Examine the impact that public policy considerations and the so-called *'Hill Immunity'* have had on liability in this context.

→ Analyse the recent decision in *Robinson* v *Chief Constable of West Yorkshire* [2018] 2 WLR 595 and its effect on the impact of policy considerations in the context of a duty of care in the prevention and/or investigation of crime.

Diagram plan

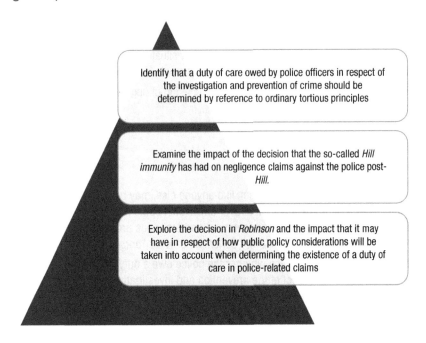

A printable version of this diagram plan is available from **www.pearsoned.co.uk/lawexpressqa**

Answer

[1] Indicate from the outset of your answer that you understand that public policy considerations have had a significant impact on case law regarding alleged police negligence.

[2] By including a reference to human rights in your introduction, you are demonstrating that you appreciate the wider impact of the decision in *Hill*. However, the question asks you about duty of care and therefore your answer should focus on this.

Lord Keith in **Hill v Chief Constable of West Yorkshire** [1989] AC 53 highlights that the police can potentially be found to owe a duty of care in negligence, however his consideration of public policy in **Hill** as the justification for excluding the possibility of a duty being owed, has formed the basis of many decisions pertaining to alleged police negligence since the case was decided.[1] The so-called '*Hill immunity,*' seemingly applicable to police officers in the investigation and prevention of crime, has caused much legal debate not only in terms of its impact on tortious principles but also in the sphere of human rights based litigation.[2] However the recent decision in **Robinson v Chief Constable of West Yorkshire** [2018] 2 WLR 595 confirms that more orthodox duty of care principles should apply in litigation involving police defendants and that decisions should be made unencumbered by any strict rule of immunity.

³ This demonstrates that you have a good understanding of the fundamental principles applicable to duty of care and how they arise in the context of the actions against the police.

⁴ You do not need to list all the cases where a duty is owed by the police to a member of the public. This sentence would be sufficient to make the point that you are trying to make.

⁵ Providing case examples supports the proposition you are making. While you could examine these cases in more detail within an answer, you need to consider whether or not this would be the most effective means of answering the question. Exploring the facts of cases such as these may help illustrate a point; however, your answer should not consist entirely of case fact examples.

⁶ Including academic opinion within your answer demonstrates that you have read more widely than your textbook and the case law. Always ensure that academic opinion is relevant to the matter you are discussing/ point you are trying to make. Inclusion of academic opinion for the sake of doing so will not be an effective use of your word count/time for answering the question.

⁷ While you have advanced McIvor's view, you still need to subject it to some evaluation in order to answer the question.

Both the cases of **Hill** and **Robinson** confirm that the police could owe members of the public a duty of care in the investigation and prevention of crime and that to assert otherwise would be inconsistent with pre-existing authority (see **Rigby v Chief Constable of North-amptonshire** [1985] 1 WLR 1242 as an example). However as was noted in **Michael v Chief Constable of South Wales** [2015] AC 1732 the duty on the police to investigate and prevent crime does not establish a general private law duty, nor does the law of tort generally recognise liability for an omission to act (**Stovin v Wise** [1996] AC 923) or for the acts of a third party. These are both issues that are acutely evident in the context of the prevention and investigation of crime as the litigation often stems from some alleged failure on the part of the police for harm caused by a party other than themselves.³ Consequently, cases where the police have been found to owe a duty of care have been relatively few and far between since the decision in **Hill**.⁴

Although the difficulties of establishing a duty of care in this context can be rationalised by reference to well-established tortious principles, this does not appear to be the basis upon which the judiciary have framed their decision making. Instead the courts have placed reliance on public policy arguments, with the possibility of defensive police practices and a detrimental impact on finite resources being the overwhelming reasons for finding that no duty is owed (**Hill; Elguzouli-Daf v Commissioner of Police for the Metropolis** [1995] QB 335; **Brooks v Commissioner of Police of the Metropolis** [2005] UKHL 24).⁵ McIvor (2010) argues that the validity of such policy arguments is a 'matter for debate' and that the courts are too 'broad-brush' in their reliance on them in police-related cases.⁶ Consequently it could be argued that cases are being decided in a manner which is arbitrarily favourable to police defendants on the basis of the '*Hill* immunity'. However,⁷ it should be noted that it is likely that the rules governing liability for omissions/acts of third parties would preclude the finding of a duty of care in these cases, even if public policy were not the prevailing justification for the courts approach in these cases.

Lord Reed, with whom Baroness Hale and Lord Hodge agreed, in **Robinson** suggests that **Hill** is not authority for the proposition that the police enjoy generally immunity from suit, nor should the courts in previous cases so readily have deferred to public policy considerations in determining liability.[8] Lord Reed indicates that the approach previously taken by the courts has stemmed from a misinterpretation of the tripartite test *Caparo Industries* v *Dickman* [1990] 2 AC 605. The Supreme Court in *Robinson* makes it clear that courts should adopt an approach based on common law, precedent and the incremental development of the law by analogy with reference to established authorities. *Caparo* repudiates the idea that there is a single test for determining the existence of a duty of care. The necessity to defer to public policy considerations, such as those explored in *Hill* and subsequent cases, will only arise in novel situations or where the courts are asked to depart from a pre-existing authority. Lord Mance, acknowledges that even established legal principles have the potential to be developed and, when they do, the courts will need to have regard to public policy considerations; however, this is unlikely to be a day-to-day concern of the lower courts. In most cases, the prior consideration of public policy obviates the need to consider it afresh in every case.

It appears that as a consequence of *Robinson* the explicit consideration of public policy will diminish in claims pertaining to alleged negligence by the police in the context of investigation and prevention of crime. *Robinson* confirms that the police will be unable to hide behind the veil of the '*Hill immunity*' and that they will be subject to the same scrutiny that any other defendant would experience. Foster and Gladwin-Geoghegan (2018) argue that *Robinson* may potentially have the effect of greater certainty and coherency in this particular area of negligence litigation; however, as highlighted above a significant increase in successful actions against the police is not likely to be forthcoming post-*Robinson.*

In conclusion, it is evident that although the courts have previously been heavily reliant on public policy arguments for determining the existence of a duty of care in relation to alleged negligence by the police in the investigation and prevention of crime, explicit consideration of such arguments is likely to diminish post-*Robinson.* The need to defer to such considerations is seemingly replaced by a more straightforward application of the legal principles pertaining to a duty of care in negligence, that are as applicable to the police as any other potential defendant.[9]

Make your answer stand out

■ Read the decision in **Robinson** in full. You should support your understanding of the case by reading academic commentary on the decision; for example, Foster, S and Gladwin-Geoghegan, R. (2018) Police Liability in Negligence: Immunity or Incremental Liability? *Coventry Law Journal* 23(1):38-47.

■ Draw on academic opinion in order to evaluate the approach the courts have taken in respect of police liability in the context of the question asked. Try:

 – McIvor, C. (2010) Getting defensive about police Negligence: the *Hill* principles, the Human Rights Act 1998 and the House of Lords. *Cambridge Law Journal*, 69: 133;

 – Tofaris, S. and Steel, S. (2016) Negligence liability for omissions and the police. *Cambridge Law Journal*, 75:128.

! **Don't be tempted to . . .**

■ Focus narrowly on **Hill** just because it features in the question. You will miss out on the opportunity to demonstrate a wider level of knowledge and understanding.

■ Produce a descriptive list of cases where negligence has been alleged against the police. While case examples may be useful for illustrating a point that you are making, the question requires you to be evaluative. A purely descriptive answer will not enable you to meet the requirements of the question.

■ Be drawn into a detailed consideration of the human rights implications of actions against the police for failures in the prevention and investigation of crime. Although you may want to demonstrate an awareness of these, the question is directing you to focus on tortious liability.

@ **Try it yourself**

Now take a look at the question below and attempt to answer it. You can check your response against the answer guidance available on the companion website (**www.pearsoned.co.uk/ lawexpressqa**).

 '. . . there is at present no general duty at common law to prevent persons from harming others by their deliberate wrongdoing, however foreseeable such harm may be if the defender does not take steps to prevent it'. *Per* Lord Goff in *Smith* v *Littlewoods Organisation Ltd* [1987] 1 AC 241 at 279.

Evaluate why this is generally the case and when a duty will be imposed in relation to a failure to act.

www.pearsoned.co.uk/lawexpressqa

Go online to access more revision support including additional essay and problem questions with diagram plans, you be the marker questions, and download all diagrams from the book.

Negligence: Duty of care for economic loss

2

How this topic may come up in exams

The law restricts when a duty of care arises in negligence for purely economic losses. This area can come up as a distinct question, independent from a more general negligence one, or within the sole examination of negligence. In this chapter we look at common essay questions only, for which you will need to know about the policy factors behind the law's restrictive approach. The topic is equally liable, though, to appear as a problem question dealing with either form of economic loss (i.e. resulting from negligent misstatements or negligent acts) or both (see Chapter 5). As such, you will need to learn the whole area, alongside the other components of negligence.

◼ Before you begin

Acquaint yourself with the following components and key issues of this topic; and familiar-ise yourself with how you would structurally progress through them all, if necessary, when attempting to answer a question on this topic.

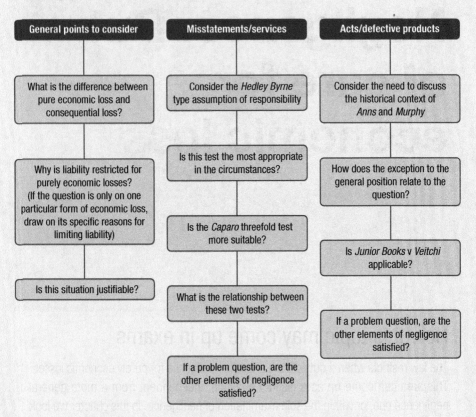

A printable version of this diagram is available from **www.pearsoned.co.uk/lawexpressqa**

 Question 1

'I think it is correct to regard an assumption of responsibility as a sufficient but not a necessary condition of liability, a first test, which, if answered positively, may obviate the need for further inquiry. If answered negatively further consideration is called for.' *Per* Lord Bingham in *Customs and Excise Commissioners* v *Barclays Bank* [2007] 1 AC 181 at 190.

In light of the above statement, critically examine the utility of an 'assumption of responsibility' as a necessary criterion for establishing a duty of care for negligently inflicted pure economic loss.

Answer plan

➜ Explain the background to the test and why it was developed.

➜ Discuss the operation of the test including what is required to establish a duty and consider the merits of the test.

➜ Evaluate the criticisms to which the test is subjected.

➜ Consider any alternatives that could be utilised instead of the voluntary assumption of responsibility test.

Diagram plan

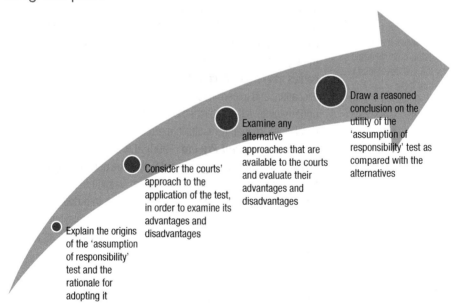

Explain the origins of the 'assumption of responsibility' test and the rationale for adopting it

Consider the courts' approach to the application of the test, in order to examine its advantages and disadvantages

Examine any alternative approaches that are available to the courts and evaluate their advantages and disadvantages

Draw a reasoned conclusion on the utility of the 'assumption of responsibility' test as compared with the alternatives

A printable version of this diagram plan is available from **www.pearsoned.co.uk/lawexpressqa**

Answer

[1] This demonstrates to the marker that you have an appreciation of the wider implications of legal uncertainty in this area.

[2] By including a sentence such as this at the beginning of your answer, you signpost to the marker how your answer to the question will develop. In order to do this, you need to have a clear plan of where you want your answer to go before you start to write.

The proposition that needs to be examined is whether or not an 'assumption of responsibility', a requirement that derives from *Hedley Byrne & Co v Heller & Partners Ltd* [1964] AC 465, is a necessary ingredient for establishing the existence of a duty of care in the context of negligent misstatements. Legal certainty in this area is particularly important for claimants and potential defendants alike, given the law's already policy-driven and restrictive approach to liability in this context.[1] In assessing the necessity of such a requirement, it will be argued that although an 'assumption of responsibility' provides a clear indication that a duty of care should be imposed, alternative approaches can be adopted where suitable to do so.[2]

In situations where a person has suffered pure financial or economic loss as a consequence of another's negligence, the law has adopted a restrictive approach to recovery. The general exclusionary rule is such that a claimant will not be able to recover for financial losses that are not consequential on another harm (*Spartan Steel & Alloys Ltd v Martin & Co Contractors* [1973] QB 27). The justification for limiting recovery in this manner is three-fold. First, the potential for far-reaching and crushing liability is great, given the complexity of the relationships that arise in the context of pure financial loss claims. A single negligent act may cause financial losses that 'ripple' throughout a complex web of economic relationships. Second, the parties have a greater opportunity to utilise contracts to determine risk allocation, and to permit recovery in negligence may have the effect of undermining well-established contractual principles. Third, pure economic loss frequently results in mere transfers of wealth (*Per* Hughes J in *Perre v Apand Pty Ltd* (1999) ALR 606:623). The claimant's loss is merely another person's gain, whereas personal injury or property damage usually involves a new loss. Despite these justifications for the general exclusionary rule, an exception to it does exist where the loss arises as a consequence of the negligent misstatement and a particular relationship between the parties exists, such as to justify the imposition of liability.[3]

[3] By including a paragraph such as this by way of explanation, you make the marker aware that you understand the rationale as to why the law developed in the way that it did in *Hedley Byrne* and provide some context to your later discussion. However, you should be mindful not to spend too long examining these policy considerations, as this is not the main thrust of the question asked of you.

[4] Although *Hedley Byrne* is a crucial case in respect of answering the question, you should not be tempted to explain the facts of the case in detail. This is not likely to add anything to your answer.

The starting point for determining the scope of the relevant relationship is the House of Lords decision in *Hedley Byrne*.[4] The basis of the test derivative from this case is that the statement maker needs to assume responsibility towards the claimant, who must then reasonably rely on the statement causing loss to result. It applies regardless of the presence of a contractual or fiduciary relationship between the parties. However, according to Lord Devlin, the circumstances are said to be akin to a contractual relationship,[5] through an assumption of responsibility, though lacking in the necessary consideration. The relationship between the claimant and the defendant is 'special' in the sense that it creates sufficient proximity between the parties to justify the imposition of a duty. Lord Reid explained in *Hedley Byrne* that the familiar test for a duty of care, which at the time derived from *Donoghue v Stevenson* [1932] AC 562, was not an adequate control for loss which arose from negligent words, and therefore the requirement of a 'special relationship' is imposed as this facilitates the overcoming of the policy considerations outlined above.[6]

In *Henderson v Merrett Syndicates Ltd* [1995] 2 AC 145, Lord Goff identified that all of their Lordships in *Hedley Byrne* spoke in terms of one party having assumed responsibility towards another and according to Lord Steyn in *Williams v Natural Life Health Foods Ltd* [1998] 1 WLR 830 there 'was no better rationalisation for the relevant head of tort than assumption of responsibility'. Lord Devlin in *Hedley Byrne* indicated that the necessary assumption of responsibility must be undertaken voluntarily and not imposed by law; however, following *Henderson* a more objective approach seems to have arisen, which considers not the defendant's state of mind, but whether objectively an assumption of responsibility can be said to have taken place based upon the facts of the particular case.[7] In *White v Jones* [1995] 2 AC 207, a case concerning whether or not a solicitor's duty of care in respect of pure economic loss extended to an intended beneficiary under a proposed will, Lord Browne-Wilkinson explained that the *Hedley Byrne* exception required the defendant to assume responsibility for the performance of the task at hand rather than legal responsibility towards the particular claimant. However, Lord Mustill dissenting in *White,* argued that in order for an assumption of responsibility to exist, a degree of mutuality was needed between the parties so that both played an active role in the transaction in question.[8] While this was evident in many of the cases that preceded *White,* no such mutuality existed between the defendant solicitor and the claimant beneficiary. Lord Mustill's dissent builds upon the opinion of Lord Griffith's in the earlier case of

[5] Highlighting that the 'assumption of responsibility' draws parallels with contractual relationships will be useful in supporting your evaluation of the test later in your answer.

[6] It is important to remember that *Hedley Byrne* was decided prior to *Caparo.* Being faced with the alternative test in *Donoghue* may justify the 'assumption of responsibility' test; however, the courts were not burdened in the same way by the time of *Customs and Excise Commissioners.* You should acknowledge this at some point in your answer.

[7] This indicates that the law has developed since *Hedley Byrne* and therefore ensures that your analysis of the test is up to date.

[8] Lord Mustill's dissenting opinion is a good starting point for your analysis of the 'assumption of responsibility' test. Dissenting opinions often offer alternative approaches that can be explored in an answer, in order to further your evaluation.

Smith v Eric S. Bush [1990] 1 AC 831, and if their perspectives are to be construed as the correct approach to what constitutes an assumption of responsibility, then the test should not have been applied to cases such as *Smith* and *White* in the way that it has been. If their approach is to be adopted, the suitability of the test to determine liability can be called into question.

[9] Up until this paragraph you have only considered the suitability of the 'assumption of responsibility' test. In order to answer the question, you need to explore its utility. This invites a consideration of any suitable alternatives such as that found in *Caparo*.

[10] Clearly you need to outline what the test involves, but the actual issue of the question does not require you to break it down in any further detail.

[11] This links back to the previous paragraph where you explained *Hedley Byrne* and the development of the 'assumption of responsibility' test.

Lord Bingham, in *Commissioners of Customs & Excise v Barclays Bank* [2007] 1 AC 181, noted that although it is correct to apply the test objectively, the further removed the test is from the actions and intentions of the defendant in question, the less difference there is between an assumption of responsibility and the three-fold test derivative of *Caparo Industries v Dickman* [1990] 2 AC 605.[9] Lord Bingham further doubted the usefulness of terms such as 'assumption of responsibility', suggesting that they are used as slogans rather than practical guides to be used to determine whether a duty of care exists. In *Caparo,* both Lord Oliver and Lord Bridge criticised the assumption of responsibility test as not helping to identify the key factors in the case. The three-stage test of foreseeability, proximity and fairness, justice and reasonableness[10] provided a more robust test for establishing a duty of care than that which had previously been advanced in *Donoghue*[11] and afforded the courts greater opportunity to focus more directly on policy issues. Such an approach was endorsed in *Spring v Guardian Assurance Plc* [1995] 2 AC 296, where a majority of the House of Lords held that an employer owed a duty of care to an ex-employee when preparing a reference and could be liable for economic loss suffered as a consequence of a reference that was negligently drafted.

[12] Adding a quotation here provides substance to the general assertion that you are making.

While there does appear to be merit and some judicial support for utilising the three-stage test in *Caparo* rather than deferring to the 'assumption of responsibility' test, this test too does not always provide a sufficient answer. Lord Walker in *Customs and Excise Commissioners* commented that it provides 'a fairly blunt set of tools'[12] with the other judges expressing similar sentiments. While each of the tests have their own merits, in the sense that the assumption of responsibility aligns with contract law and the *Caparo* approach permits a broader consideration of policy considerations, neither alternative is wholly adequate as a test for determining the existence of a duty of care in the context of negligently caused pure economic loss.

[13] Referring back to the quotation in the question allows you to draw together your arguments in your conclusion. Make sure that you specifically address the question asked of you in your conclusion in order to provide a meaningful ending to your answer.

In conclusion, Lord Bingham in the quote outlined above[13] does not appear to be suggesting that the 'assumption of responsibility' test or the three-stage test in *Caparo* should be considered as alternative rivals tests. The tests should be considered mutually supportive of one another rather than mutually exclusive and used to check the conclusions drawn as a consequence of an application of either approach. Both approaches have different merits and criticisms; however, it appears from the decision in *Customs and Excise Commissioners* that the further away the parties are from a relation akin to a contractual relationship and particularly in situations where the alleged negligence arises from the provision of a service, the greater the necessity to call upon the three-fold test in *Caparo* to determine the existence of a duty of care.

✓ Make your answer stand out

■ Explain briefly what the policy reasons are that make the law seek to limit when a duty arises for these types of losses.

■ Read the articles such as Barker, K. (1993) Unreliable assumptions in the modern law of negligence. *Law Quarterly Review,* 109:461; Murphy, J. (1996) Expectation losses, negligent omissions and the tortious duty of care. *Cambridge Law Journal,* 55(1): 43–55; Hedley, S. (1995) Negligence – pure economic loss – goodbye privity, hello contorts. *Cambridge Law Journal,* 54(1): 27–30; and Stanton, K. (2006) Professional negligence; duty of care methodology in the twenty-first century. *Professional Negligence,* 22: 134, in order to gain some substance for your argument.

■ Highlight specific strengths and weaknesses with the 'assumption of responsibility' test and the *Caparo* test and evaluate these, in order to produce a balanced and reasoned argument in response to the question.

! Don't be tempted to . . .

■ Labour the facts of the cases that you refer to. You need enough to show how the application of the test did, or did not, have merit to that particular situation but that is all.

■ Stray into examining in depth the merits of recoverability for economic losses; remember the question is about the specific test used to find a duty.

■ Chart the history of the development of the duty of care concept, especially in a narrative form.

Question 2

'The Court of Appeal applied what it called the "three-fold test" proposed by Lord Bridge in *Caparo Industries plc* v *Dickman* [1990] 2 AC 605 . . . Mr Brindle QC, who appeared for the bank, said that this was the wrong approach. One should ask whether the bank had assumed responsibility for monitoring the account.' *Per* Lord Hoffmann in *Customs & Excise Commissioners* v *Barclays Bank plc* [2007] 1 AC 181, [32]–[34].

Evaluate the application of these tests by the courts in determining when a duty of care will be owed in relation to negligent misstatements and whether the existence of both is detrimental to the law.

Answer plan

➡ Explain and evaluate what policy factors influence this area of law.

➡ Outline the initial approach of the courts to establishing the duty from *Hedley Byrne & Co. Ltd* v *Heller & Partners Ltd* [1964] AC 465.

➡ Assess the creation of the test from *Caparo Industries plc* v *Dickman* [1990] 2 AC 605 and whether its development is based on sounder principles.

➡ Draw on *Customs and Excise Commissioners* v *Barclays Bank plc* [2007] 1 AC 181, evaluate the law and whether any inconsistencies from having two approaches can be reconciled.

Diagram plan

Set out the policy basis to the law

- Explain why a restrictive approach is taken
- Evaluate the merit of the policy factors

Discuss the traditional method of establishing liability

- Analyse the voluntary assumption of responsibility test from *Hedley Byrne*
- Explain the expanded use of the test and whether it was still justifiable

Compare that with the test from *Caparo*

- Explain why the test was developed and how it operates
- Consider if it has a stronger basis

Assess the current state of the law

- Consider whether the existence of both tests is detrimental and, if so, how
- Discuss how the courts have sought to reconcile the two tests to resolve matters

A printable version of this diagram plan is available from **www.pearsoned.co.uk/lawexpressqa**

Answer

[1] Show from the start that you understand the area fully; know what the debate is getting at; and what you are required to consider.

[2] Whenever you are giving the rationale for a legal principle always ensure you evaluate its merit rather than simply state it, even if the question does not say to specifically evaluate that point, as you will still pick up marks and show you understand the law. In terms of this question, it is needed here to establish whether, regardless of what test is used, there is a sound basis for the law's overall approach.

[3] This may seemingly add nothing, but its purpose is to link what you are about to say back to the case that you have just discussed and highlight to your marker what the authority is for what you are saying without repeating the case.

[4] Illustrate how the principle worked in the case to show your understanding of it. This can also help your answer avoid coming across as overly descriptive as to what the law is.

[5] However, don't forget this significant fact from the case. While the court recognised the duty, it did not find one on the facts. It is a good sign as to whether you have read, and properly understood, the case.

The issue raised by the quote is what test should be used when deciding when a duty will be owed for negligent misstatement causing purely economic loss. While recoverable, such losses are dealt with more restrictively than personal or property injuries. This is controversial as a person suffering significant financial damage may be left without redress even though all other aspects of negligence are satisfied. Therefore, the basis of liability needs clarity and certainty, and to be based on sound principle.[1] By having seemingly different tests, without explanation of their relationship, the law has lacked these qualities and has risked causing injustice if each test reaches a different result, or undermining itself if each is stretched beyond its normal bounds to reach the same outcome as the other. However, it is submitted that the tests have now been reconciled and the law has a clear, consistent and just basis going forward.

No duty for such losses existed prior to *Hedley Byrne & Co. Ltd v Heller & Partners Ltd* [1964] AC 465. However, in recognising such a duty, the House of Lords stressed that it would be on a restrictive basis as the policy factors for previously denying a duty still had force. The concern is ensuring that the statement maker is not disproportionately, and unfairly, burdened with liability. This is legitimate as people can express definitive opinions in certain situations without considering the influence, due to the situation, that those words will have.[2] Additionally, words can be quickly disseminated to a wider audience so that the people who ultimately suffer the loss may differ from those to whom the statement was made and whom the maker may not know. This may explain why the person may not have taken sufficient care initially when making the statement. As such, their Lordships held[3] for a duty to be imposed what must be established is an assumption of responsibility by the defendant towards the claimant, which was reasonably relied on by the claimant, and the defendant knew that their skill and judgement was being relied on (the assumption of responsibility test). This worked in *Hedley Byrne* because the defendant bank knew that the credit worthiness rating was for the purpose of enabling the claimant to make a business decision,[4] albeit liability was ultimately excluded.[5]

[6] While this expansion came after a period when the 'three-fold' test from *Caparo* was in the ascendancy, it is worth dealing with how the original approach was taken in these expanded situations here, before looking at the latter test, as it is all part of how the original test operates. If you take a chronological approach your evaluation of the application of the assumption of responsibility test risks being disjointed.

[7] Use his Lordship's reasoning as well as it contrasts nicely with the criticisms made by Lords Mustill and Griffiths, which you can flow onto neatly before setting out the three-fold test. Additionally, by using Lord Browne-Wilkinson in addition to Lord Goff you also highlight the lack of agreement by the majority, which strengthens the point that is ultimately being made.

[8] Your aim in this section is to not only show the development of the assumption of responsibility test, but also to set a platform for the rest of your answer and link it back to the question. The statement shows there are different tests and implies judicial inconsistency and disagreement, which is what you are highlighting here. You can then use this to support why a second test was needed and then discuss that test, in that context.

Problems started to arise though as the test was expanded.[6] It was first developed to apply to the negligent provision of services on the grounds that what underpins the test is the claimant entrusting the undertaking of their affairs to the defendant. When the parties have a direct relationship, this can be justified and overcome the policy concern noted above, but where the relationship is more indirect there are legitimate doubts. In **Henderson v Merrett Syndicates** [1995] 2 AC 145, A had contracted with B to perform a service for the benefit of C in the knowledge that it was for C's benefit. That A knew that C was benefiting from the service created a sufficient closeness between the parties to justify the suggestion that A had assumed responsibility towards C and thus keep liability limited in scope.

The closeness of relationship in **Henderson** can be contrasted with **White v Jones** [1995] 2 AC 207 where a negligent failure to redraft a will meant the claimants inherited nothing. As the contract was with the deceased and the claimants would have had no knowledge of it, it is difficult to see an assumption of responsibility which, despite finding a duty, was recognised by Lord Goff. His Lordship felt practical justice required the assumption of responsibility to the deceased be extended to the claimant. Lord Browne-Wilkinson[7] suggested that the phrase 'assumption of responsibility' meant for the task performed, and not in relation to any legal obligation. There was a strong dissent by Lord Mustill[8] who argued that for an assumption of responsibility to exist there needs to be mutuality between the parties from both playing an active role in the transaction. Lord Mustill argued that in previous cases this was the case as, at the very least, B had contracted with

[9] What you are writing here naturally fits with your argument at this stage and placing this particular point at the end of the paragraph allows you to then go seamlessly into the *Caparo* test and the next part of your answer.

A at the instigation of C. Criticisms of the test predated its expansion and Lord Mustill's dissent built on earlier criticisms of the test by Lord Griffiths in **Smith v Eric S. Bush** [1990] 1 AC 831.[9] Lord Griffiths held that 'assumption of responsibility' only has any real meaning if it refers to when the law deems the maker of a statement to have assumed responsibility towards the person who acted upon the advice, i.e. they had assumed a legal obligation to them. This highlights the lack of clarity as to what a key component of the test refers to.

Lord Griffiths had preferred what became known as the 'three-fold' test from **Caparo.** This test was a response to the perceived weakness of the assumption of responsibility test and involves the claimant demonstrating that their injury was foreseeable to the defendant; there was sufficient proximity between them and; overall, it is fair, just and reasonable to impose a duty. The judges in **Caparo** acknowledged though that the test was limited and lacked precise definition.[10] Resultantly, it leaves a large degree of discretion in the courts' hands. While inherent flexibility can be advantageous, it puts claimants firmly at risk of policy decisions denying their claim. Ultimately, this test could be said to have equal weaknesses as the assumption of responsibility test in not providing certain application.[11]

[10] Highlight how the judges have acknowledged it is not perfect. This gives your evaluation of the merits of the test extra depth and allows you to substantiate your point with judicial support.

[11] As you are discussing a different test and explaining that it came about in light of criticism of the previous test, you need to assess the merit of this test. Link it back to your earlier discussion by considering whether it deals with any of the problems you discussed in relation to the assumption of responsibility test.

Therefore, the situation was detrimental as two tests existed, each with limitations and no clear guidance as to which should be used and when. The position has since been resolved in **Customs and Excise Commissioners,** which made clear that an assumption of responsibility is simply a sufficient basis for finding a duty of care, but not necessary. Whether there has objectively been such an assumption is simply a first question which, if answered negatively, calls for a consideration of the three-fold test. Lord Bingham noted both tests are compatible, although each has a more appropriate realm of application. An assumption of responsibility can objectively be said to exist where there is akin to a contractual relationship. More remote relationships may still warrant a duty, but based on the three-fold test which can give it a sounder basis. While the judges acknowledged there was no one single touchstone of liability, the case does at least provide certainty as to the interplay between the test and clarifies the process.[12] Unnatural applications of the concept of assumption of responsibility, beyond when it can be said to realistically exist, are avoided. However, by then having recourse to the three-fold test,

[12] Although you are about to go into your conclusion, do not wait to give a view on what the case decided and its impact on the law. It needs to be stated at the time you discuss the point to have more strength. The supporting basis for the proposition can be viewed in conjunction with it and thus it also helps to maintain a strong structure.

flexibility is provided in order to achieve a just outcome while allowing the law to develop into novel situations in a controlled manner.

In conclusion, the current position accommodates both tests in a logical way while retaining the sound basis for finding duties restrictively. While there could still be some uncertainty to the law, it is in a much stronger position now.

✓ Make your answer stand out

- Make sure that you have read *Customs and Excise Commissioners* v *Barclays Bank plc* [2007] 1 AC 181 and have a good understanding of the different judicial opinions within it. Draw on a variety of these to reinforce the points you are advancing as to the law's operation.
- Consider whether the tests are that dissimilar and the extent that cases could have been decided the same way using either test.
- Demonstrate a wide range of academic opinion in your arguments by reading articles such as Stapleton, J. (1991) Duty of care and economic loss: a wider agenda. *Law Quarterly Review*, 107: 249; Murphy, J. (1996) Expectation losses, negligent omissions and the tortious duty of care. *Cambridge Law Journal*, 55(1): 43–55; and Hedley, S. (1995) Negligence – pure economic loss – goodbye privity, hello contorts. *Cambridge Law Journal*, 54(1): 27–30.
- Consider economic loss from negligent acts briefly in order to make a wider statement as to the coherence of the overall law, and the judicial approaches taken to economic losses.

! Don't be tempted to . . .

- Provide a full history of the duty concept even in relation to economic loss. Stick to a tight structure or you will risk running out of time.
- Extensively cover the facts of each case. Demonstrate that you know what happened and give enough detail to enable you to comment on whether the development was justified, even only on the facts.
- Get side-tracked by the issue of the injunction in *Customs and Excise Commissioners* v *Barclays Bank plc* [2007] 1 AC 181.
- Discuss in any detail economic loss for negligent acts other than a brief comparative comment, as mentioned above, as that is distinct from the specific direction in the question.
- Similarly go on to discuss the other elements of negligence, as the question is specifically on the duty aspect.

Try it yourself

Now take a look at the question below and attempt to answer it. You can check your response against the answer guidance available on the companion website (**www.pearsoned.co.uk/lawexpressqa**).

> 'Quite careful people often express definite opinions on social or informal occasions, even when they see that others are likely to be influenced by them; and they often do that without taking that care which they would take if asked for their opinion professionally, or in a business connection.' *Per* Lord Reid in *Hedley Byrne & Co. Ltd* v *Heller & Partners Ltd* [1964] AC 465 at 482. ·

> Critically evaluate the extent that tort law will impose a duty of care for negligently made statements and whether this reluctance is justified.

www.pearsoned.co.uk/lawexpressqa

 Go online to access more revision support including additional essay and problem questions with diagram plans, you be the marker questions, and download all diagrams from the book.

Negligence: Duty of care for psychiatric injury

How this topic may come up in exams

Psychiatric injury is an aspect of negligence concerned with mental harm which has been caused through the negligent act of another. However, it has its own specific criteria for establishing whether a duty of care is owed. For these reasons, it is a common exam question in its own right, separate and distinct from the more normal questions on negligence and physical injury. You must ensure that you are familiar with the different rules for establishing liability and the distinctions that the law makes between the different categories of individuals within a problem question (see Chapter 5). The law has also been heavily criticised, with various proposals offered regarding reform. This also makes this topic equally favourable with examiners as an essay question.

■ Before you begin

Acquaint yourself with the following components and key issues of this topic; and familiarise yourself with how you would structurally progress through them all, if necessary, when
attempting to answer a question on this topic.

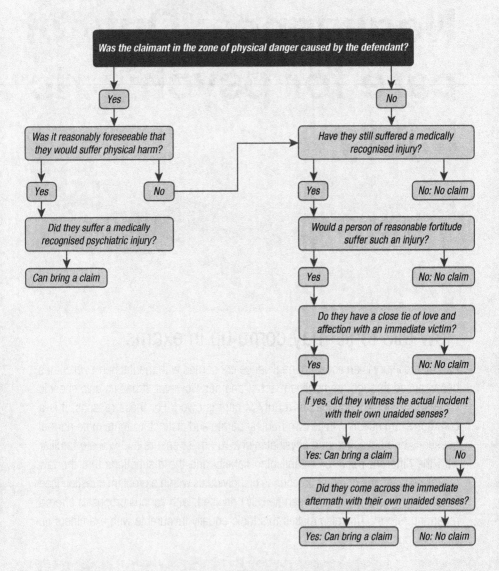

A printable version of this diagram is available from **www.pearsoned.co.uk/lawexpressqa**

 Question 1

'. . . primary victims need only prove reasonable foreseeability of *some personal injury*. They were not to be constrained by having to prove the foreseeability of *psychiatric* illness or by the additional, policy-based proximity limitations . . . differentiating between "primary" and "secondary" victims is itself beset with difficulty' (Teff, H. (1998) Liability for negligently inflicted psychiatric harm: justifications and boundaries. *The Cambridge Law Journal*, 57. 91–122 at 93).

Critically examine the requirements for primary and secondary victims in the context of negligently inflicted pure psychiatric injury and whether the distinction between them is justifiable.

Answer plan

→ Define psychiatric injury.

→ Explain the distinction between primary and secondary victims.

→ Critically examine the additional limitations imposed upon secondary victims in order to establish a duty of care.

→ Examine whether or not the current approach of the law is justified, with reference to any proposals for reform.

Diagram plan

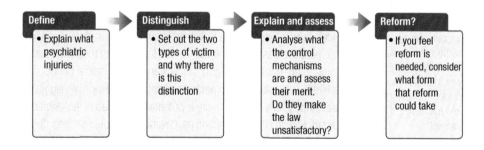

A printable version of this diagram plan is available from **www.pearsoned.co.uk/lawexpressqa**

Answer

[1] Try to demonstrate your non-legal knowledge as it is important to highlight the context in which legal principles have developed. You can use the fact of medical advances in relation to psychiatric injury later in your answer, in order to question whether or not the current approach of the law is justifiable.

Liability for psychiatric injury has evolved over the years, as advancements in medical understanding of psychiatric injury have developed.[1] While psychiatric injury is considered a form of personal injury, the law draws a clear distinction between physical injury and injury that is purely psychiatric in nature, with different rules applying to each. Notwithstanding the potentially incapacitating nature of mental illness, the law has adopted a highly restrictive approach, based upon public policy considerations in respect of the latter form of harm. Lord Steyn in **White v Chief Constable of the South Yorkshire Police** [1999] 2 AC 455, remarked that the law governing compensation for psychiatric harm was a 'patchwork quilt of distinctions'. This is exacerbated by the differing approach of the courts in respect of 'primary' and 'secondary' victims. The differing approach of the courts to different categories of victim will be assessed, in order to examine whether or not the current distinctions drawn are justifiable.

[2] Although subtle, this sentence highlights that you recognise that the burden of proof of establishing actionable harm rests with the claimant.

[3] You should offer some comparison between the approach of the law in respect of actionable physical injury and actionable psychiatric injury. This sets you up to critically evaluate the law in the remainder of the paragraph.

[4] This demonstrates that you are able to consider the practical implications of the point that you are discussing, rather than simply considering the law in the abstract.

In order for psychiatric injury to be actionable, the claimant must establish that they are suffering from a medically recognised psychiatric injury.[2] The law will not compensate for mere grief or sorrow (**Hinz v Berry** [1970] 1 All ER 1084) and a minimum threshold for psychiatric harm must be overcome. This is true regardless of whether the particular claimant is considered to be a primary or secondary victim and differs from the approach taken in actions arising from physical injury where no such threshold is applied.[3] This requirement can be perceived as one of the ways of the law meeting the need to place limitations upon the number and extent of admissible claims. Teff (1998) supports this approach as intelligible, however highlights the fact that as any physical injury is potentially actionable, this additional restriction on claims regarding psychiatric injury could be regarded as anomalous. However, in reality the likelihood of a claimant embarking on potentially costly and time-consuming litigation in respect of a very trivial physical injury is low.[4]

In determining whether or not a duty is owed to a claimant, the law categorises them as either primary or secondary victims. Teff (1998) indicates that such a distinction poses difficulty, which is a sentiment

[5] It is important to provide a balanced evaluation of the law; however, by beginning your consideration of the distinction between primary victims and secondary victims in this way, you are demonstrating to the marker, how you will frame the remainder of your answer.

echoed by the Law Commission who have described the distinction as more of a 'hindrance than a help'.[5] Primary victims must themselves be exposed to a reasonably foreseeable risk of physical injury (*Page* v *Smith* [1996] 1 AC 155). Provided that physical injury to the claimant is reasonably foreseeable, the claimant would be successful even if their psychiatric injury was not. Lord Lloyd in *Page* held that there was no justification for treating physical and psychiatric injury any differently in the context of such claims. It is the foreseeability of some risk of injury to the claimant which invites the imposition of the ordinary duty of care not to cause personal injury.

[6] Providing a brief reference to the Hillsborough disaster, you have given some context to *Alcock* which will support some of the points raised in your answer. A detailed account of exactly what happened at Hillsborough will, however, extend beyond what is required for this purpose and is unlikely to significantly enhance your answer.

Those claimants who are not in the reasonably foreseeable zone of physical danger but, nevertheless, suffer a recognised psychiatric illness, may be considered as secondary victims. In contrast to their primary victim counterparts, secondary victims have a significantly higher burden to overcome in order to establish that they are owed a duty of care. While the defendant must take their victim as they find them where primary victims are concerned, secondary victims must be of 'customary phlegm' in order to succeed (*Bourhill* v *Young* [1943] AC 92). Additionally, they must satisfy the control mechanisms from the leading case of *Alcock* v *Chief Constable of South Yorkshire Police* [1992] 1 AC 310, which arose out of major disaster at the Hillsborough Stadium in Sheffield.[6] This puts secondary victims in a much less favourable position than primary victims and, as a consequence, the justification for such a distinction can be questioned.

[7] This demonstrates that you understand the operation of the control mechanisms. This point is quite often lost in an answer where each of the control mechanisms is considered in turn.

Although *Alcock* identifies three control mechanisms, it is important that the courts consider these holistically rather than as individual requirements.[7] The first control mechanism is that the claimant must have a close tie of love and affection with the immediate victim of the incident. *Alcock* identifies that in the case of parents and children, and spouses there is a rebuttable presumption that such a tie exists. In all other relationships, a sufficiently close tie must be proven by the claimant (see *McCarthy* v *Chief Constable of South Yorkshire Police,* unreported, 11 December 1996). Although this mechanism is premised upon the idea of reasonable foreseeability, as is the case in respect of primary victims, the operation of this mechanism has faced criticism. Weir (1992)[8] argued that the mechanism risks

[8] Try to demonstrate variety in the academic opinion that you use in order to demonstrate wider reading.

causing 'embarrassment' to claimants who face cross-examination of the closeness of their relationship.

The second control mechanism requires temporal and spatial proximity to the incident or its immediate aftermath (*McLoughlin* v *O'Brien* [1983] 1 AC 410). While the extension made in *McLoughlin* to include the immediate aftermath can be perceived as a relaxation of the strictness of the control mechanisms, it invites an arbitrary drawing of a line between sufficient and insufficient proximity. While the line must be drawn somewhere, this has led to seemingly inconsistent applications of the law to subsequent cases (*Alcock; McLoughlin; Galli-Atkinson* v *Seghal* **[2003] Lloyd's Rep. Med.** 285), which supports the notion that the law in relation to secondary victims is unsatisfactory.

The third control mechanism is that the psychiatric injury must have resulted as a consequence of perceiving the incident or its immediate aftermath with one's own unaided senses. It requires the injury to arise from the sudden shock of witnessing the incident rather than gradual exposure over a more extended period of time. While in *North Glamorgan NHS Trust* v *Walters* [2003] PIQR 16 a mother was able to recover for psychiatric injury arising from a series of events culminating in the death of her son, the courts have more consistently been much stricter in their approach (*Wild* v *Southend University Hospital NHS Trust* [2016] PIQR 3; *Liverpool Women's Hospital NHS Foundation Trust* v *Ronayne* [2015] EWCA Civ 588). Given that a claimant must have a medically recognised psychiatric condition in order to bring an action, it is arguable that secondary victims should not be further restricted by a 'shock' requirement. It is arguably reasonably foreseeable that a sufficient injury would occur in situations where the assault on the claimant's mind was more gradual in nature. The impact of such injuries have the potential to be great for the particular claimant and therefore there must be strong justifications for limiting liability in the way that this control mechanism does.

The development of the law in relation to psychiatric injury, and in particular the control mechanisms, is underpinned by a number of different policy considerations which were explained by Lord Steyn in *White.* Lord Steyn identifies that the complexity and diagnostic uncertainty of mental injury claims may be a cause for concern. However, this is not an issue that is unique to secondary victims. Neither is the consideration identified by Lord Steyn that litigation may act as a disincentive to rehabilitation or recovery. Stapleton (1994a)[9] explains that the judiciary are concerned with preventing the prolongation or deterioration of the claimant's condition through the stress of the adversarial process and concern over compensation. Teff (1998) asserts that there is little evidence to support that this has in fact been a major concern of the courts. Consequently, it appears as though the distinction between primary and secondary victims is difficult to justify on either of these two bases. Lord Steyn does, however, place particular emphasis on the danger of wide-ranging liability (floodgates) and of an unfair burden being placed upon defendants as a consequence of disproportionate tortious conduct, as providing justification for restricting liability. These factors are of particular concern in the context of secondary victim claims, due to the potential for a single incident to cause psychiatric injury to a much wider range of people, as compared with only those who are physically injured or where physical injury would be reasonably foreseeable, a more restrictive approach to liability is arguably required.

[9] In examinations, include citation of academic opinion in order to strengthen the arguments that you are making and demonstrate that you have undertaken further reading. A citation such as this helps the marker identify the source that you are relying on. That said, you can save time in an examination by abbreviating your citation in this way. In courseworks you should ensure that you utilise the proper referencing style outlined in the assessment brief.

While the justifications for adopting a more restrictive approach to liability in relation to secondary victims as compared with primary victims may be defensible, there have nevertheless been widespread calls for reform of the law. The Law Commission proposed that second and third control mechanisms be removed due to the injustices that can arise. The first control mechanism would be amended to a statutory list of relationships where a conclusive presumption would apply; those not within the list would still need to prove sufficient proximity. Although the proposals may address some of the concerns with the law outlined above, it is important to note that they have not been adopted on any formal basis.

Overall, it is submitted that difficulty does arrive from the distinction between primary and secondary victims in the context of negligence claims. Although distinguishing between the two categories of claimant may be justifiable on the grounds of public policy as outlined above, the mechanisms that the law utilises in order to limit liability in respect of the latter is unsatisfactory in nature. Reform of the law in this area is not only desirable but necessary in order to address the problems that arise.

✓ Make your answer stand out

- Contrast the approach taken in respect of physical injuries and discuss in more depth whether such a distinction between types of injury is warranted.

- Expand your reading beyond your textbooks and the case law. There is a wide array of academic opinion on this area that you can use to support and substantiate the arguments that you are making.

- Expand on the options for reform. Although the question does not expressly ask for a discussion regarding reforming the law, the quote does imply that reform is needed. Your starting point should be the Law Commission (1998) Report *Liability for Psychiatric Illness*, No 249.

! Don't be tempted to . . .

- Just focus on the requirements for establishing a duty, you need to evaluate why the law requires those points for this type of duty.

- Simply describe what criticisms and reforms exist. While you will pick up marks for this knowledge, to get the higher marks you need to consider whether the criticisms have merit and whether a reform will make things better. Give an opinion as to what you think.

- Focus exclusively on case law. There are a number of academics who have questioned the merit of the law and/or offered reform proposals. Draw on these to build up just how large the consensus is on the proposition within the question.

🖎 Question 2

'There is no authority which decides that a rescuer is in any special position in relation to liability for psychiatric injury.' (*Per* Lord Hoffmann in *White* v *Chief Constable of South Yorkshire Police* [1999] 2 AC 455 at 509)

Evaluate the approach to rescuers seeking damages for negligently inflicted psychiatric injury taken by the House of Lords in this case and the merit of the decision that was taken.

Answer plan

→ Provide a brief factual overview of the case and set out the decision taken.

→ Analyse the reasons given by the majority for not recognising a duty of care to those who are not at risk of physical injury and evaluate their merit.

➡ Contrast that to the reasoning of the minority and explain why they would have recognised a duty.

➡ Discuss the justification of the current position and whether a different approach should be adopted in the future.

Diagram plan

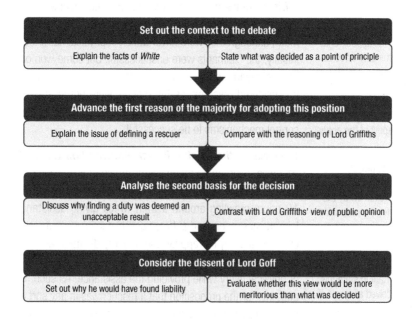

Set out the context to the debate	
Explain the facts of *White*	State what was decided as a point of principle

Advance the first reason of the majority for adopting this position	
Explain the issue of defining a rescuer	Compare with the reasoning of Lord Griffiths

Analyse the second basis for the decision	
Discuss why finding a duty was deemed an unacceptable result	Contrast with Lord Griffiths' view of public opinion

Consider the dissent of Lord Goff	
Set out why he would have found liability	Evaluate whether this view would be more meritorious than what was decided

A printable version of this diagram plan is available from **www.pearsoned.co.uk/lawexpressqa**

[1] It is questionable that they do, or even did prior to the debate within this case. As such, it is important to phrase this in a way which shows it is not conclusive, but recognises the possibility. It is useful to raise it though as it provides context for the debate as to whether rescuers should have a special position for psychiatric injury. You can then pick up on the point later in your answer if you choose.

Answer

Rescuers have been thought to hold[1] a special position with regards to the tort of negligence and the issue here is the merit of the decision in *White* v *Chief Constable of South Yorkshire Police* [1999] 2 AC 455 where this idea was rejected in the context of a claim for psychiatric injury. The rationale behind the majority's decision is evaluated before assessing the merits of the dissenting opinions. It is argued that while within the context of the factual background to the case the decision is understandable, and denying rescuers a special position can be justified, overall the decision in terms of legal principle was unmerited and lacked principle.

[2] By setting this out you have a yardstick from which to determine whether the decision of the case was correct. The history of the case provided an important basis for the decision of the majority.

[3] Obviously, there were two grounds to the appeal, one regarding the duty owed as employee and one on the basis of their rescuer status. As the question is focused on rescuers, you need to focus on just that aspect of the appeal.

[4] You need to give the brief facts to explain why the case was being relied on by the claimants for the proposition under discussion.

[5] It is important to state this, as the perceived absence of authority allowed the majority to come at the matter as they did on policy grounds. It also sets up a contrast to Lord Goff, which can be evaluated later.

[6] As Lord Griffiths' reasons for dissenting on this point are at complete odds with Lord Hoffmann's, raise them now as a way of testing the merit of the majority's view rather than as advancement of a distinct argument against the decision later.

Before an assessment of the decision can be made, it is necessary to outline the background from which it originates, as the decision was unarguably influenced by the context in which it was made.[2] The case arose from the Hillsborough disaster and is inextricably linked to *Alcock v Chief Constable of South Yorkshire Police* [1992] 1 AC 310. While *Alcock* concerned unsuccessful claims for psychiatric injury by the relatives of those that had died, the claimants in *White* were the policemen who suffered such injuries through their involvement in the disaster and the assistance they gave in its aftermath, although they were never at risk of physical harm themselves. Initially, the claimants were unsuccessful, but some won on appeal. The defendant appealed in turn, with one ground being[3] that, even if considered rescuers, as the officers were not in any reasonably foreseeable physical danger, they would have to satisfy the *Alcock* control mechanisms to be successful.

The case of *Chadwick v British Railway Board* [1967] 1 WLR 912 was relied on as the basis for arguing that rescuers were in a special category and free of control mechanisms. Chadwick spent 12 hours crawling around a train wreck giving assistance to the injured passengers and suffered psychiatric injury as a result.[4] However, in allowing the appeal, the majority deemed Mr Chadwick to be simply what is now considered a primary victim as he was at risk of physical injury while providing the assistance. As such, it was not authority for the proposition that a rescuer was in any sort of special position regarding psychiatric injury.[5] Lord Hoffmann acknowledged the law could be extended to cover the situation at hand; however, he noted two reasons for not doing so. First, he noted a rescuer is currently clearly understood as being someone who puts themselves in physical danger. If the term was extended to cover those not at risk of physical injury it would be difficult to distinguish them from mere bystanders. By contrast, Lord Griffiths[6] held that, while a distinction is needed between providing immediate assistance at the scene and participation once the victim is safe, this could easily be determined on the facts of each case. Therefore, Lord Griffiths would have dismissed the appeal and allowed the law to be extended, provided it was still reasonably foreseeable that the rescuer in question would suffer psychiatric injury through their participation in the event. This is arguably the better view as it permits control to be maintained, but allows for flexibility where merited. It also reflects advances in

[7] The point here is to raise the issue of whether, if medical professionals struggle to distinguish the two types of injury and look at the overall idea of personal injury, the law should be making such a firm distinction. This gives you another basis to explore the merit of the current legal position and what was decided.

[8] While essentially the same as Lord Hoffmann's, if you include the opinion of Lord Steyn you demonstrate your knowledge of the whole case and provide variation of material in support of your argument.

[9] As the majority were so clearly swayed by the factual background to the case and the decision in *Alcock*, it is important to have raised this beforehand. By doing so you give yourself a platform from which to fully evaluate the reasoning given in the case.

[10] Therefore, your answer will benefit from Lord Goff's reasoning being looked at separately from Lord Griffiths'.

[11] It is quite central to explaining Lord Goff's opinion that you highlight the different way that he saw the question to be asked in the case. Therefore, you need to state what the question was in his view in order to fully demonstrate your understanding of his reasoning.

medical knowledge,[7] noted previously in *Page v Smith* [1996] AC 155, meaning it is difficult to distinguish physical and psychiatric consequences of trauma, and focus instead on personal injury as an overall concept.

Lord Hoffmann's second reason was based on public policy. He felt that if the claimants were better off than those in *Alcock,* ordinary people would be offended and think it unfair that similar cases were not being treated alike. This was supported by Lord Steyn who considered it would be an 'unedifying spectacle'.[8] Lord Griffiths again disagreed that the public would find it offensive. The important point was their suffering of a recognised psychiatric illness alongside their involvement as events unfolded, as opposed to mere grief and bereavement and assistance after the event. In view of the background context of the decision, it is hard to argue with the concerns of the majority.[9] However, approaching the matter ignorant of the *Alcock* decision and looking simply at the direct facts of *White* it is hard to deny the merit of the approach advocated by Lord Griffiths.

In also dismissing the appeal, Lord Goff offered a different basis[10] which is arguably more forceful. He highlighted how Mr Chadwick did not actually rescue anyone, but simply brought aid and comfort. Additionally, he noted that while Mr Chadwick had faced some physical danger, it was treated as irrelevant by the judge who attributed his injuries to the whole horror of the event. Lord Goff felt each point was significant as the first meant that we need not be restricted by the meaning of rescuer, while the second indicated that there was no reason to single out for compensation only those who had done rescue acts where those acts were only incidental to the wider incident which, overall, caused the psychiatric injury. His Lordship suggested that requiring a rescuer to be objectively at risk of physical injury was, in fact, contrary to authority. This meant that the majority were wrong in viewing the question as to whether the law should be extended, rather than whether the law should be restricted.[11] Consequently, the majority were viewed as imposing an artificial barrier against recovery for foreseeable psychiatric injury. Furthermore, Lord Goff felt the majority views were misconceived with their concerns of public opinion being offended if the claimants succeeded. The function of tort is to correct wrongs by having the wrongdoer compensate the person

[12] As Lord Goff was basing his opinion firmly on tort principles, you need to provide some explanation as to the underlying principle and function of tort law. This will strengthen your discussion of Lord Goff's opinion and show the depth of your understanding of tort law generally.

[13] The law is widely deemed to be unsatisfactory in this area and lacking principle so it is important to look at the merits of each side in the case and how well they sit with the overall principles of tort and past case law.

they injure.[12] That some claimants will fail to satisfy the necessary requirements of their case was no reason to restrict all claims of that type. The focus should be on the individual parties in each case, but with the same principles applied in each instance. The position as Lord Goff saw it would defeat the claim by a policeman who was a mere witness to event, but the position advanced by the majority would, while also defeating such a claim, deny a relative who had attempted a rescue. It is hard to argue with this reasoning, particularly as it retains principle within the law[13] which the majority conceded had been lost in their view.

To conclude, it is now settled that a rescuer who is at no risk of physical injury must satisfy the *Alcock* control mechanism to be successful. While denying rescuers special status has merit, and the decision in fact suggests that they do not have such status for physical injury either, the overall outcome of the case leaves the law in an unjustifiable and unprincipled state, a point in fact conceded by the majority. From an emotional perspective, the decision is understandable in that parity was being sought with the claimants in *Alcock*; however, for the benefit of the law as a whole, the view of the minority from the case is preferable.

✓ Make your answer stand out

- Explore the point raised by Lord Hoffmann in *White* that rescuers do not even receive special treatment in cases of physical injury.

- Extend the discussion regarding the validity of distinguishing between physical and psychiatric injuries in light of medical advances.

- Tailor your answer to suit your view; if you actually disagree with the minority, end your answer with the views of the majority and why they are more justified. This will ensure that your answer finishes strongly.

- Offer your own view as to what the law should be in order to be in a better state if you feel that to be the case. If you have identified a problem, try to solve it. Do make sure that you substantiate any opinion by expressing the basis for that opinion.

- Draw on the wealth of academic literature on the topic in order to support the different positions that you are considering, for example Geach, N. (2012) Re-establishing the search for principle: the dissent of Lord Goff in *White* v *Chief Constable of South Yorkshire Police* [1999] 2 AC 455, in N. Geach and C. Monaghan (eds.) *Dissenting Judgments in the Law*. London: Wildy, Simmonds & Hill Publishing.

Don't be tempted to . . .

■ Dwell too long on setting out the factual backdrop to the case and provide too much detail. You just need to provide some context as to why the majority reached the decision that they did.

■ Ignore the opinions of the dissenting Law Lords on the basis that their view is not the law. The question asks you to evaluate the merit of the decision, so it is essential to consider the alternative viewpoints in the case.

■ Give an in-depth account as to control mechanisms applied to secondary victims. The question gives some scope to mention them in order to show your knowledge, but you would be straying too far from the issue of the question if you provide a detailed overview. You can show your understanding of them, and the question, by not mentioning them in depth.

@ Try it yourself

Now take a look at the question below and attempt to answer it. You can check your response against the answer guidance available on the companion website (**www.pearsoned.co.uk/lawexpressqa**).

'The concerns about recovery for nervous shock are real, but the available techniques for controlling it are not only artificial but bring about the law into disrepute.' Stapleton (1994a) In restraint of tort, in P. Birks (ed.), *The Frontiers of Liability.* Oxford: Oxford University Press.

Critically analyse the requirements for making a successful claim for psychiatric injury and the control mechanisms that the courts utilise to limit such claims. Your answer should refer to academic criticism of the law and proposals for reform.

 www.pearsoned.co.uk/lawexpressqa

Go online to access more revision support including additional essay and problem questions with diagram plans, you be the marker questions, and download all diagrams from the book.

Negligence: Breach, causation, remoteness and defences

4

How this topic may come up in exams

While these all naturally come together in a problem question, as shown in Chapter 5, as with the duty concept each is examinable as an individual essay. For breach questions you will need to ensure that you know what are the factors the courts consider, and be able to evaluate how and why they are used, as well as when they will be adapted. Causation is very popular for essay questions as it has many different complex subsections. Therefore, you will need a firm understanding of the judicial reasoning in causation cases, and be able to evaluate whether those opinions have merit. Ensure you have also read sufficient academic opinion to support your argument. Remoteness and defences are less likely as individual essays.

Before you begin

Acquaint yourself with the following components and key issues of this topic; and familiarise yourself with how you would structurally progress through them all, if necessary, when attempting to answer a question on this topic.

Breach
- What standard of care is expected of the defendant?
- Does the defendant profess to have a particular expertise which justifies an application of *Bolam*?
- Is the situation one where a medical practitioner has failed to inform the patient of a risk, in which case *Montgomery* should be applied?
- Has the defendant fallen below the standard of care expected, taking into consideration any of the following where relevant:
  - likelihood of harm
  - magnitude of harm
  - social utility of the defendant's conduct
  - cost/practicability of avoiding the harm.

Causation in Fact
- Is the injury that has been caused one that is actionable?
- Is the situation one of the distinct, alternate or cumulative causes?
- Depending on the type of cause, has the breach of duty caused, materially contributed to or materially increased the risk of injury, on the balance of probabilities?
- Are there any consecutive causes to the injury and can any of these be classed as an intervening act?

Causation in Law (Remoteness)
- How has *The WagonMound No.1* changed the test of remoteness?
- Is the injury one which is of the type, kind or class which is reasonably foreseeable?
- Has there been an intervening act which would render the injury too remote?

Defences
- Has the defendant voluntarily assumed the risk of injury?
- Is the injury one for which liablity can be excluded or limitated and is such an exclusion or limitation applicable?
- Is the claim substantially based upon an illegal act by the claimant?
- Has the claimant contributed to his injury through his own negligence?

A printable version of this diagram is available from **www.pearsoned.co.uk/lawexpressqa**

🖋 Question 1

'It is unsurprising that the courts have found difficulty in the subsequent application of *Sidaway*, and that the courts in England and Wales have in reality departed from it; a position which was effectively endorsed, particularly by Lord Steyn, in *Chester* v *Afshar.* There is no reason to perpetuate the application of the *Bolam* test in this context any longer.'
(*Per* Lord Kerr and Lord Reed in *Montgomery* v *Lanarkshire Health Board* [2015] AC 1430 at [1462–1463])

Explain the development of the reasonable patient and 'test of materiality' approach adopted by the courts in *Montgomery* and evaluate the impact that the courts' rejection of the *Bolam* test has on medical negligence litigation.

Answer plan

➡ Explain the *Bolam* test and its function in determining a breach of duty.

➡ Outline the development of the test of materiality using cases such as *Sidaway*, *Pearce* and *Chester.*

➡ Explain the reasonable patient approach and 'test of materiality' as outlined in *Montgomery*, including the therapeutic privilege exception.

➡ Highlight the impact that *Montgomery* will have on what is expected of a medical professional in the context of adequately informing patients of risks of and alternatives to treatment.

➡ Consider the overall impact of the decision in *Montgomery* on medical negligence litigation.

Diagram plan

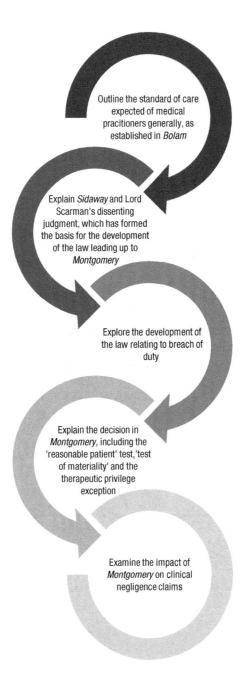

Outline the standard of care expected of medical pracitioners generally, as established in *Bolam*

Explain *Sidaway* and Lord Scarman's dissenting judgment, which has formed the basis for the development of the law leading up to *Montgomery*

Explore the development of the law relating to breach of duty

Explain the decision in *Montgomery*, including the 'reasonable patient' test, 'test of materiality' and the therapeutic privilege exception

Examine the impact of *Montgomery* on clinical negligence claims

A printable version of this diagram plan is available from **www.pearsoned.co.uk/lawexpressqa**

Answer

The duty of care in negligence is to take reasonable care in the circumstances of the case, with the standard of care expected of a particular defendant determined by law. Where the alleged negligence concerns a defendant who holds themselves out to have a particular skill such as in the case of medical professionals, the defendant will be judged according to a person having the same skills and expertise that the defendant professes to have (**Bolam v Friern Hospital Management Committee** [1957] 1 WLR 582). However, under **Bolam** professionals can avoid a finding of negligence if they are able to demonstrate that a responsible body of opinion from within the profession would have acted in the same way, even if others would not have done so. This is provided that the body of medical opinion is capable of withstanding logical analysis (**Bolitho v City and Hackney Health Authority** [1998] AC 232).[1]

The application of the **Bolam** test has been particularly controversial in the context of informing patients of risks associated with medical treatment. The decision in **Sidaway v Bethlem Royal Hospital** [1985] AC 871 confirmed the application of the **Bolam** test in this context and supported the paternalistic approach of the courts that is arguably perceived in the context of claims against medical professionals. Disclosure of risk was held to be primarily a matter for clinical judgement and fell within the realms of the doctor, rather than the patient, knows best. This was with the caveat that a failure to inform a patient of a 'substantial risk of grave adverse consequences' may lead the court to justifiably come to the conclusion that no prudent medical professional would fail to disclose it. Lord Scarman delivered a powerful dissenting opinion in the same case, urging for the adoption of the 'prudent patient' test.[2] This test focused on what the prudent patient, in the patient's position would want to know and is a clear exposition of patient autonomy and the right to make a fully informed choice.

Over time the majority approach in **Sidaway** has steadily been eroded. Lord Woolf MR in **Pearce v United Bristol Healthcare NHS Trust** [1999] ECC 167, advocated for a threshold that requires practitioners to disclose significant risks which would affect the judgement of a 'reasonable patient', which appears quite patient-centred. However, Lord Woolf MR deferred to what the medical professionals perceived to be a significant risk, thus implying that under **Pearce,** the opinion of medical

[1] Ensure that you accurately outline the test from *Bolam* and the gloss on this test added by *Bolitho*. You will likely refer back to *Bolam* throughout the remainder of your answer, therefore it is important to set it out precisely at the beginning.

[2] Ensure that you clearly indicate that Lord Scarman provided a dissenting judgment in the case of *Sidaway* and the premise for his dissenting opinion. Lord Scarman's dissenting opinion has shaped the development of the law up until *Montgomery* and therefore it must be mentioned in your answer.

[3] Although this may appear like an older and therefore potentially out-of-date article to utilise, when asked to discuss the development of the law, it is important to consider academic commentary throughout the period of development.

professionals still retained significant weight in determining the existence of a breach of duty. Nevertheless, Brazier and Miola (2000: 111) argue that this amounted to a substantial body-blow to *Bolam* in this context.[3] Judicial support for patient autonomy in treatment decisions was also evident in *Chester* v *Afshar* [2005] AC 134 and although this case is important in the context of causation, Lord Steyn's rhetoric supports the perspective that medical paternalism in this context is no longer supreme and aided in shifting the balance in favour of a patient-focused approach to determining the existence of a breach of duty, premised on concepts of patient autonomy and informed consent.

[4] Although the facts of the case provide some context to the case of *Montgomery* you shouldn't explain them in excessive detail as they are not directly relevant to the question asked of you.

The decision in *Montgomery* v *Lanarkshire Health Board* [2015] AC 1430 has confirmed the inapplicability of *Bolam* in relation to informing a patient of risks associated with medical treatment. The Supreme Court unanimously found in favour of the claimant Ms Montgomery, due to Dr McLellan's failure to inform her of the risk of 'shoulder dystocia' associated with a vaginal delivery of her baby.[4] They did so on the basis that a patient is entitled to decide on risks to their health that they are willing to run and that this decision should be informed by information regarding material risks associated with treatment and any reasonable alternative treatment. It is therefore incumbent upon a medical practitioner to take reasonable care to ensure that a patient is adequately informed. The Supreme Court went on to outline the test of materiality, which is 'whether in the circumstances of a particular case, a reasonable person in the patient's position would be likely to attach significance to the risk, or the doctor is or should reasonably be aware that the particular patient would be likely to attach significance to it.'[5] The benefits of, risks of, and alternatives to treatment are not to be regarded as purely a matter for professional judgement and instead a patient-centred approach, reminiscent of Lord Scarman's dissent in *Sidaway,* will be utilised to determine the existence of a breach of duty.

[5] Although this is a long quotation, it is difficult to articulate it in a more concise manner without losing accuracy. Ensure that you are using the appropriate reference style for quotations if you are writing a coursework assignment.

[6] Although the question asks you to focus on the 'reasonable patient' test and the 'test of materiality' it is important to address the therapeutic privilege exception outlined in *Montgomery* as this is relevant to the operation of these tests.

The courts have, however, retained the therapeutic privilege exception[6] which permits a medical professional to withhold information from a patient if he reasonably considers that its disclosure would be detrimental to a patient's health. It would appear as though reliance on the therapeutic privilege exception would require some examination of the defendant's conduct in the *Bolam* sense. However, the courts have warned that the therapeutic privilege exception should be narrowly applied and not be used as a means of subverting the general rule laid down in *Montgomery* by enabling the doctor to prevent a patient from making an informed choice, where the doctor believes that the patient is liable to make a choice that is not in their best interests.

Consequently, the decision in **Montgomery** is a landmark decision in relation to breach of duty and informed consent, due to it formally overruling the decision in **Sidaway** and narrowly construing any exceptions to the legal principle that it lays down. Commentators such as Sokol (2016) suggest that the decision will have important implications for medical practitioners; however, Farrell and Brazier (2016: 85) argue that **Montgomery** will make little difference in the healthcare practice and consent.[7] The UK General Medical Council guidance[8] on the issue of consent, is largely reflective of the reasonable patient approach and has been for some time, therefore medical practice will be unlikely to appreciably alter. Arguably, the Supreme Court in **Montgomery** has merely endorsed an approach that was already perceived to exist by medical practitioners and lawyers alike.

The decision in **Montgomery** is also narrow in its scope, in the sense that its application is confined to cases concerning an alleged breach of duty by reason of a failure to adequately advise a patient of the risks that treatment may entail and the alternative strategies for treatment that are available. The **Bolam** test will continue to be utilised in the context of diagnosis and treatment as these properly fall within the remit of professional expertise. Therefore, although **Montgomery** can be perceived as a significant step forward in relation to informed consent, it does not constitute an overhaul of the manner in which negligence actions against medical professionals will be determined.

[7] By providing differing academic opinion, you pave the way for the critical evaluation required by the question.

[8] Referring to the GMC guidance demonstrates an understanding of the law in practice.

✓ **Make your answer stand out**

- Ensure that you evaluate the decision in *Montgomery* within the context of negligence claims.

- Consider the practical impact that the decision will have in relation to medical practice. In order to do this, you will need to consider the General Medical Council's guidelines on 'Consent: patients and doctors making decisions together'.

- Ensure that you read beyond the case law. Although *Montgomery* is the focus of your answer, draw on the opinions of academics or practitioners such as Farrell, A. and Brazier, M. (2016) Not so new directions in the law of consent? Examining *Montgomery* v *Lanarkshire Health Board*. *Journal of Medical Ethics*, 42(2): 85, or Sokol, D. (2015) Update on the UK law on consent. *BMJ*, 350: h1481.

! Don't be tempted to . . .

- List every case that you can think of regarding informed consent and breach of duty. You need to identify the main cases that have influenced the development of the law until the rejection of **Bolam** in **Montgomery.**

- Cover all aspects of negligence or, more specifically, breach of duty; the question is particularly concerned with breach of duty in the context of actions against medical professionals.

📝 Question 2

'In a case where medical science cannot establish the probability that "but for" an act of negligence the injury would not have happened but can establish that the contribution of the negligent cause was more than negligible, the "but for" test is modified, and the claimant will succeed.' (*Per* Waller LJ in *Bailey* v *Ministry of Defence* [2009] 1 WLR 1052 at [46].)

Evaluate the instances when a court will depart from the 'but for' test in favour of an alternative test and consider whether the law is satisfactory.

Answer plan

→ Outline the standard 'but for' test.

→ Demonstrate its standard application in scenarios consisting of distinct, alternative possible causes of injury.

→ Highlight what problems there can be with the application of the 'but for' test.

→ Chart the development of the 'material contribution' test through to the 'material increase in risk' test and evaluate their use in situations where the 'but for' test is deemed inappropriate.

→ Conclude by assessing the current state of the law.

Diagram plan

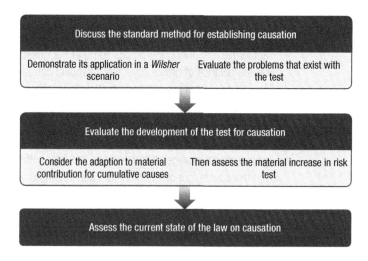

Discuss the standard method for establishing causation

Demonstrate its application in a *Wilsher* scenario Evaluate the problems that exist with the test

Evaluate the development of the test for causation

Consider the adaption to material contribution for cumulative causes Then assess the material increase in risk test

Assess the current state of the law on causation

A printable version of this diagram plan is available from **www.pearsoned.co.uk/lawexpressqa**

Answer

The issue to address is the test used for determining causation in negligence and how it is modified depending on the circumstances. Strict adherence to the traditional approach has led to many claimants going uncompensated, whereas in certain circumstances claimants benefit from a relaxation of the rules. It will be argued that this discrepancy in the law can be justified and so the law is satisfactory.

The standard approach for determining causation was devised in **Cork v Kirby Maclean** [1952] 2 All ER 402, and is to apply a simple test to the facts. One asks whether, 'but for' the negligent act, the claimant would have suffered their injury. This requires looking at whether, on the balance of probabilities, the negligent act was the most likely cause of the claimant's injury. Where there is an over 50 per cent chance that the negligent act was the cause, it is treated as the 100 per cent cause. Where it is shown that the injury was likely to have occurred even without the negligence, the defendant cannot be deemed the factual cause of the injury. **Hotson v East Berkshire AHA** [1987] AC 750 illustrates this, with

[1] It is the decision of the case and its reasoning here which you need to illustrate your point, so there is no need to give a fuller factual account.

the judge holding that as there was only a 25 per cent chance that without the negligence the condition would have been avoided, the injury was already in place prior to the negligence.[1] In **Bonnington Castings Ltd v Wardlaw** [1956] AC 613, Lord Reid noted the authorities supported the proposition that the question is whether on the balance of probabilities the defendant caused or materially contributed to the injury. Although **Wardlaw** concerned cumulative causes, the issue of material contribution to the injury applies where the cause is one of several distinct factors as seen in **Wilsher v Essex AHA** [1988] AC 1074. Here a prematurely born baby was given excessive oxygen by the hospital and later suffered blindness, but there were four other completely separate risks which the baby was exposed to which could have caused the blindness. Lord Bridge framed the question throughout as one of showing that the excess oxygen administered to the baby was the cause or material contribution of the blindness. However, the problem was the presence of the other factors, which meant that it could not be shown that 'but for' the contribution of the negligent cause, the injury would not have occurred. The application of the 'but for' test for the material contribution of injury in such a case was affirmed in **Bailey v Ministry of Defence** [2009] 1 WLR 1052.

[2] The fact that these cases are set in a different context is important as to why the same policy factors as *Wilsher* have not been applied. Therefore, you need to flag up this difference in setting.

[3] Do not forget this qualification to the decision as this forms part of the justification to the decision.

[4] By referring to Lord Rodger in *Fairchild*, you have high level authority for the statement that you are making.

As **Wilsher** shows, the test has been rigorously applied in medical negligence cases: however, in cases of negligent exposure to industrial illnesses,[2] the courts have been willing to relax the 'but for' test to overcome causal uncertainties. In **Wardlaw,** while the fact that a material contribution would suffice as opposed to actually causing the injury, the issue was complicated by the fact that the case concerned a cumulative-cause scenario. Wardlaw contracted pneumoconiosis from inhaling silicon dust while at work. There were two sources of inhalation, an innocent cause from using a pneumatic hammer, which could not be avoided, and a negligent cause by his employer who had failed to maintain the extraction plant. Wardlaw succeeded as, while it could not be said that 'but for' the negligence the injury would not have occurred – indeed the evidence showed it was insufficient to have caused it – the evidence showed that his employer's contribution to him contracting the illness was more than negligible.[3] In **Fairchild v Glenhaven Funeral Services Ltd** [2002] UKHL 22 Lord Rodger expressly stated[4] that the 'but for' test is departed from in such situations.

The approach was developed further by **Mcghee v National Coal Board** [1973] 1 WLR 1. McGhee, through his job, was non-negligently exposed to brick-dust and then negligently not provided with washing facilities, which prolonged the exposure while he travelled home. Subsequently, he developed dermatitis which medical evidence showed was from the exposure. However, the evidence only showed that the prolonged exposure increased the risk of dermatitis but not that this negligent exposure had caused it. Lord Reid felt that there was no distinction between a material contribution and a material increase in risk, although this was rejected in **Fairchild.** Lord Wilberforce justified liability on the basis that where a person creates a risk by breaching a duty, and injury ensues from within the area of risk, he should bear the loss unless he can show there was another cause. This was a matter of justice as the employer should be taken to foresee the possible injury and thus bear the consequences.[5] At first glance this might seem unfair on the defendant who becomes liable for injury which it is unclear that he caused. However, it certainly achieves justice for the claimant and would seem to be grounded in tort principles, such as ideas of corrective justice and loss distribution. A wrong has been done with a foreseeable outcome; the employer is in a better position to bear such a loss through insurance and could prevent liability through better working practices, another aim of tort.

Therefore, a shift in approach has been undertaken by the courts in relation to causation and the application of the 'but for' test, with departure permitted where, as Lord Rodger states in **Fairchild,** 'it is inherently impossible for the claimant to prove exactly how his injury was caused'. The principle, started in **Wardlaw** and developed in **McGhee,** can be applied where the claimant has proved all they can, with the causal link of the injury needing scientific investigation which cannot be concluded because science itself is uncertain as to the cause.[6] **Wilsher** appeared to make a distinction between industrial cases and medical cases. While justified on the grounds of protecting NHS funds, this has now rightly been removed by **Bailey** which stated that there is no policy reason for not applying **McGhee** in cumulative-cause medical cases, which does provide some consistency.[7]

However, **Bailey** did retain a distinction between cases where the cause is cumulative but flowing from essentially the same substance or where there are distinct, alternative causes as in **Wilsher.** In the

[5] This is still part of Lord Wilberforce's reasoning which you need to set out before considering whether *McGhee* was an acceptable departure from the traditional position.

[6] Although a judicial quote has just been stated on how/when the principle operates, you ought to demonstrate that you understand it by explaining it and developing the point.

[7] It is important to explore why the distinction existed and the nature of that distinction, i.e. you comment on whether it is right or wrong that *Bailey* has exposed the medical profession to potentially more litigation.

[8] Refer to your previous comment to justify your point without repeating in full what you have already said.

[9] If you are arguing that there is a distinction, you need to highlight why this is the case and then argue whether there is a good reason for it, or not.

former, to alleviate the evidential uncertainty the 'but for' test is departed from, and possibilities are considered rather than probabilities. As noted above,[8] this is justifiable under tort principles, but it raises questions as to why the same tort principles are not applied to a *Wilsher*-style case. However, the key distinguishing factor is that in *Wilsher* there were several independent causes.[9] No commonality existed and so it is hard to say that the hospital's negligence even contributed to the injury; the uncertainty is too great. Imposing liability would be too unfair and thus justice is ensured between the parties in question; no wrong needs correcting.

✓ Make your answer stand out

- Evaluate the merits of the single agent theory as the basis for continuing to distinguish *Wilsher* v *Essex AHA* [1988] AC 1074 from *McGhee* v *National Coal Board* [1973] 1 WLR 1. Look at the opinion of Lord Hoffmann in *Fairchild* v *Glenhaven Funeral Services Ltd* [2002] UKHL 22, who did not think it was satisfactory, although he did change his mind in *Barker* v *Corus UK Ltd* [2006] 2 AC 572.

- Offer a view about whether material contribution is different to material increase in risk; if you think it is, are both equally justifiable?

- Include academic opinion throughout to support your discussion. Consider: Lee, J. (2008) Causation in negligence: another fine mess. *Professional Negligence,* 24: 194 and Bailey, S. (2010) What is a material contribution? *Legal Studies,* 30: 167.

- Analyse the specific approach taken in mesothelioma cases drawing on *Fairchild* v *Glenhaven Funeral Services Ltd* [2002] UKHL 22, *Barker* v *Corus UK Ltd* [2006] 2 AC 572 and *Sienkiewicz* v *Greif (UK) Ltd* [2011] UKSC 10 and the Compensation Act 2006, section 3.

- Consider the potential overlap with issues for loss of a chance.

! Don't be tempted to . . .

- Focus your answer solely on mesothelioma and the discussion of such principles in cases such as *Fairchild* v *Glenhaven Funeral Services Ltd* [2002] UKHL 22, *Barker* v *UK Ltd* [2006] 2 AC 572 and *Sienkiewicz* v *Greif (UK) Ltd* [2011] UKSC 10. The question is framed more generally than that.

- Leave out a discussion of the policy factors which underpin why each case was decided in the way it was. These are needed to more fully assess whether the decisions reached in the cases as to test of causation to apply are justifiable for those situations.

📝 Question 3

'The common law imposes duties and seeks to provide appropriate remedies in the event of a breach of duty. If negligent diagnosis or treatment diminishes a patient's prospects of recovery, a law which does not recognise this as a wrong calling for redress would be seriously deficient today.' (*Per* Lord Nicholls in *Gregg* v *Scott* [2005] 2 AC 176 at 185E.)

Critically evaluate whether the law on causation is 'deficient' and loss of a chance should be an actionable head of damage.

Answer plan

➡ Outline the factual background of *Gregg*.

➡ Set out the majority's view, evaluating the compatibility of each judge's reasoning.

➡ Discuss whether the decision leaves the law 'deficient'.

➡ Evaluate whether the opinion of Lord Nicholls satisfactorily counters the majority's concerns.

➡ Conclude which view is more justifiable.

Diagram plan

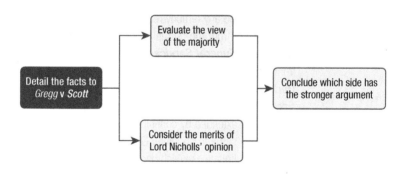

A printable version of this diagram plan is available from **www.pearsoned.co.uk/lawexpressqa**

Answer

[1] By stating these points here, you are showing that you are aware of the context in which the debate is taking place and providing the marker with insight into the reasoning that will form the basis of your argument.

Whether loss of a chance is an injury which warrants being an actionable head of damage in negligence is an important issue, as recognising such harm would give effect to a fundamental principle of tort, namely corrective justice. However, it would potentially increase litigation against the NHS and lead to defensive medical practices.[1] It will be argued that theoretically the stronger argument is that it should be adopted while equally any practical complaints can be overcome.[2]

In *Gregg v Scott* [2005] 2 AC 176, the defendant misdiagnosed a lump under the claimant's arm as harmless when in fact it was cancerous. The misdiagnosis was revealed nine months later when Gregg visited another GP after the lump had grown.[3] Resultantly, the cancer spread, reducing Gregg's chances of recovery from 42 per cent to 25 per cent, therefore no injury had occurred which was caused by Scott. On the balance of probabilities, there was no chance of recovery to lose. Gregg unsuccessfully appealed on two grounds, the second being that loss of a chance should be an actionable injury itself.

[3] Save yourself time by being brief with the factual background to the case. This is needed just to provide the context to the debate on the issue in the House of Lords.

Lord Hoffmann dismissed this ground[4] for lacking a principled basis. He regarded the law as deeming everything to have a determinate cause, even if that cause is not known. A lack of knowledge and evidential difficulty do not make the cause indeterminate. He considered economic loss cases could be explained owing to an act of an independent third party, which was not the case here; it was simply whether the defendant caused the injury.

[4] You need to state what position each of their Lordships was coming from as this was a majority decision.

[5] This indicates that you have read the case in full and know the full range of arguments advanced before their Lordships.

Responding to counsel's argument that a wrong required remedying,[5] he argued any remedy required widening the limited exception for departing from the normal rules of causation from *Fairchild v Glenhaven Funeral Services Ltd* [2003] 1 AC 32 and departing from *Wilshire v Essex AHA* [1988] AC 1074 and *Hotson v East Berkshire AHA* [1987] AC 750; yet the arguments had not changed since those cases. Gregg argued that the *Fairchild* principle could be narrowly extended by confining it to cases in which the claimant had already suffered an injury. Lord Hoffmann felt this was artificial and akin to limitations which had 'disfigured' the law on psychiatric injury. Such a restriction had no underlying principle to it, nor did the alternative restriction of limiting the principle to cases where medical knowledge of the cause was lacking. While Lord Hoffmann was adamant that the claim should not succeed, no reason was advanced against the latter restriction and it was the complete opposite of how Lord Nicholls saw that issue.[6]

[6] This sentence allows your answer to flow naturally into how Lord Nicholls saw the matter.

[7] Make sure you show that you are aware that he was not in the majority, to give the context of why he took the opposite view.

[8] Starting with this part of his opinion straightaway gives weight to the comparative evaluation which you should be seeking to provide in your answer, as it is in direct contrast to the argument which you have advanced.

Lord Nicholls, allowing the appeal,[7] felt the matter was, in principle, 'clear and compelling';[8] actionable loss should cover the loss of a favourable outcome rather than just the lost outcome itself. He argued this would 'match medical reality' and recognise what, in practice, the patient had before the negligent act and thus what has been lost. He further argued that the extent of the duty owed by doctors is to exercise care and skill when diagnosing and treating patients. This is hollowed by stating that just because a favourable outcome was originally less than 50 per cent it can be negligently reduced; there would be no need to exercise the requisite care on a patient in such a position.

Underlying this reasoning was the recognition that tort's principal objective is to provide redress where a duty has been breached. The principle of corrective justice centres on injuries being corrected by the payment of compensation; it is hard to see even on grounds of distributive justice why the former should be departed from. Lord Nicholls argued that leaving a claimant without redress in this situation would leave the law deficient and, notwithstanding Lord Hoffmann's view, 'open to reproach' in light of the differing approach taken to loss of financial opportunities.

He furthered countered Lord Hoffmann's argument by considering that it is not always true that the patient's actual condition at the time of the negligence will determine the answer to the hypothetical question which must be asked as to what would have happened 'but for' the negligent act. As such, **Gregg** was not covered by authority as Lord Hoffmann suggested. In **Gregg,** the answer to the latter question was laced with uncertainty and could only be answered by recourse to statistics expressed in percentage terms. Reflecting this, there were no theoretical grounds for holding that compensation could not be awarded for the diminution of recovery. By restricting the development to where the claimant already has the illness complained of, he felt it also left the **Fairchild** principle unaffected.[9]

[9] As you are seeking to rebut the arguments of the majority and show why it should be actionable, you must show how Lord Nicholls countered the arguments of the majority and tie it back to the points you advanced earlier.

It does appear that tort is placing financial interests above the chance of achieving personal well-being, which is strange considering that claims for pure economic loss are tightly restricted. The justification could lie in the practical difficulties in adopting this change. Lord Nicholls addressed some of these implications, although not in as much depth as the theoretical arguments. He simply stated that the fear of floodgates was not a convincing enough reason for departing from the principal objective of tort. In terms of increased costs to the NHS, he felt, while a formidable argument, it was 'unacceptable' and by keeping the development to the tightly defined circumstances which he did and insisting on a significant reduction in the chance of recovery this would combat the issue. Finally, regarding claims that defensive medical practices would result, he noted that doctors are already aware that they face being sued if they are negligent and thus this argument was unimpressive.

It could be said that Lord Nicholls' failure to go into more depth weakened his opinion and he certainly does not counter the argument of Lady Hale that nearly all claims based on loss of an outcome could be changed to a loss of a chance of that outcome. This would result, if both were retained, in the defendant always being liable, as the claimant would always have the fallback position of a proportionate claim. This could be unfair, but it misses the fact that they have been at fault and, therefore, based on corrective justice principles, it is not necessarily an unfair situation. A stronger argument was that for some claimants this could be a negative development. If both types of claims could not be retained and the latter were adopted, then claimants who currently get 100 per cent compensation would suddenly get less. This is detrimental to claimants but arguably fairer for defendants and would further best recognise the medical reality of the situation.

[10] Throughout your answer you will have been looking at the merits of both sides of the argument. However, in your conclusion it is essential, in order to fully answer the question, to come down on one side.

In conclusion, in principle a lost favourable outcome should be actionable.[10] *Gregg* differed from *Hotson;* the eventual outcome 'but for' the negligent act was not determined at the time of that act. Even Lady Hale's concerns could be argued as having some positive consequences, with any issues as to quantifying damages being resolved in practice. Potential implementation difficulties should not prevent the law's development in a fair manner consistent with fundamental principles. The potential impact on the NHS needs to be monitored, with Parliament stepping in if it proves detrimental.

 Make your answer stand out

- Look at the basic objective of tort in order to determine which view in *Gregg* v *Scott* [2005] 2 AC 176 was right.
- Explain the extent of the principle in *Fairchild* v *Glenhaven Funeral Services Ltd* [2003] 1 AC 32.
- Draw on the arguments of academics such as Reece, H. (1996) Losses of chances in the law. *Modern Law Review,* 59: 188.

■ Consider whether loss of a chance needed to be actionable if the majority had been persuaded by the quantification argument within the first ground of appeal. On this point, read Gore, R. (2012) Loss of chance, Lord Hope's dissent in *Gregg* v *Scott* [2005] UKHL 2, in Geach and Monaghan (eds.), *Dissenting Judgments in the Law.* London: Wildy, Simmonds & Hill Publishing.

! Don't be tempted to . . .

■ Put too much factual background surrounding the illness and misdiagnosis and get too technical in terms of medical terminology.

■ Cover all the points raised by their Lordships in *Gregg* v *Scott* [2005] 2 AC 176 as you will simply run out of time for your answer.

■ Dwell on the first ground of appeal, the quantification argument, as the question centres on the second ground. Therefore, in light of the point above you do not need to worry about Lord Hope so much in this question.

🖎 Question 4

'The *Polemis* rule works in a very strange way. After the event a fool is wise. But it is not the hindsight of a fool; it is the foresight of the reasonable man which alone can determine responsibility.' (*Per* Viscount Simonds in *Overseas Tankship (UK) Ltd* v *Morts Dock & Engineering Co. Ltd (The Wagon Mound (No. 1))* [1961] AC 388 at 424)

In light of this statement evaluate the judicial approach to the issue of remoteness of damage.

Answer plan

➜ Outline the requirements and operation of the test in *Re Polemis.*

➜ Discuss what problems arose through the test's use.

➜ Highlight the approach adopted in *The Wagon Mound (No. 1).*

➜ Evaluate the requirement for change and whether it has solved the highlighted problems.

➜ Have there been adverse consequences because of the change?

Diagram plan

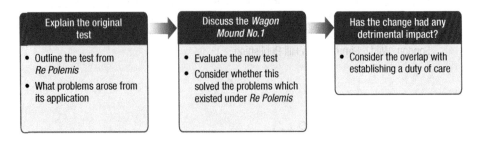

A printable version of this diagram plan is available from **www.pearsoned.co.uk/lawexpressqa**

Answer

For any claim to be successful in tort, the injury suffered must not be too remote from the act of the defendant. Therefore, the issue is how the courts should best go about determining whether negligent acts will be deemed to be the legal cause of injury. This has implications for claimants as, even if the defendant factually caused the injury, they may still not receive compensation. The current approach will be evaluated to explain why it is better than the original approach from **Re Polemis** [1921] 3 KB 560.

Remoteness is the law's attempt to limit liability on policy grounds even where the defendant has factually caused the injury.[1] This restriction is justified[2] as liability is based on the risk that the negligence creates. If the injury is outside of this risk, it is unfair to impose liability. The issue, therefore, is how the law determines whether the injury was within the scope of risk for which liability should result.

Originally, following **Re Polemis,** remoteness was determined by looking at whether the injury was a direct consequence of the negligent act regardless of its foreseeability. In the case, a ship was destroyed when, through the negligence of the stevedores, a rope from a sling led to a wooden plank dropping into the ship's hold, which in turn caused a spark because the hold contained benzine vapour.[3] The court acknowledged that this outcome was not a foreseeable consequence of the negligent act. However, it held that provided the outcome was a direct cause of the negligence, it was irrelevant whether the defendant could anticipate that outcome. Foreseeability

[1] Before you can discuss whether the approach to remoteness is appropriate, you need to explain what this aspect of negligence is about and what it attempts to do.

[2] By then discussing whether the actual purpose of remoteness is justified, you have more scope to argue that perhaps the law should be different; would a change in approach allow the law to be more justifiable, or strengthen its overall purpose?

[3] You need the key facts in order to highlight how the test operates, and then you can decide whether the approach is fair or not by using these as an illustration.

of the consequences went towards negligence not compensation. What would amount to 'direct' was not explained, and questions could be asked about how someone is meant to guard against such an outcome if they do not know what they may be liable for. However, the decision itself can be said to be fair; a negligent act was performed which caused damage. As such, liability should ensue as that damage was caused by the negligence, thereby sanctioning negligent behaviour and awarding compensation for loss suffered, which are two functions of tort.[4] The decision could also be justified owing to the circumstances of the time. As Davies (1982) noted, the case was tried during a slump in the shipping industry[5] and so the decision would have been a further blow to a struggling shipping industry if liability was not found. While not stated as a reason within the case, Davies argues it must surely have played a part; owing to the importance of shipping at the time this seems a fair assessment.

Although no criticism regarding excessive liability was made following the decision, negative comment did emerge after **Donoghue v Stevenson** [1932] AC 562 established a general principle for imposing a duty of care in novel situations. Academic criticisms over excessive liability were also combined with judicial comments, subsequent to **Donoghue,** which were at odds with **Re Polemis** and which never wholeheartedly endorsed the principle.

This culminated in the Privy Council[6] decision of **The Wagon Mound (No. 1).** Viscount Simonds felt that the **Polemis** approach overcomplicated matters with a prime example being a defence based around intervening acts. Furthermore, he felt that the basis of **Re Polemis,** whereby the issue of foreseeability related to liability rather than whether compensation was payable, was false. He noted that liability is founded upon the consequences of the act, not the act itself. Therefore a new approach was adopted whereby the question to ask is simply: was the injury of a type which was reasonably foreseeable to occur from the negligence? His Lordship felt that it was unjust to impose liability simply because an injury is a natural consequence, especially if completely unforeseeable.[7] Although he noted the opposite was true, where injury is reasonably foreseeable, even if an indirect consequence of the act, liability is fair and just. To hold otherwise would be at odds with principles of civil liability that a person is only liable for the probable causes of his/her acts, while still leaving minimum standards to be observed by society.

[4] Give your own view on whether the test has merit. Your purpose here is to help set up the debate later in your answer about whether a change was needed.

[5] The point of highlighting this is so you can give some context to the decision and then also argue whether, even if the principle behind the case is flawed, there is still some justification to the decision. You are looking to provide an explanation for the case.

[6] By including reference to this you could explore how binding this decision should be.

[7] As you are stating that the law was changed, you need to explain what his reasoning was. This then allows you to evaluate whether the reasoning, and by extension the change, was justifiable.

Interestingly, he did not feel that many cases would be decided any differently, and that in fact where damage was a direct or natural consequence of the act it would be reasonably foreseeable. However, by insisting on reasonable foreseeability as the limitation of liability, it meant that liability was kept within the bounds of common conscience. It is significant that the problems with *Re Polemis* began to emerge following the change to imposing duties in *Donoghue*; indeed Viscount Simonds states that to base remoteness on *Re Polemis* would be a departure from the sovereign principle of *Donoghue.* This ignores that *Re Polemis* was pre-*Donoghue* and decided at a time when the duty concept was narrowly applied to particular relationships. A wider test of remoteness only became an issue when the application of the duty concept was widened in *Donoghue.* However, this development means it is more logical to treat compensation the same as culpability with both based on foreseeability. The injury suffered must be within the scope of any duty owed, otherwise the act cannot be said to be negligent. If duty is restricted on this basis, it is indeed unjust to still award compensation for injury which, while a cause of the act, was not something which the defendant could have foreseen and so taken steps to prevent.

[8] Even if you feel that the change was justified, you ought to explore what the consequences have been. Just because something has merit in theory you still need to look at how it works in practice.

However, the equating of remoteness with reasonable foreseeability has created an overlap with the imposition of the duty of care.[8] This was seemingly accepted by Viscount Simonds, as he states that culpability dependent on reasonable foreseeability is determined by reference to the foreseeability of what actually happened. This raises the question as to why this separate element of the tort is needed.[9] Arguably, for remoteness to have any independent purpose, notwithstanding the opinion of Viscount Simonds, hindsight must play a part.[10] If the aim of remoteness is to determine whether the injury was one that was within the risk to which a duty was owed, then hindsight must be used to establish what risks were created by the act of the defendant. Otherwise, the test advanced by his Lordship does not work.

[9] The point here is to question whether the purpose of the element which you identified earlier is being carried out following this change.

[10] This ties your answer back to address the suggestion of Viscount Simonds in the quote.

In conclusion, while it was in fact *Donoghue* that caused the problems for *Re Polemis* and not the test itself, the argument has merit: it is clear that with the approach to duty of care firmly established, a test based on foreseeability makes more sense. While this approach does raise questions about the overall need for such a test, it creates an extra precaution against liability, helping to ensure that liability and the resultant compensation only occur where justified.

✓ Make your answer stand out

- Read the article by Davies, M. (1982) The road from Morocco: *Polemis* through *Donoghue* to no-fault. *Modern Law Review*, 45(5): 535–55 to gain more depth for your argument around *Re Polemis & Furness, Withy & Co. Ltd* [1921] 3 KB 560.
- In particular, expand on the background context to *Re Polemis & Furness, Withy & Co. Ltd* [1921] 3 KB 560 and whether, in fact, it could be argued that *Donoghue* v *Stevenson* [1932] AC 562 was the problem.
- Make sure you use part of your answer to address the point in the quote that hindsight has no place in the test of remoteness.
- Ensure that you consider whether the direct consequence test has merit, as this enhances the overall evaluative nature of your answer.

! Don't be tempted to . . .

- Get too tied down with the facts of either *Re Polemis & Furness, Withy & Co. Ltd* [1921] 3 KB 560 or *The Wagon Mound (No.1)* [1961] AC 388. The key points can be used to illustrate the application of the particular test, but you will lose time if you go into too much depth.
- Start a more in-depth account of duty of care and what was said in *Donoghue* v *Stevenson* [1932] AC 562 and why it was said.

🔖 Question 5

'[There] is a need in the law of tort for a principle which permits judges to deny recovery to a [claimant] on the ground that to do so would undermine the integrity of the justice system.'
(*Per* McLachlin J in *Hall* v *Hebert* (1993) 101 *DLR* (4th) 129, 179)

In light of this statement, critically discuss the occasions when negligence denies recovery to a claimant by allowing a defendant a defence to the claim and the extent to which this is justified.

Answer plan

→ Consider each defence in turn and explain the circumstances in which each operates.

→ Assess whether there is justification for denying recovery by the claimant based on the principles of each defence.

→ Evaluate the requirements of each as you do so.

Diagram plan

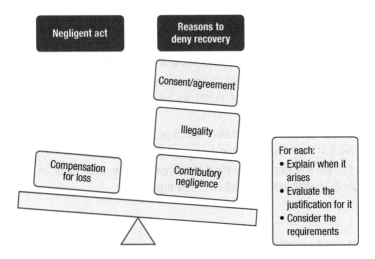

A printable version of this diagram plan is available from **www.pearsoned.co.uk/lawexpressqa**

Answer

As negligence liability is determined by fault, once that is proven, qualifying a person's liability may be difficult to justify. An evaluation of the different defences demonstrates that policy factors provide the justification for their application. However, it is argued that applying contributory negligence more broadly at the expense of the others would produce the fairest outcome in view of the overall principles underlying liability in negligence.

[1] Academically, it is worth acknowledging the debate and assessing the merits of each view, but demonstrate that you are aware of the practical implications of the defence more by highlighting that, in practice, it makes no difference to the individual relying on it. Look to question whether the exceptions undermine the defence or are justified in their own right as this stops your answer just becoming a description of the defence's operation.

The main reason for denying compensation is that, notwithstanding the defendant's fault, the claimant consented to the injury or the risk of it. If one voluntarily invites the risk, they cannot complain if it materialises. Therefore, such a defence makes good sense and is just (***Smith v Baker & Sons*** [1891] AC 325). What is unclear is whether the defence operates by removing the existence of the duty or negating liability for the breach. However, in any event, the overall outcome is the same with the courts determining the final issue on the facts of the case before them.[1]

To justify denying recovery, there must be informed consent as to the nature of the risk of negligent injury (***Nettleship v Weston*** [1971]

2QB 691). It must be shown that the claimant had full knowledge of the extent of the risk that they faced, and that they agreed to that risk. In the absence of an express agreement, it can be implied through a deliberate course of conduct (*Smith*). Secondly, the legal consequences of the risk must be assumed voluntarily (*Nettleship*). Therefore, the defence generally has no applicability in cases involving employees and rescuers, on the basis they act out of compulsion, not their own volition. This is justifiable on policy grounds, as otherwise employers would never be responsible for the safety of their workplaces and rescuers may be deterred from acting.[2] Perhaps more controversially, the defence does not apply to suicides. While seemingly a clear, voluntary act of risking death, applying the defence hollows the specific duty owed by the defendant (*Reeves* v *Metropolitan Police Commissioner* [2000] 1 AC 360). This might seem strange in light of the defence denying the existence of a duty and, as Weir (2006) noted, it is at odds with the concept of personal autonomy. Yet, the non-application of the defence is justified, as the duty is to prevent that very outcome from occurring and the negligence allowed it to in fact occur.

The defence is further limited by statutes.[3] First, section 149 of the Road Traffic Act 1988 provides that a passenger does not consent to the risk of injury by entering a vehicle. As the driver must have insurance for this scenario, it is fair to leave the burden of liability there.[4] The Unfair Contract Terms Act 1977 (UCTA) also limits the defence's application for liability arising out of things done, or to be done, in the course of a business, and on business premises. Liability for negligently caused death or personal injury can never be excluded or limited (s. 2(1)); however, other injuries can be if the relevant clause is reasonable (s. 2(2)). Further, under section 2(3), agreement or awareness of a term purporting to exclude or limit liability for negligence is not to be taken as voluntarily assuming the risk. Policy underlies this; the consent cannot be said to be voluntary as it is extracted from the person who needs to enter the contract and, as such, lacks equality of bargaining power to negotiate the term.

Illegality by the claimant is another reason for denying them recovery. While there is seemingly an obvious public policy justification to the defence, the claimant was injured engaging in criminal activity,[5] the rationale has not, however, always been clearly and consistently

[2] As you have set out previously that the defence is a justified means of denying a claimant recovery overall, you need to offer some explanation of why it is right that it does not apply against all categories of claimant.

[3] The logical place for you to discuss these is after the main discussion on consent, as they restrict the situations when that defence could be said to operate.

[4] Make sure you offer some form of explanation about why the defence is limited by the statute when at a first glance it appears it should apply. The same applies to the legislation governing contracts. Sections 62 and 65 of the Consumer Rights Act 2015 provides the same in relation to consumer contracts.

[5] While your answer will go on to explore how the defence operates and on what basis, make sure you explain why it is needed. This is particularly important with this defence, which has been criticised historically for its lack of coherence.

[6] The purpose here is not to provide the whole history of the defence, but to show that you are aware of its development and the concerns that have fuelled it. Keeping this brief allows you to focus on what the law is now, and whether it is justified now, while benefiting from knowing its past.

[7] This is a good example to use as it is a case which was hard to explain previously as the claim seemed to be founded on the illegal act, which used to be the stated basis for denying recovery.

[8] This shows that you are aware of the change brought about by the Act more succinctly than giving a fuller account of the background to the defence. You can then get on more quickly to how the defence operates.

[9] Include this as an option for the purposes of assessing whether the justice system could be better served in this way rather than having the current different defences. If you agree with the proposition it will allow you to bring your answer together nicely and flow into your conclusion. If you don't agree, mention this at the beginning of this section before explaining why it is not a better approach.

explained, and applied. This led the Law Commission to seek parliamentary clarification for many years. However, following *Gray v Thames Trains Ltd* [2009] UKHL 33 they now believe that the law has been clearly explained.[6] The defence has two forms, with each having a differing policy basis. The narrow form is where the claimant seeks to avoid a penalty imposed on him/her by the criminal law due to his/her illegal act, such as compensation for lost earnings, damage to reputation and general damages for imprisonment. The wider form is where the claimant seeks to recover compensation for the consequences of his/her criminal act, such as compensation to cover their liability for unlawfully killing someone. This latter form was explained by Lord Hoffmann as being justified on the ground that compensating the claimant for the consequences of his/her criminal behaviour would offend public notions of the fair distribution of resources. Alternatively, the narrower form is based on the idea that it would simply be inconsistent to compensate someone for the losses incurred by their going to prison for their criminal behaviour. In the wider sense, the issue becomes one of causation and the question is: was the damage caused by the criminal act; or while the criminal act provided the opportunity for the damage to occur, the tortious act was the immediate cause? This focus on whether the criminal act was incidental to the accident helps retains the legitimacy of the defence, while providing a better rationale for cases such as *Revill v Newbery* [1996] QB 567 where a burglar received compensation for having been shot.[7]

The final way of denying recovery is through the principles of contributory negligence. Following the Law Reform (Contributory Negligence) Act 1945, this is now a partial defence.[8] Damages are reduced to reflect the amount that the claimant contributed to their injury through their negligence; three factors must be proven (*Fookes v Slaytor* [1978] 1 WLR 1293). First, the injury must result from the claimant exposing him/herself to a particular risk. Secondly, his/her negligence contributed to his/her injury; and finally that there was fault on the claimant's part. A reduction will be made regardless of the difficulty ascertaining the exact scope of the contribution (*Capps v Miller* [1989] 1 WLR 839). In *Vellino v Chief Constable of Greater Manchester* [2001] EWCA Civ 1249 Sedley LJ, dissenting, considered that applying this defence is a far more appropriate tool for ensuring justice than applying a full defence to deny liability completely.[9]

While perhaps no longer needed in light of the changes to the illegality defence in **Gray,** this view has force as if the defendant is not liable for the full extent of the injury, it is justifiable to limit damages to the extent to which they are, but the fault of the defendant is still recognised by still requiring compensation.

In conclusion, even though the injury may be the defendant's fault, it is right that defences are applied to deny the claimant compensation. However, relying more on contributory negligence at the expense of the full defences would better strike the required balance between recognising the defendant's fault while also taking account of the claimant's own role in events.

 Make your answer stand out

- Explore in more depth whether contributory negligence is a more justified approach to the issue of denying recovery than the other defences. In particular, explore the dissent of Sedley LJ in more detail.
- Compare the approach and use of defences in this country to other jurisdictions to lend depth to your evaluation.
- Draw on academic writing to substantiate the points that you are making. Consider reading Goudkamp, J. (2017) *Tort Law Defences.* Hart Publishing: Oxford.

! Don't be tempted to . . .

- Just describe each defence; offer some evaluation of why each is needed if liability is based upon the defendant's fault and whether it is justified.
- Discuss the requirements for establishing liability in negligence; it is not needed and will use up time better spent evaluating the merits of the defences.

Try it yourself

Now take a look at the question below and attempt to answer it. You can check your response against the answer guidance available on the companion website (**www.pearsoned.co.uk/lawexpressqa**).

'It is important that the elusive conception of causation should not be frozen into constricting rules.' *Per* Laws LJ in *Rahman* v *Arearose Ltd* [2001] QB 351 at [29].

Evaluate how and when the law has adopted more flexible rules on causation in cases of negligence.

www.pearsoned.co.uk/lawexpressqa

 Go online to access more revision support including additional essay and problem questions with diagram plans, you be the marker questions, and download all diagrams from the book.

Negligence: Combined issue questions

5

How this topic may come up in exams

In the previous chapters we looked at how the aspects of negligence may arise individually as essay questions. Here we combine all of these aspects for problem scenarios. In such a question all aspects of the tort will need to be addressed and skill is needed in identifying the weight which should be given to each aspect. As this is a way of testing your knowledge and understanding of the entire tort, they are very common but, provided you work through the tort logically, they should not be feared. Don't forget questions may be focused on the restricted duty situations; some examples are also included here.

Before you begin

Acquaint yourself with the following components and key issues of this topic; and familiarise yourself with how you would structurally progress through them all, if necessary, when attempting to answer a question on this topic.

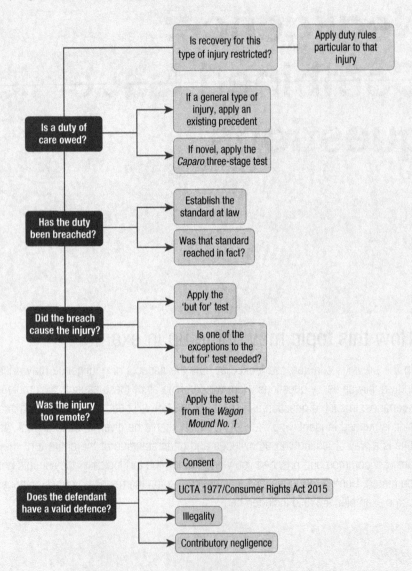

A printable version of this diagram is available from **www.pearsoned.co.uk/lawexpressqa**

🖋 Question 1

Mick had recently purchased a new sports car and, feeling excited, took it out to see how fast he could get it to go. Having got the car up to 90 mph, he saw something in the road and slammed on the brakes. Unfortunately, he lost control and hit the central reservation.

An ambulance arrived and rushed him to Keefstone Hospital where his condition was stabilised. However, following the operation, a nurse from the hospital failed to rehydrate Mick sufficiently, which left him weaker than he would have been.

Subsequently, because of a pre-existing condition which Mick had, a complication developed which required further major surgery. Owing to his increased weakened state, Mick suffered a heart attack. The evidence shows that the heart attack could have been naturally caused because of the trauma of the second surgery, but this is inconclusive; in any event, his weakened state would have heightened the risk of this occurring.

Advise Mick as to whether he has a claim in negligence for his injuries.

Answer plan

➡ Confirm the existence of a duty of care owed by the hospital.

➡ Explain whether, and if so how, it has been breached.

➡ Evaluate the difficulty Mick may face with regard to causation and the non-applicability of the 'but for' test.

➡ Discuss whether, regardless of the lack of firm evidence, Mick could still prove causation.

➡ Consider whether the heart attack is too remote from the breach.

➡ Discuss whether there is a possible defence because of Mick's own negligence in speeding initially.

Diagram plan

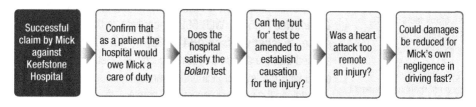

A printable version of this diagram plan is available from **www.pearsoned.co.uk/lawexpressqa**

Answer

[1] As there can be a lot of issues surrounding a negligence problem question, spell out the key issues within the scenario early to show that you have fully understood the question.

In advising Mick on his action for negligence, the rules relating to causation will need particular focus as, on the traditional rules, it seems as if the hospital's act is not the factual cause of his injury.[1] However, it will be argued that Mick's case may warrant a relaxation of these rules and he is likely to be successful in his claim.

[2] The *Caparo* test only applies to novel situations and, therefore, you should not mention it when you have a scenario which is covered by precedent, as it suggests you do not fully understand its operation. While there are more long-standing authorities for the point, factually the situation is the same as *Bailey* so you can justifiably use *Bailey*, which is then easier when you refer to it again.

The first aspect of negligence which needs to be satisfied is that the hospital must have owed Mick a duty of care. As this is not a novel situation, precedent must be relied on to determine the matter, which clearly shows in this situation a duty is owed: for example, ***Bailey v Ministry of Defence*** [2008] EWCA Civ 883 which is factually similar to Mick's case.[2] Therefore, the hospital can be said to have owed Mick a duty of care in relation to his operation and the subsequent treatment which would follow.[3]

[3] Make sure that you explain what the duty of care in the instant case is and the extent of that duty, because this will be relevant in terms of determining breach and whether the damage is too remote.

Once a duty is imposed, it then needs to have been breached. This occurs when the defendant's conduct falls below a reasonable standard. Here it will need to be shown that the standard of the operation and aftercare was unreasonable owing to a failure to sufficiently rehydrate Mick following the operation.[4] Mick should be advised that there are two legal questions to ask: what is the required standard and, on the facts, does the conduct fall short of the standard? In terms of the first question, the legal standard is normally to take such care as is reasonable in the circumstances (***Paris v Stepney BC*** [1951] AC 367) and determined objectively. However, when the issue is one of professional negligence, as is the case here in dealing with a surgical operation, the standard is altered to take account of the professional status of the defendant (***Bolam v Friern Hospital Management Committee*** [1957] 1 WLR 582), regardless of their level of experience (***Wilsher v Essex AHA*** [1988] AC 1074).[5] Mick should be advised that the standard required becomes whether the defendant acted with the level of skill and competency expected of someone undertaking the activity in question. Therefore, the question is simply whether a reasonable nurse would have provided the level of rehydration which was given to Mick. While we are not told whether others would have provided the same level of rehydration, owing to the risks brought by the level provided and following a major operation, it is unlikely to be the standard of a reasonable nurse.

[4] So that you can fully explore whether there has been a breach, you need to highlight, out of the facts, what the potential act is which breached the duty.

[5] Even though the question does not mention the extent of the nurse's experience, show that you are aware of the potential issue by advising Mick briefly how this will not affect his claim.

[6] As this part of the claim is inconclusive at this stage, and you are offering advice, emphasise that this aspect is conditional on the previous requirement. This will also illustrate your understanding by showing that you are not making firm opinions when the evidence does not necessarily confirm the view.

[7] This is the main focus of this question so you should factor in most time for this part of your answer.

[8] Even if you recognise straightaway that this is not a 'but for' scenario, you should follow a logical progression through what the law requires. Therefore, set out how this normally applies first rather than jumping to the relaxed rules.

[9] As there have been two operations, identify which one is in issue here, particularly as the first operation appeared successful.

[10] Quoting the facts will strengthen the suggestion that the principle applies.

[11] By stating this, you allude to knowing the issues around the overlap between duty and damage since they are both based on foreseeability following the *Wagon Mound (No. 1)* case.

If a breach is found,[6] the next issue to advise Mick on is whether this left him so significantly weakened as to cause or materially contribute to his heart attack[7] (*Bailey*). Normally, causation is determined on the balance of probabilities by reference to the 'but for' test[8] (*Cork v Kirby Maclean* [1952] 2 All ER 402): 'but for' the negligent rehydration would the injury have been suffered? On the facts this cannot be said to be so, as the heart attack may have been caused through non-negligent means, the trauma of the second[9] operation. However, this is a cumulative cause scenario whereby, because of evidential difficulties, the 'but for' test is not applied. Under *Bonnington Castings Ltd v Wardlaw* [1956] AC 613, provided there is a negligent contribution which is more than negligible, it will suffice as a causative factor. While the hospital may claim that the evidence here does not even show that the lack of hydration made any contribution to the heart attack, this may not matter. The *Wardlaw* principle was developed in *McGhee v National Coal Board* [1973] 1 WLR 1 so that causation can be satisfied where the evidence shows the negligence caused a material increase in the risk of the harm suffered. This is the situation here as we are told that the risk of the heart attack was 'heightened'[10] by Mick's increased weakened state that resulted from the rehydration failure. It was doubted, following *Wilsher,* that this relaxation of the causation rules would apply to medical negligence cases and instead was limited to industrial cases. However, following *Bailey* the distinction is between distinct, independent causes as in *Wilsher,* or cumulative causes as in *Wardlaw.* It was held that there was no sufficient policy reason for not applying the relaxed rules for the latter scenario even where it is medical negligence. On the authority of *Bailey,* and especially in light of the similarities, it would appear that there is sufficient factual causation.

Even if the breach was the factual cause of Mick's injury, it must also be the legal cause. This means that the injury suffered must be of a type which was reasonably foreseeable (*Wagon Mound No. 1* [1961] AC 388) and not too remote. Arguably, this is satisfied here as a heart attack is a foreseeable occurrence in such incidents and could be said to show that a duty is recognised in this situation.[11] The fact that Mick was suffering a pre-existing condition which necessitated the second operation will also not matter as an 'eggshell skull' rule applies in negligence (*Smith v Leech Brain & Co. Ltd* [1962] 2 QB 405), meaning that the hospital must take Mick as they find him.

[12] Demonstrate that you appreciate this by stating it as you introduce it.

Therefore, it appears that Mick would have a valid claim for negligence; however, he should be advised that the hospital may seek to rely on the partial[12] defence of contributory negligence; if successful, this would mean any compensation is reduced to take account of his own negligence. They may argue that the only reason Mick was in hospital was through his own negligence: speeding, which caused the initial crash. However, while Mick may satisfy the first requirement of *Fookes* v *Slaytor* [1979] 1 All ER 137 that the injury resulted from a risk which Mick exposed himself to, his negligence needs to contribute to the injury suffered. The evidence does show that the heart attack was contributed to by his non-negligently caused weakened state following his operation and this could be traced back to him crashing his car. Therefore, this could be a contributing factor to his injury; however, Mick should be advised that as the injury occurred following the negligence and the second operation, not the operation following the crash, a contributory finding may be unlikely. Finally, the hospital must show negligence on Mick's part which, as noted, is easily satisfied as he was speeding.

[13] Remember to use consistent wording: earlier it was couched in less than absolute terms so do not make it concrete now.

To conclude, Mick was owed a duty of care by the hospital which seems[13] to have been breached; this is likely to be deemed to have caused the injury under the principle from *McGhee.* As this injury is not legally too remote, Mick is likely to succeed in his claim; however, this would be subject to a possible reduction for his own negligence in crashing his car initially.

 Make your answer stand out

- Explain how, even though the negligence was the act of an individual nurse, the hospital will be vicariously liable (*Cassidy* v *Ministry of Health* [1951] 2 KB 762).
- Discuss the issue of the skill and experience of the nurse.
- Consider the potential counter to the *Bolam* principle which the hospital could make under *Bolitho* v *City & Hackney Health Authority* [1997] 3 WLR 1151.
- Evaluate the policy factors flowing from the decision in *Bailey* v *Ministry of Defence* [2008] EWCA Civ 883 and its potential impact on the health service.

Question 2

Alf and Bert are a pair of low-level criminals who specialise in home break-ins and carjackings. One day the pair had planned to steal a car by staging an accident. Alf pretended to collapse in the road as Eddie was approaching, and made out that he was having a heart attack. Panicking, Eddie slammed on the brakes, stopped and rushed out to help. As he did, Bert rushed out from behind a parked car and bundled Eddie over. Alf and Bert then jumped into the car. As Alf had recently learned to drive they had agreed that he would be the getaway driver. However, just as this was happening PC Wedgewood drove around the corner on patrol. Seeing as Eddie appeared OK, he gave chase after Alf and Bert.

Realising that the pair were being followed by the police Bert starting yelling at Alf, 'Drive faster and lose the copper, you idiot!' Alf sped up, but the pair started to bicker about the best way of escaping and so neither was looking at where they were going. As such, Alf did not see that he was coming up to a pedestrian crossing and sped through it without stopping. Reg was crossing the road at that point and dived out of the way. However, he landed awkwardly on his shoulder and elbow and due to an unknown condition suffered multiple fractures and permanent loss of mobility. A person without the condition would just have suffered bruising.

Eventually, Alf took a corner at too much speed and lost control of the car. The car slid off the road and crashed into a lamp post on the near-side pavement. The lamp post made impact with the front passenger door, causing severe injuries to Bert.

Advise Alf on his liability for the injuries suffered by Reg and Bert.

Diagram plan

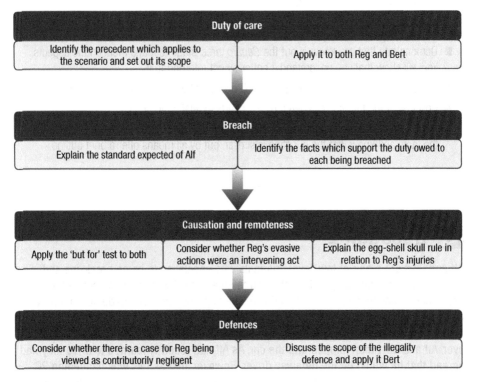

A printable version of this diagram plan is available from **www.pearsoned.co.uk/lawexpressqa**

Answer plan

→ Confirm that Alf, as the driver, owes a duty of care to other road users as well as his passengers.

→ Establish that even though he is an inexperienced driver he is judged to the same standard as a normal driver and so there were breaches of his duty to both Reg and Bert.

→ Apply the 'but for' test in order to identify the causes of each injury and consider whether Reg's actions were an intervening act.

→ Consider the principle of remoteness and draw on the 'eggshell skull' rule to explain how Reg's injuries will still be considered legally caused by Alf.

→ Evaluate what defences could be relied on by Alf.

Answer

[1] When faced with a question which just says 'Advise X', it is worth spelling out in your first line that you have correctly identified the exact thing that you should be advising the person on.

[2] As there is a precedent regarding the duty in this situation, there is no need to talk about *Caparo*.

[3] While perhaps not the key question for liability in the question, it would be the key question for Alf personally, as for someone unfamiliar with the law; a natural response would be to highlight their lesser experience than the average motorist. This is why it warrants a bit more treatment than you might otherwise be inclined to give.

[4] As this standard is detrimental to Alf's chances of defeating the claim, you should advise him why this is the situation and, in doing so, you will show that you have more than a superficial knowledge of the law.

[5] It is useful here to briefly remind the marker that you know what the scope of the duty owed is; you then need to draw on the facts to illustrate how it was breached. You can save time and not compromise your structure by dealing with duty and breach in relation to both Reg and Bert at the same time.

The issue involves advising Alf on his potential liability in negligence (as the driver) for the personal injuries suffered by Reg and Bert following each incident. This will involve looking at the standard of care required by drivers and the impact on liability of the fact the injury occurred involving a stolen car.[1] It will be argued that Alf has clearly breached the duty of care owed to Reg and Bert, and that this has caused each one injury. However, while he may have a defence against Bert due to the illegality of the incident, he will still be liable to Reg as the injury will not be deemed too remote.

As the car's driver, Alf owes a duty of care to all other road users who may be reasonably foreseeably injured if care is not exercised (*Langley v Dray* [1998] PIQR P314).[2] This duty covers both passengers and pedestrians and so the first element of negligence is satisfied.

The key question, however, is what standard is expected of Alf in order to discharge his duty, especially considering he has only recently passed his test and so has less experience than most drivers.[3] Under *Blyth v Birmingham Water Works Co.* (1856) 11 Ex 781, the expected standard is determined objectively by assessing what the reasonable person would do in the situation; and the reasonable person possesses the standard of foresight, which eliminates the idiosyncrasies of the person whose conduct is in question. This means Alf's inexperience is irrelevant and he will be judged by the same standard expected of someone with more experience (*Nettleship v Weston* [1971] 2 QB 691). This may seem unjust to inexperienced drivers; however, it is necessary in order to overcome the difficulties of determining an individual standard for each and every driver.[4] Therefore, as held in *Langley,* Alf is expected to drive with such care and skill so as to avoid exposing other road users to unnecessary risk of injury. By speeding, not looking where he is going, driving through a red light and generally not paying attention it is clear that Alf has not met the standard of a reasonable driver.[5] As such, Alf has breached the duty owed to both Reg and Bert.

The next consideration is whether each breach of duty was the cause of each injury. Causation is a question of fact whereby it is asked whether, on the balance of probabilities, the injuries would have happened 'but for' Alf's breach (*Cork v Kirby Maclean* [1952] 2 All ER 402). This seems satisfied as, if Alf was not speeding and was

75

[6] Take them in this order as Bert's situation is more clear-cut whereas there is a bit more to say on Reg.

paying attention, he would not have lost control of the car and hit the lamp post, thus injuring Bert. In relation to Reg, Alf could argue that his injuries were caused by Reg jumping out of the way.[6] However, as jumping out of the way of an oncoming car is reasonably foreseeable, Alf should have sought to prevent Reg needing to do it, and clearly Reg would not have needed to if Alf was driving to a reasonable standard. As such, Reg's actions will not be considered an intervening act.

The breach also needs to be the legal cause of the injuries, meaning that the injuries were of a kind, type or class that were reasonably foreseeable (***Wagon Mound (No. 1)*** [1961] AC 388). Again there is no issue with this in relation to Bert's injuries; these were clearly foreseeable due to how Alf was driving. However, Reg's injuries were worse than would be expected due to an unknown condition. This means Alf needs to be advised of the 'eggshell skull' rule. This provides that the defendant must take the claimant as they find them and they will be liable for the entire harm caused, even where it is greater than expected owing to a particular condition of the claimant. This might seem at odds with the principle from ***Wagon Mound (No. 1),*** but it has been held to still apply (***Smith v Leech Brain & Co. Ltd*** [1962] 2 QB 405). As the injury was a type which was still foreseeable, the fact that Reg's condition meant the injury was far more severe will not limit liability.

[7] Normally, because this is only a partial defence, it should be dealt with last; however, as there is no question of the full defences applying it makes sense to deal with it first, as it follows on from the previous paragraph and allows you to finish with Reg. There will be more success against Bert so you can then clearly focus on that in detail.

[8] We do not have much detail in the facts to support this discussion so take care to read what you have been given and draw on what you can to construct as good an argument as you can.

In relation to Reg's claim, the only possible defence that Alf could rely on would be the partial defence of contributory negligence.[7] This reduces the amount of damages payable where just and equitable to reflect the level of negligent contribution to the injury made by the claimant (Law Reform (Contributory Negligence) Act 1945, s. 1). For Reg to be negligent using the pedestrian crossing he would need to have been forbidden to cross at that time due to, for example, pedestrians having a red light. However, the facts suggest that Alf should have stopped and if that was the case, on top of his speeding, it would seem unlikely that Reg was negligent here.[8]

[9] Obviously, there are other actions which Alf may face to which the following may not apply, so it is worth clarifying the scope of the application of the defences.

[10] As the section will bar the application of the defence, there is no more that needs to be said other than this. Do not go on and explain what the defence involves, let alone apply the requirements to the scenario, as it will be a pointless exercise.

Alf should have more chance of avoiding liability in negligence[9] against Bert. Under section 149 of the Road Traffic Act 1988, Alf will not be able to claim that Bert voluntarily assumed the risk of such injury by getting in a car which was being used as a getaway vehicle.[10] However, where Alf may have success is in relying on the full defence of illegality which absolves Alf of all liability. The wider form of the defence, as identified by ***Gray v Thames Trains Ltd*** [2009] UKHL 33, applies where the compensation is sought as a consequence of the claimant's own illegal act. The

[11] Try always to be specific about who said what you are about to advance from the case, as it shows greater knowledge.

[12] Even if you think that the illegality defence would certainly apply, you should still discuss this, as there is a possibility the other defence would not be applied. Further, by doing so you show that you know not only about this issue, but also how it relates to the other defences.

[13] While you will always have a conclusion in negligence problem questions, as there are several issues, sum up events by recapping what you have discussed throughout.

question is whether the criminal act caused the injury, or simply provided the opportunity for it to occur with the tortious act being the immediate cause. This seems more of a case of the former and this is supported by *Ashton* v *Turner* [1981] QB 137, which also concerned an injury suffered by the passenger in a getaway vehicle. As Lord Hoffmann noted in *Gray*,[11] allowing recovery in such circumstances would offend public notions of the fair distribution of resources. Even though Alf lost control and was at fault for the injury, it would be permissible to deny recovery by Bert. If a court were to hold that the claim was not substantially based on the crime, Alf should be advised that he may be successful in pleading contributory negligence on the part of Bert.[12] In terms of what reduction would be made, Alf should be advised that under the Act damages cannot be reduced by 100 per cent, even if it was Bert's idea to take the car and drive in that way (*Pitts* v *Hunt* [1991] 1 QB 24).

In conclusion,[13] Alf should be advised that he owed both Reg and Bert a duty of care which was clearly breached. As those breaches caused the injuries, he would be liable notwithstanding that the extent of Reg's injuries were worse than could have been foreseen. However, owing to the illegality of the situation, Alf will have a defence against Bert.

 Make your answer stand out

- Read *Langley* v *Dray* [1998] PIQR P314 and draw on the judgment of Stuart-Smith LJ to support your discussion of the nature of the duty owed by motorists and the reasons for it.
- Consider the validity of the 'eggshell skull' rule.
- Explain the policy factors which justify defences to an action for negligence when liability has been made out.
- Mention how Alf could also face a claim from Eddie for trespass.

! Don't be tempted to . . .

- Show your wider knowledge of the tort by raising aspects which are not applicable to the scenario. For example, there is no need in relation to causation to discuss anything more than the 'but for' test.
- Repeat things you have already discussed by taking each claim independently of the other from the outset and, therefore, having two paragraphs on duty and breach.
- Explain in detail why there is illegality at the heart of the issue.

Question 3

Paddy Chandler was a long-term alcoholic and was recently told that, owing to his lifestyle, he only had about a 45 per cent chance of living more than three years. After an unexpected bet came off, he decided to check himself into the Ladbroke Hills Private Medical Centre for a liver transplant in order to prolong his life expectancy. Prior to the operation he had spoken to Dr Done, an employed doctor at the Centre, who talked him through the procedure that would be used. Reflecting the seriousness of the situation, a new and innovative procedure was to be used which, while not having wide-scale endorsement, has been supported by a leading expert in the field in a national medical journal.

However, because he believed that Paddy really ought to have the operation, Dr Done chose not to inform Paddy that the operation carried with it a 5 per cent risk that the new liver may not be accepted by his body, which could result in death.

Following the operation, it became apparent that the new liver had not been accepted and Paddy was informed that with some medication the condition could be managed, but he would only have a 20 per cent chance of living longer than three years. Paddy has indicated that, if he had been informed, he might not have gone ahead with the operation.

Advise Paddy as to whether he has a successful negligence action against the medical centre.

Diagram plan

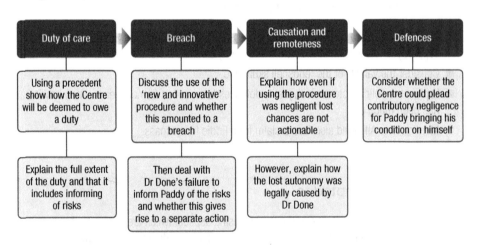

A printable version of this diagram plan is available from **www.pearsoned.co.uk/lawexpressqa**

Answer plan

➡ Explain quickly how a duty of care is owed by the Centre in this situation and set out the full scope of the duty.

➡ Identify the two potential breaches and deal with each, assessing whether they were breached.

➡ Explain how, even if the duty with regard to the operation procedure was breached, it is non-actionable.

➡ Apply the causation rules to the personal autonomy breach and explain how the approach is taken by the courts.

➡ Address any appropriate defences that the Centre may have.

Answer

[1] It is important to highlight early that you have spotted that this is not simply a loss of chance problem scenario and that in fact it is arguably more to do with *Chester* v *Afshar* [2004] UKHL 41. To avoid your answer getting messy, clearly separate out the two issues and then explain to the reader this is what you are doing so they know and thus do not lose track of what you are saying by trying to work out why you are saying it.

[2] By inserting this word, and after citing *Cassidy,* you show that you are aware of the applicability of the doctrine of vicarious liability to this situation, without getting sidetracked by a fuller explanation of it.

In advising Paddy on whether he has a claim against the Centre in negligence, the full extent of the duty owed by the Centre will be established and then the two possible ways any action may be taken will be considered. It will be argued that while it would appear that he has not suffered any actionable injury, merely a lost chance of living more than three years, the presence of the issue of personal autonomy in the matter means that he should have some basis for succeeding in any action.[1]

The first point to establish is that authorities such as ***Cassidy*** **v** ***Ministry of Health*** [1951] 2 KB 343 clearly show that through the doctor–patient relationship the Centre will vicariously[2] owe a duty of care to Paddy when treating and operating on him. It is also important to advise Paddy that there is an additional aspect to the duty, which is to warn Paddy of any significant risks involved (***Montgomery* v *Lanarkshire Health Board*** [2015] UKSC 11). This duty has long been recognised as important (***Sidaway* v *Board of Governors of***

[3] By including this part of the sentence you can show your knowledge of the principle and how long it has been recognised, while also demonstrating that you are aware that there has been a departure from the reasoning in *Sidaway*, you can then explain that in more detail in the more appropriate place later on in your answer.

the *Bethlehem Royal Hospital* [1985] AC 871) even though the view of how it operates has altered over time.[3]

The next issue, therefore, is whether the duty owed to Paddy was breached by the Centre. In taking the duty covering the actual performance of the operation, the standard must be that of the level of skill and competency expected of a person undertaking that activity and with the level of skill that the defendant professes to have (*Bolam v Friern Hospital Management Committee* [1957] 1 WLR 582). While Paddy may argue that the new procedure is not widely endorsed, this is not necessary. Provided the Centre can show that Dr Done acted in accordance with a respectable body of medical opinion, which can withstand logical scrutiny (*Bolitho v City and Hackney Health Authority* [1997] 3 WLR 1151), this standard will be deemed to have been reached. The fact that a leading expert has supported the procedure in a national journal would suggest that the procedure was in line with a respectable body of opinion.

[4] Even if you strongly conclude that the use of the procedure was non-negligent, it is worth adding an additional paragraph on this point – to show that you have recognised that there is a similarity here to *Gregg*, but that you understand the legal position and, therefore, that an action by Paddy on this basis would not work.

Paddy would have a problem though in that, even if it is accepted the use of this new procedure was negligent, he has suffered no actionable injury. Prior to the operation, he only had a 45 per cent chance of living over three years. After the operation he had a 20 per cent chance. Therefore, this makes his position nearly identical to that in *Gregg v Scott* [2005] 2 AC 176 where the House of Lords held that the claimant in fact lost nothing as, on the balance of probabilities, the outcome in question would not have happened, there was no chance to lose. Further, it was held that a reduction in the chance itself should not be an actionable head of injury.[4]

[5] As you discuss how the law has moved on and changed in relation to what needs to be shown, it is beneficial to explain why the change arose. You can then comment on its justification.

However, as explained, the scope of the Centre's duty was wider than merely carrying out the operation in a non-negligent manner. It extended to warning Paddy of the risks which the operation entailed. It was noted in *Montgomery* that the importance of personal autonomy has increased in line with patients no longer being seen as passive recipients of medical care and more as consumers with greater levels of medical knowledge themselves.[5] Therefore, to discharge the duty, a doctor must take reasonable care to ensure that the patient is aware of any material risks involved in any recommended treatment, and of any reasonable alternatives. Paddy should be advised that whether a 5 per cent risk is material is dependent on whether a reasonable person in his position would attach significance to it and Dr Done could justify non-disclosure of the risk if it would have been seriously detrimental to Paddy's health to inform him of the risk. Therefore, more information about why the decision was made and what Paddy may have done with the information is needed. Ultimately though, while the facts suggest that Dr Done was acting to ensure a needed operation occurred, reflecting the emphasis on patients' rights and informed consent, it is likely that the failure to inform Paddy will be deemed a breach.

Paddy should then be advised that the breach of the duty to inform must then be deemed to have caused the injury suffered. As stated, his injury is simply a non-actionable reduction in his chance of survival. Even proceeding on the basis that the injury was the lost ability to make an informed choice, this presents some difficulties because on conventional principles it must be shown that, on the balance of probabilities, 'but for' the negligence, the injury would not have occurred. The issue here is that Paddy may well have proceeded and, therefore, the risk would still have materialised, and the breach would not be the factual cause of the injury. Even if he would not have proceeded, the risk here was not created by the breach but was present regardless and notwithstanding how the operation was performed.[6] However, as Lord Steyn accepted in *Chester* after referring to the academic work of Professor Honoré,[7] the situation which Paddy finds himself in cannot be fitted within normal causation principles, but policy and corrective justice support vindicating his personal autonomy. Otherwise, the duty owed would be stripped of its content and would, in Lord Hope's view in *Chester,* be particularly useless for a patient like Paddy who cannot say what they would have done if they had been properly advised.[8]

Therefore, while it could be argued that factually the injury was not caused by the breach of the duty to warn, as Lord Hope highlighted, the injury was caused in the legal sense. It is on this basis that there would not appear to be any issues regarding remoteness of damage, namely that the injury was a kind, type or class that was reasonably foreseeable (*Wagon Mound (No. 1)* [1961] AC 388). The injury suffered was the failure of the new liver to be accepted by Paddy's body, the risk of which, as in *Chester,*[9] was exactly what he should have been informed of by Dr Done.

[6] By highlighting this you further distance this part of your answer from the previous discussion, as it shows that passing the *Bolam* test has no bearing on this aspect of Paddy's situation.

[7] Professor Honoré was cited by both Lord Steyn and Lord Hope in the majority in *Chester* in support of their opinions; therefore, a small reference such as this allows you to demonstrate your knowledge of their opinions and the wider academic thinking on this issue.

[8] In the latter part of this sentence, use the facts from the question to identify Paddy with the reasoning of Lord Hope to make your application stronger as well as, again, showing an in-depth knowledge of the judicial reasoning which impacts on this point.

[9] Refer to *Chester* to reinforce your argument that legally the breach should be seen as the cause of an actionable injury, i.e. the lost autonomy.

[10] Your aim here is to just briefly raise the possibility, reflecting your awareness of the similar facts between Paddy's situation and that in *St. George*. This also shows that you understand the point by applying it in dismissal of the potential argument by the Centre.

[11] Make sure that you reinforce that the success of any action brought by Paddy would be solely for this injury.

Finally, Paddy should be advised that there does not appear to be any defences which the Centre could rely on to counter any claim. The only possible argument[10] would be that his alcoholism put him in a position whereby he needed treatment and, therefore, this behaviour makes him contributorily negligent. However, following *St George v Home Office* [2008] EWCA Civ 1068, as this was a lifestyle choice made prior to the creation of the duty of care, it cannot be considered for the purposes of reducing any compensation.

In conclusion, while there may be causation issues in Paddy's situation, there has been a clear breach of the Centre's duty to inform Paddy of the operation's risk. This denial of personal autonomy should, on the basis of cases such as *Montgomery* and *Chester*,[11] mean that Paddy would have an action for this loss.

✓ **Make your answer stand out**

- Explain in a bit more detail the issue of vicarious liability.
- Make sure that you clearly distinguish the two potential breaches by the Centre of their duty of care to Paddy.
- Ensure that you have read *Montgomery* v *Lanarkshire Health Board* [2015] UKSC 11 so that you can discuss the change in judicial approach to assessing a breach of the duty to inform patients and the validity of the change.
- Make more reference to academic opinion on the issue of causation and informing patients of risks. A selection of academic articles can be found in the opinion of Lord Steyn in *Chester* v *Afshar* [2004] UKHL 41.
- Draw on the dissenting opinion of Lord Hoffman in *Chester* v *Afshar* [2004] UKHL 41 to give balance to your argument. He expands on this in Hoffman, L. (2005) Causation. *Law Quarterly Review*, 121: 592–603, which is also worth reading in relation to wider issues of causation.
- Add some of the reasons why loss of chance as in *Gregg* v *Scott* [2005] 2 AC 176 is held to be non-actionable.

! **Don't be tempted to . . .**

- Get into too much of an in-depth discussion on whether a lost chance should be an actionable claim. As the law stands it is not; show that you are aware of the differing views in cases such as *Gregg* v *Scott* [2005] 2 AC 176 but remember that this is a problem question on the whole of negligence and not an essay on that specific issue.
- Explain the history of the development of the duty of care.
- Gloss over aspects of negligence which are not in issue; all must be referred to.

⚜ Question 4

Owing to a recent flurry of burglaries in the area, a group of local residents decided to form a neighbourhood watch team. The purpose of the team was to set up a patrol around the area to act as a deterrent by approaching people who looked to be up to no good and to contact the police at the first hint of any criminal activity.

One of the members, Brandon, had that day gone away for the night and, having realised he had left a downstairs window open, sent a text to Mac, a friend but non-member, asking him to close it for him. However, Mac was busy getting ready to go out and thought there would be nothing to worry about as the neighbourhood watch patrol would go past Brandon's house regularly, and it was only for one night.

That evening, it was Keith's turn to do the patrol. Keith had already worked a long day at the factory where he was employed and so felt tired. As he approached Brandon's house he saw someone climbing through the window but just wanting to get home to watch TV he did nothing, thinking it was just someone who had locked themselves out.

The next day, Brandon returned home to see his house had been burgled with all of his belongings taken. The burglar has never been caught.

Brandon now seeks your advice on whether he could bring a claim against Mac or Keith, as he holds them responsible for what happened.

Diagram plan

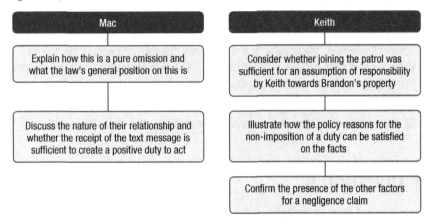

A printable version of this diagram plan is available from **www.pearsoned.co.uk/lawexpressqa**

Answer plan

➜ Set out the general position regarding omissions and deal with Mac's potential liability first.

➜ Consider if there is an assumption of responsibility by Mac towards Brandon which warrants imposing a positive duty to act.

➜ If so, assess whether the duty was breached and confirm the other elements of negligence.

➜ Assess the potential liability of Keith on the same basis.

Answer

The issue to determine is whether Brandon has a claim in negligence, even though Mac and Keith have not performed any positive acts. This is important, as usually the law only permits this in limited situations and thus, if they do not fit those, Brandon will be left without redress for his loss. It will be argued that Mac does not owe a duty, but Keith may well be held liable.

As indicated, the general position in negligence is that a duty of care will not be imposed in relation to omissions (**Smith v Littlewoods Organisation** [1987] 1 AC 241). It is clear in relation to Mac that this is a case of a pure omission as opposed to being a failure to act as part of a wider positive course of conduct, such as not stopping at a

[1] The point is to show that you are aware of the distinction between the two, and using the facts to confirm what we are dealing with here. This is important as the law does impose duties in the latter type of situation.

[2] At this point you are explaining why Brandon is unlikely to succeed in making a claim against someone. As the point of the question is to advise him on the law, you have to make sure you state the reasons why he would not have a claim. If you imagine him in front of you, he would be asking why not, so tell him.

[3] Whereas before you were highlighting how the reasons were not satisfied, now you need to use the facts to show how they have been overcome, as this is what will justify the courts imposing a duty on Keith.

[4] The presence of an assumption of responsibility will generally warrant imposing a duty of care; however, the same facts would also generally satisfy the *Caparo* test. A negative finding of an assumption of responsibility does not preclude reference being made to *Caparo* and so it is worth highlighting it here to reinforce why you feel Keith is likely to owe a duty in this situation.

red light, which will carry a duty.[1] Mac received the text message but clearly omitted to do anything about it and so this is the former category and within the general rule. However, exceptions to this position were outlined by Lord Goff in *Smith*. Of these, the most likely to be applicable is that Mac assumed responsibility for Brandon's property. Brandon could argue that by asking Mac to close the window and highlighting the present danger a duty should be imposed. However, Brandon should be advised that this is unlikely to be accepted, as there was no confirmation by Mac that he would do so. Had Mac done so, then a duty would be present, as Brandon would have had trust and confidence in Mac's words, which would justify a finding of an assumption of responsibility. In the absence of a reply confirming he would act, the political reason given by Lord Hoffmann in *Stovin v Wise* [1996] AC 923 for not imposing a duty for omissions is not addressed. The reason is that it is a greater invasion of a person's freedom to compel them to act than it is to require them to take care of others when they have chosen to embark on a course of conduct.[2] This can only be justified when there is an element of proximity between the parties, which their friendship alone is unlikely to create.

Brandon should be advised, however, that he may be more successful in a claim against Keith. While, again, this is a case of a pure omission, the reason for the greater likelihood of success is that Keith is a member of the neighbourhood watch patrol and was meant to be keeping an eye out for burglars that night. By accepting this role, Keith assumed responsibility towards those residents who are covered by the patrol, which includes Brandon. As such, the political reason stated above is overcome; he has volunteered to act and failed to do so.[3] The moral reason advanced by Lord Hoffmann for not imposing a duty is also satisfied. This is based on the idea that there could be an indeterminate class of potential defendants in an omission situation, raising the question of why it is justifiable to pick out the actual defendant for liability. However, here, as Keith was performing the patrol that night, it is morally right to pick him out for liability over others.

Those factors which suggest an assumption of liability also suggest that the tripartite *Caparo* test[4] for imposing a duty is satisfied here. It is clearly foreseeable that, if Keith omitted to approach the person climbing through the window, at the time of widespread burglaries, harm could be caused to the property in question. While it was stated in *Smith* that mere foreseeability is not sufficient to create a duty to prevent criminal acts by a third party, the facts indicate that the key requirement of proximity exists between Brandon, as a resident under the patrol's remit, and Keith who was undertaking the patrol. These factors combined, by addressing the policy concerns for imposing a duty, mean that it would be fair, just and reasonable to impose a duty on Keith.

[5] The duty of care is only one part of negligence and, while this is the focus of the question, it is important that you cover all the aspects, although naturally these will not need as much depth.

As it seems likely that Keith will owe duty of care, Brandon now needs advising as to whether the rest of the elements for a claim in negligence are satisfied.[5] By not doing anything when he saw the person climbing through the window, it would seem apparent that Keith failed to reach the standard of care expected of a reasonable person: the likelihood of harm was increased and thus Keith should have approached the person, or at least contacted the police, as that was part of the patrol's remit.

'But for' this breach, Brandon's loss of property would also not have occurred. If he had approached the person and/or called the police, the incident would have been prevented or the person apprehended and, therefore, the causal link required is established. While usually the deliberate wrongdoing of a third party will be deemed an independent cause of the loss (*Weld-Blundell* v *Stephens* [1920] AC 956) exceptionally, where for example the duty in question is to prevent that third party from doing the wrong, as here, it shall not be classed as an intervening act (*Dorset Yacht Club* v *Home Office* [1970] AC 1004). The scope of the duty also means there is not any issue of remoteness. Here the loss suffered by Brandon is stolen property and so it is of a type that was reasonably foreseeable as required by *Wagon Mound (No. 1)* [1967] 1 AC 617.

[6] By this stage of your answer, if you have time, you could name the defences but it is not necessary. As they are clearly not applicable to Keith, there certainly is no need to discuss them in detail. Therefore, by treating them like this, you show that you understand the full extent of them, which is more important than showing that you simply know them.

However, Brandon should be advised that, if successful, any compensation received may well be reduced on the grounds of contributory negligence. This is because he was aware of the danger of being burgled by leaving his window open, as shown by his text to Mac. However, it is unlikely that any of the full defences[6] to a negligence claim can be relied on by Keith.

In conclusion, Brandon should be advised that he is unlikely to succeed with any claim against Mac, as this is a situation of a pure omission for which the law does not generally impose duties. Owing to the lack of proximity between the two, the policy reasons for the law's approach are not surmounted. However, Keith's position in the patrol is likely to have created an assumption of responsibility which justifies a duty being imposed on him. As the other negligence factors are present, this means that a claim against Keith should succeed.

✓ **Make your answer stand out**

- Expand on the why the law is reluctant to impose duties of care for pure omissions.
- Read Markesinis, B.S.(1989) Negligence, nuisance and affirmative duties of action. *Law Quarterly Review*, 105: 104 and refer to this in support of your arguments.
- Explain in more depth, drawing on the cited case, the issue of intervening acts and why they will not break the chain of causation.
- Discuss more fully the partial defence of contributory negligence and apply the elements of it in more detail to the facts.

! **Don't be tempted to . . .**

- List every exception to the rule; just highlight the ones which are most applicable. Otherwise you risk indicating that you do not fully understand them.
- Focus entirely on the duty issue because of the prominence of the omission issue in the question. To obtain the highest marks you will need to address the question in full which, here, is to advise Brandon on a claim in negligence as a whole.

📝 Question 5

Donald is a law student who was due to sit his final exam. As long as he passed the exam he had been assured of a pupillage at a prestigious barristers' chambers. As he did not want to risk being late by using public transport, Donald chose to drive to the exam. Donald passed his test the year before, but had not driven much as he lacked confidence driving on busy roads and he was conscious of setting off his anxiety problem. On the day of his exam though, he felt there was more risk in not driving.

On his journey, Donald stalled at a busy junction and consequently was the victim of road rage from another driver. Donald started to feel more and more anxious, but carried on driving so as not to be late for the exam. However, he ended up having a full-blown panic attack which caused him to drive, at speed, into the back of a car driven by Nigel who had had stopped at a red light. Nigel suffered a broken leg and also hit his head against the side of his car.

Nigel was taken to the Clintonville General Hospital and seen by Dr Hilary. Dr Hilary was a junior doctor with no specialism in head and brain injuries; however, due to a lack of experienced staff there was no one present who could assist in performing the appropriate assessment. As Nigel was conscious, Dr Hilary felt that the trauma to Nigel's head was unlikely to have caused any significant head injury and so decided to treat his broken leg first rather than sending him for a CT scan. This was in fact contrary to the official NHS guidelines and an experienced doctor would have appreciated the need to have a scan immediately. Subsequently, Nigel suffered a seizure due to suffering internal bleeding in the brain which would have been revealed by a CT scan. His condition continued to worsen and Nigel ended up in a vegetative state.

Advise Donald and the hospital on the extent to which either will be held liable for Nigel's injuries.

Answer plan

➡ Establish that Donald owed Nigel a duty of care.

➡ Evaluate the implications of Donald's condition and the panic attack and whether this will lead him to being held in breach of duty.

➡ Confirm the absence of any issues regarding causation and remoteness in relation to the initial injuries resulting from the crash.

➡ Consider the intervention of Dr Hilary and whether this amounts to *novus actus interveniens* and explore the consequences if it is.

➡ Advise on the quantification of damages that will be payable.

Diagram plan

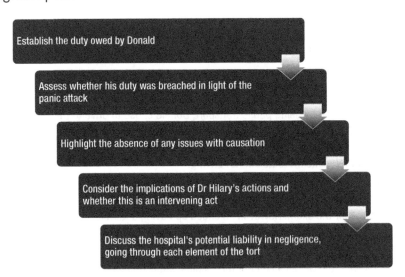

A printable version of this diagram plan is available from **www.pearsoned.co.uk/lawexpressqa**

Answer

The issue regarding Nigel's injuries concerns the interrelationship between Donald's acts and the hospital's and application of the law on intervening acts. This is important to determine, as it will impact on the level of liability which may be imposed on both parties. It will be argued that, as the action of Dr Hilary was an independent event, it will break the chain of causation with regard to Donald's liability.

First, as a motorist, Donald owes a duty of care to other road users such as Nigel (**Langley v Dray** (1998) PIQR P314).[1] The question is whether this duty to Nigel was breached. The standard of care to be exercised is that of the reasonable competent driver regardless of their level of experience and, therefore, it is irrelevant that Donald had not long passed his test and had driven little in that time (**Nettleship v Weston** [1971] 2 QB 691). The fact that Donald hit Nigel 'at speed'[2] despite approaching a red light suggests a clear breach. However, Donald's situation is complicated by his anxiety attack before the accident, as this could be classed as a disabling event which would affect the level of care and skill expected of him. The case of **Mansfield v Weetabix Ltd** [1998] 1 WLR 1263 involved a driver who suffered a medical condition that impaired his driving ability, leading to a crash,[3] which seems to be[4] what happened here. The court held that there was no reason in principle why a person should not be deemed negligent where the disabling event was gradual, as opposed to a sudden event, provided they were unaware of the condition. As such, it is in fact of little help to Donald[5] as he knew of his condition as this was why he had little driving experience. That knowledge compounds his decision to continue driving despite feeling 'more and more anxious'. If Donald was not having an anxiety attack at the time of the crash and he was going at an appropriate speed he may avoid being found in breach. More information is obviously needed in this regard; however, based on what we have been told it would seem that Donald would be in breach of his duty of care to Nigel due to **Mansfield,** irrespective of the speed he was travelling at when approaching the red light.

If Donald is held to be in breach of his duty,[6] applying the standard 'but for' test from **Cork v Kirby Mclean** [1952] 2 All ER 402, on the balance of probabilities, 'but for' Donald's negligence, he would not have hit Nigel and caused those initial injuries. These injuries are also

[2] Make sure that you highlight you are using the facts of the question to substantiate your point.

[3] State enough of the facts to highlight the connection with Donald's situation, but do not go into a full-blown account.

[4] Strictly speaking, from the facts we do not know for certain that this was definitely the case and so you should not write this sentence as if it was.

[5] It is still important to discuss the case in order to demonstrate your knowledge and understanding by applying it to the facts in order to rule out its applicability to Donald. Remember that cases and principles may be relevant to the discussion even if not ultimately applicable in terms of the likely outcome of the scenario.

[6] While likely that he is, reflect the possible doubt in your choice of words.

89

of a type which was reasonably foreseeable (*Wagon Mound (No. 1)* [1961] AC 388) thus they are not too remote. From the facts there would not seem to be any possible defence that Donald could rely on.

[7] By calling it 'alleged', you maintain consistency with your previous discussion. At this stage you will not have determined that it was negligence.

The issue, however, is the extent of Donald's liability and whether he will be liable for Nigel's ultimate condition and injury following the seizure. In negligence the defendant is liable for the reasonably foreseeable damage caused by his breach. While it could be said Nigel was only in the hospital because of Donald's alleged[7] negligence, an act by a third party can break the chain of causation. For the court to make such a finding and limit the extent of Donald's liability, the actions of Dr Hilary must not be a natural and probable consequence of Donald's own act (*Knightly v Johns* [1982] 1 All ER 851), nor a foreseeable act (*Lamb v Camden LBC* [1981] QB 625). It appears that the internal bleeding would have been caused in the crash when Nigel hit his head and so his ultimate condition could well be viewed as a natural and probable consequence of Donald's negligent driving. However, we are told that the seizure was caused by the continuing, untreated bleeding on Nigel's brain. Negligent medical treatment can be said to be foreseeable, meaning Donald would be liable for the full extent of Nigel's injuries. That said, Donald should be advised that where medical treatment is so grossly negligent as to be an irresponsible treatment of the injury initially caused, the treatment would be an intervening act (*Webb v Portsmouth Hospitals NHS Trust* [2002] PIQR P8). Dr Hilary's failure to follow official NHS protocols in relation to head traumas and check for injury, in the circumstances, can be considered to be below the standard of care to be expected by a medical professional.[8] It could also said to be irresponsible treatment in that the hospital did not have specialist staff on duty who could have conducted the treatment in the appropriate manner. Donald should, therefore, be advised that the actions of Dr Hilary are likely to be seen as a new intervening act[9] which would mean that he would not be liable for the subsequent injuries resulting from that intervention.

[8] This is obviously the language to be used when discussing breach. You need to use it here because it is only a highly negligent breach of duty by the hospital that will break the chain of Donald's liability.

[9] You could use the Latin phrase if you know it, but this will suffice. Arguably, it is better as it shows you understand what the Latin means.

[10] By highlighting this you demonstrate your broader knowledge on non-delegable duties and vicarious liability without going off on a tangent. It also allows you to explain that a duty is owed briefly and enable you to focus more on the key issues of breach and intervening acts.

[11] Normally, you would establish the duty first but, in this instance, it makes sense to discuss the negligence on the part of the hospital prior to confirming the duty, as this is crucial to there being an intervening act for the purposes of Donald's liability which necessitates looking at the hospital's duty.

Therefore, the hospital needs to be advised on its own liability to Nigel. A hospital owes a primary, non-delegable duty of care to all its patients (*Gold v Essex County Council* [1942] 2 KB 293) and so it does not matter what employment status Dr Hilary has within the hospital.[10] As discussed above,[11] the duty seems to have been breached. Even if the hospital were to argue a lower level of care is reasonable in light of Dr Hilary only being a junior doctor and having less experience, this would not succeed due to **Wilsher v Essex Area Health Authority** [1988] AC 1074. Further, there is unlikely to be a reasonable body of medical opinion which would have made Dr Hilary's clinical decision in light of the official NHS guidelines on how to act in such a situation, and on that basis, certainly not one capable of withstanding logical scrutiny (**Bolitho v City and Hackney Health Authority** [1997] 3 WLR 1151). There appear to be no issues surrounding causation or remoteness in relation to the hospital and as it would have no defence, the hospital would be liable in negligence for Nigel's current state.

To conclude, Donald should be advised that he faces being held liable for damages reflecting the initial injuries suffered by Nigel. The chain of causation regarding Nigel's condition was broken by the intervention of Dr Hilary and so the hospital should be advised that they would be liable for the subsequent injuries. As these acts and the resulting injuries are more independent than concurrent, the Civil Liability (Contribution) Act 1978 will not apply (**Rahman v Arearose Ltd** [2001] QB 351) and each party will be liable for the amount of compensation quantified to reflect the harm that they individually caused.[12] However, Donald should be advised that the quantification of his amount of compensation will not be curtailed by the hospital's subsequent tort if Nigel would have suffered any future, ongoing losses as a result of his negligence (**Baker v Willoughby** [1970] AC 467).

[12] You will not be expected to offer a specific percentage for each, but your answer will be incomplete if you do not advise them on how the court may go about apportioning their respective share of compensation. In real life, having advised them they face liability, this would be of real importance to them.

✓ **Make your answer stand out**

■ Contrast the situation from *Knightly v Johns* [1982] 1 All ER 851 with regards to foreseeable third party acts with the case of *The Oropesa* [1943] 1 All ER 211 and use that to add depth to your discussion of Dr Hilary's actions.

■ Consider any policy implications of classing the actions of Dr Hilary as an intervening act.

■ Support your discussion of whether Donald breached his duty to Nigel with reference to academic articles such as McDonald, B. (2005) Blameless? *Public Interest Law Journal*, 35: 15–17.

■ Discuss in more detail the issue of quantification of damages and mention the criticisms of the approach in *Baker v Willoughby* [1970] AC 467 by the House of Lords in *Jobling v Associated Dairies* [1982] AC 794.

■ Provide more of an explanation as to why on the basis of *Rahman v Arearose Ltd* [2001] QB 351 the Civil Liability (Contribution) Act 1978 will not apply.

! Don't be tempted to . . .

- Get into a full discussion of cases such as *Bolam* v *Friern Hospital Management Committee* [1957] 1 WLR 582 and *Bolitho* v *City and Hackney Health Authority* [1997] 3 WLR 1151, despite this question involving medical negligence. By this stage of your answer, your time is likely to be nearly up and so you should concentrate on completing the answer, which you risk not doing by going into those cases. The breach is quite evident here and so such a discussion is not really necessary.

- Explain at length how a duty is owed in both cases; simply state one is owed on the facts, and provide a relevant authority to support the point.

Question 6

One morning, Ben was driving home after a long night shift as a hospital porter. It was raining heavily and visibility was poor. Although Ben was very tired and knew that he should pull over until the rain had cleared, he wanted to get home and so carried on driving.

Ivana was riding her motorcycle into town. As she approached a zebra crossing, she noticed a man, Gurdeep, waiting to cross. She broke steadily and allowed him to cross the road. Ben, who was driving behind Ivana, didn't notice the motorcycle in front of him brake and had to slam his brakes on, in order to try and avoid hitting Ivana. Due to the wet weather Ben was unable to stop his car in time and skidded into Ivana, knocking her from her bike and causing her severe injuries. His car narrowly missed Gurdeep, who jumped towards the pedestrian footpath when he heard Ben slam his brakes on. The emergency services attended the scene and Ivana was transferred by ambulance to the local hospital.

Gurdeep suffers from panic disorder which, until the accident, was controllable through antidepressants and cognitive behavioural therapy. Although Gurdeep suffered no physical injury, the incident exacerbated his panic disorder, causing him to have frequent panic attacks after event.

Alice, a friend of Ivana's sister, Magdalena, happened to be in a nearby shop when the incident occurred. She called Magdalena in order to let her know that Ivana had been in an accident and had been taken to hospital. Magdalena and Ivana are very close to one another. They had both moved to the UK together over 10 years ago, leaving their families behind in order to study at University. They have lived together since their arrival in the UK. When Magdalena arrived at the hospital she found Ivana unconscious. Her injuries were visible to Magdalena and Magdalena broke down at the sight of her. Magdalena has suffered from post-traumatic stress disorder since the day of the incident.

Advise Gurdeep and Magdalena whether or not they could make a claim against Ben in these circumstances.

Diagram plan

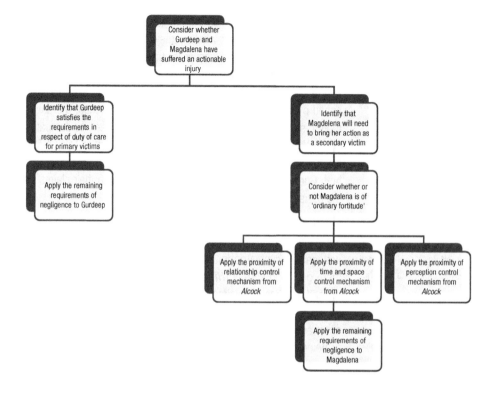

A printable version of this diagram plan is available from **www.pearsoned.co.uk/lawexpressqa**

Answer plan

➜ Gurdeep – identify that Gurdeep may potentially be a primary victim for the purposes of negligently inflicted pure psychiatric injury, and work through the requirements, applying each to Gurdeep's situation.

➜ Magdalena – identify that Magdalena would need to establish her claim as a secondary victim for the purposes of negligently inflicted psychiatric injury. Work through each of the control mechanisms and apply them to the facts of the question.

Answer

The issue that both Gurdeep and Magdalena need to be advised in respect of the incident is whether they have satisfied the relevant criteria required by law to recover for the psychiatric injury that they will argue is caused by the Ben's negligence. Both should be advised that recovery for pure psychiatric injury is an area of law heavily influenced by policy considerations and, as a consequence, the law is more restrictive in terms of establishing a duty of care, as compared with a claimant who has suffered physical injury such as Ivana.[1] This is particularly the case in respect of Magdalena. It will be argued that both Gurdeep and Magdalena may be successful in their claims on the basis of the facts provided.

In order to bring a successful action in negligence, both Gurdeep and Magdelena will need to establish that they have suffered an actionable psychiatric injury.[2] The law does not compensate for mere grief and sorrow (***Hinz v Berry*** [1970] 1 All ER 1084) and instead requires the claimant to establish that they have suffered a medically recognised psychiatric injury. Both Gurdeep's panic disorder and Magdalena's post-traumatic stress disorder are capable of being considered as a medically recognised psychiatric injury according to the American Diagnostic and Statistical Manual of Mental Disorders (DSM-5) (2013);[3] however, they should be advised that it is likely they will need to adduce expert medical evidence in support of this.

Turning to Gurdeep's potential claim,[4] he should be advised that he will need to establish that Ben owed him a duty of care in respect of the injury that he sustained. Following ***White v Chief Constable of South Yorkshire*** [1999] 2 AC 455, in order to recover as a primary victim, he must have been placed in reasonably foreseeable physical danger as a consequence of the defendant's negligence, or have been put in a position where he would have reasonable grounds to believe that he was so endangered (***McFarlane v EE Caledonia Ltd*** [1995] 2 All ER 1). As Ben's car narrowly missed Gurdeep at the pedestrian crossing, this indicates that Gurdeep was either in the relevant zone of reasonably foreseeable physical danger or would have reasonable grounds to believe that this were the case. Consequently, a duty of care would be owed.

[1] Highlighting this in your introduction indicates that you understand that the law is more restrictive in nature in respect of the two potential claimants that you have been asked to advise.

[2] As this requirement is common to both Gurdeep and Magdalena and is a matter of preliminary importance, it is appropriate to deal with both potential claimants together.

[3] This demonstrates the breadth of your understanding; however, you should remember that you are not being asked to provide medical advice. You should indicate what advice you would provide to the claimants in respect of the evidence that they should adduce.

[4] Although you previously considered Gurdeep and Magdalena's potential claims together in the same paragraph, the facts indicate that Gurdeep will be able to recovery as a primary victim, whereas Magdalena will be able to recover as a secondary victim. It is therefore appropriate to consider each of the potential claimants separately from this point onwards.

5 As the question asks you to consider Gurdeep's potential claim, your answer should not focus entirely on the duty of care issue. Although this is likely to be the most contentious issue in a question relating to psychiatric injury and therefore will be the focus of an answer, you must not neglect to consider the remaining requirements for an action in negligence.

6 When asked to advise the claimant, try to consider the arguments that a defendant would make in their defence. This not only enables you to more fully advise the relevant party, but demonstrates your ability to evaluate the application of the law to the factual scenario that you are presented with.

7 When answering this question, some students may choose to address this issue earlier in their answer when considering the duty of care. You need to make the decision as to which approach works best for you in terms of structural sense and clarity.

8 It is important to remember to highlight the significance of having this type of victim status as it demonstrates a greater level of understanding.

9 Although 'customary phlegm' has been used before, phrasing it in this way for the second time will help to demonstrate your understanding of what is meant by it.

In order to successfully claim in negligence, Gurdeep will also need to demonstrate that Ben's actions breached the relevant duty of care and that the breach in question caused the injury sustained by Gurdeep.[5] The standard of care expected of Ben is that of a reasonably competent driver, regardless of his level of skill or experience (*Nettleship v Weston* [1971] 2 QB 691). Ben's failure to pay due care and attention to the road and stop when Ivana engaged the brakes on her motorbike will amount to a clear breach of duty. Provided that Gurdeep's psychiatric injury arose from his fear for his own physical safety, there appear to be no issues in respect of factual causation. However, Ben may contend[6] that the psychiatric injury suffered by Gurdeep was too remote, due to the fact that he was suffering from a pre-existing medical condition prior to the incident.[7] However *Page v Smith* [1996] AC 155 confirms the application of the 'eggshell skull' rule in this context. Gurdeep's pre-existing medical condition, namely the panic disorder, will not preclude him claiming for the extent that Ben's negligence made the condition worse, as Ben must take his victim as he finds them. As there do not appear to be any relevant defences to Gurdeep's claim, it is likely that Gurdeep will be successful in his action against Ben.

Turning to Magdalena's potential claim, she too will need to demonstrate that she is owed a duty of care by Ben. However, unlike Gurdeep, she will be required to overcome the more restrictive requirements applicable to secondary victims as she does not meet the requirements of a primary victim, due to not being involved in the incident itself (*White; Page*).[8] Magdalena will need to demonstrate that the post-traumatic stress disorder that she suffered arose despite her being of 'customary phlegm' (*Bourhill v Young* [1943] AC 92). Although, we do not know for certain that Magdalena was of reasonable fortitude,[9] the fact that she suffers from post-traumatic stress disorder from the day of the incident, implies that she does not have any pre-existing condition that would make it likely that she is not of reasonable fortitude. On the basis that Magdalena is of reasonable fortitude, she requires advice in respect of the control mechanisms that must be satisfied in order to establish a duty of care, as outlined in *Alcock v Chief Constable of South Yorkshire* [1992] 1 AC 310.

The first control mechanism that needs to be considered is whether the claimant had a sufficiently close tie of love and affection with the immediate victim of the incident, which in this case is Ivana. In order for a duty of care to be owed, the claimant's injury must be reasonably foreseeable to the person who caused the initial incident. It is the closeness of the relationship between the immediate victim of the incident and the secondary victim that gives rise to the necessary foreseeability and warrants, in part, the imposition of the duty. The aim of such a requirement is to prevent an excess of claims and liability that is disproportionate to the conduct concerned. Magdalena should be advised that sufficient closeness is presumed between spouses and parents/children; however, in all other relationships a sufficiently close relationship must be proved by the claimant. Lord Ackner in **Alcock** acknowledged that such closeness will be determined on a case-by-case basis and therefore the fact that Ivana and Magdalena are sisters will not necessarily preclude Magdalena from successfully claiming.[10] Magdalena will need to adduce evidence such as the fact that they had moved to the UK away from their families and lived/supported each other for over 10 years in support of her claim. These facts support the conclusion that they had a sufficiently close tie of love and affection; however, this will ultimately be a matter for the court to determine and a failure to persuade the court in this regard will result in an unsuccessful action.

On the basis that Magdalena is able to establish a sufficiently close tie of love and affection,[11] the next issue is whether or not there was sufficient proximity in time and space to the incident or the immediate aftermath. Magdalena should be advised that she would have insufficient proximity to the incident itself, as she did not attend the scene of the accident and instead proceeded to the hospital as a consequence of the phone call from Alice. However, Magdalena could assert that she had sufficient proximity with the immediate aftermath of the incident through her attendance at the hospital (**McLoughlin v O'Brien** [1983] 1 AC 410). Although in **Alcock** the claimant who identified his brother-in-law at the mortuary some eight hours after the incident was unable to recover, Magdalena should be advised that her situation is more analogous to that of **McLoughlin.** In this case a mother was informed of a car crash, involving her family, two hours after it happened. She then immediately proceeded to the hospital where her family had been taken. Upon arrival she was informed that one of her children was dead, which, together with seeing the extent of the injuries of the rest of her family, caused her to suffer psychiatric injury.[12] Lord Wilberforce noted that the claimant in

[10] It is vital that you do not assume that just because Magdalena does not fall within the categories identified by the court as having a close tie of love and affection, she has no chance of claiming. This is not what was determined by the court in *Alcock*. You need to draw on the facts to support why she may still be able to satisfy this requirement.

[11] Because it cannot be conclusively determined whether or not there will be sufficient proximity of relationship, beginning your next paragraph in this way demonstrates that you acknowledge that the claim may already have failed at this point.

[12] Although students are often discouraged from simply reciting the facts of a case in their answer, a brief account of the facts of *McLoughlin* is required to lay the foundation of your argument in respect of Magdalena's case.

McLoughlin witnessed her family in the same state that they would have been had she seen them at the side of the road. This, coupled with temporal proximity, was sufficient to meet the requirements of the control mechanism. Similarly in Magdalena's case, she appears to have witnessed her sister in the same condition that she had been in at the side of the road, as she was unconscious and her injuries were clearly visible. Although the exact time between the incident and Magdalena witnessing her sister's injuries is not know, the facts imply that it was only a short period of time that elapsed, more akin to that in *McLoughlin* than in *Alcock.* On this basis, it appears as though Magdalena would be able to demonstrate sufficient spatial and temporal proximity.

The final control mechanism in *Alcock* relates to the means by which the psychiatric injury is caused. According to *Alcock* the psychiatric injury must be caused by the claimant's perception, with their own unaided senses, of the incident itself or its immediate aftermath. Being informed of the incident by a third party will be insufficient for the purposes of this proximity requirement. Magdalena first hears of the incident by virtue of the phone call from Alice and if her psychiatric injury arises as a consequence of this call, there will be insufficient proximity and no duty of care will be owed.[13] However, it does not appear as though her psychiatric injury arises at this point, rather Magdalena's post-traumatic stress disorder arises as a consequence of witnessing her sister in the hospital. If Magdalena is able to establish that this is the case and the courts accept that there is a sufficiently close tie of love and affection between Magdalena and Ivana, then it appears likely that Magdalena will be able to establish that Ben owes her a duty of care.

[13] When exploring different possibilities, you should discuss the impact of those possibilities on the likelihood of Magdalena being able to bring a successful action.

As was the case with Gurdeep,[14] it is clear that Ben has breached his duty of care towards Magdalena. Provided that Magdalena's psychiatric injury is caused by her witnessing her sister in the hospital and she is considered to be of ordinary fortitude, as discussed above, establishing causation should be straightforward. As no defences appear to be applicable in this instance, it is likely that Magdalena will be successful in her claim.

[14] As you have already discussed these matters in more detail in respect of Gurdeep, there is no need to simply repeat what you have already written.

In conclusion it appears as though on the facts both parties have actionable claims, and a chance of succeeding in them. However, more evidence is needed, particularly in respect of Magdalena, in order to fully determine whether or not a duty of care is owed to them.

✓ Make your answer stand out

- Highlight your knowledge of cases by relating the facts of the question to what in fact happened in particular cases; this will then strengthen your various arguments as you will have actual authority for applying the legal principles in that way.

- Demonstrate the policy rationale underpinning the law on psychiatric injury during your answer. Advise the parties not only about what the law is, but also why. This will also demonstrate that you have a deeper understanding of the topic.

- The question does not ask for any comment on reform of the law, and in seeking advice an individual will be more concerned with what the law currently is. However, as this area has been heavily criticised, both by academics and the judges themselves, it is beneficial to touch on the issue, at least in your conclusion, as this will show that you are aware of the debate. References to academic opinion will also have the benefit of adding depth to your level of analysis and evaluation.

! Don't be tempted to . . .

- Assume that as Ivana was only Magdalena's sister, there could not be a close tie of love and affection.

- Only consider issues pertaining to a duty of care in respect of each of the potential claimants. As the question asks you to advise in respect of potential claims and there is a strong possibility that both will be successful in establishing that a duty of care exists, you must go on to consider the remaining requirements for negligence.

- Provide a detailed account of all of the different categories of claimant in psychiatric injury cases; just keep to those that are directly applicable.

📝 Question 7

Henry, a financial adviser, undertakes work for Clown's Bank plc, although he also does independent work for himself. When he is doing work for Clown's Bank, he is provided with an office and administrative staff; the Bank also has control over the range of financial products he may offer and provides him with a basic wage plus bonuses. However, he does have the opportunity to make extra profits from any non-investment products that he sells to the customer and he can determine the level of risk to expose the customer to.

One night in the Ducker and Diver Arms public house, somewhere Henry is known to work out of when he is working late, Henry is approached by Gideon, whom he met through his work with the Bank. Gideon explains that he has inherited £1 million and requires investment advice. Henry explains that he has had six pints of strong Belgian lager and so is not really in the right frame of mind and tells Gideon to come to the Bank tomorrow. As Henry leaves he shouts back: 'Royal Bank of Wales – that's a company on the up; we'll discuss them tomorrow.'

Thinking that this was Henry's investment advice, and as he has always acted on his advice and never lost out, he decides to save time and rather than see Henry goes online and invests the whole sum in Royal Bank of Wales. Two weeks later the Royal Bank of Wales receives an urgent government bailout and their shares became worthless, with Gideon losing his investment.

Gideon now seeks to sue Clown's Bank for his economic loss, owing to what he feels was a negligent misstatement by Henry. Advise the Bank.

Diagram plan

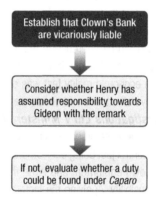

A printable version of this diagram plan is available from **www.pearsoned.co.uk/lawexpressqa**

Answer plan

➜ Determine whether Henry is an employee acting in the course of his employment for vicarious liability purposes.

➜ Evaluate whether there is an assumption of responsibility towards Gideon by Henry, by making the statement that he did.

➜ Consider the social environment in which the statement is made.

➜ Discuss whether, in the event there is no assumption of responsibility, a duty towards Gideon may be found under the *Caparo* tripartite test.

Answer

The issue to be determined is whether Clown's Bank vicariously owed a duty of care towards Gideon in relation to his economic losses. Such a finding would be financially significant and, despite the law's reluctance to find such duties on policy grounds, there are instances where one will be found.[1] However, it is argued that, while it is possible that they have responsibility for Henry, the situation is not such as to overcome the law's policy concerns and warrant finding a duty.

[1] Your point here is to show that you appreciate the practical consequences for the Bank of finding a duty in this situation as they are, effectively, your client. The other task is to give an indication of knowing the context within which the law operates, i.e. one limited on policy grounds, which you can then develop in the main body of your answer.

First, it needs to be established whether the Bank is in fact responsible for Henry's acts if a duty of care is found. The Bank should be advised that they will be vicariously liable if it can be shown that Henry is an employee and was acting in the course of that employment when he made the statement. Henry's employment status is blurred by the fact that he works independently of the Bank, as well as acting for them. Historically, whether a person was an employee was determined by reference to the level of control that he was under.[2] However, this did not fully reflect emerging employment relationships, so an economic reality test was developed. This requires looking at the overall situation for evidence of a contract of service (*Market Investigations Ltd v Minister of Social Security* [1969] 2 QB 173). This case proposed a non-exhaustive list of factors to consider, with control just being one. Others were whether the person provided their own equipment and hired their own staff and their degree of responsibility. Applying the factors to Henry, they suggest that he is likely to be classed as an employee. While Henry has some individual responsibility, he is provided with an office and administrative staff by the Bank who also dictate what he can offer clients; significantly, they pay his wages and bonuses. Therefore, overall, this suggests that there is a contract of service.

[2] You want to briefly show that you know what the test was historically, especially as this is still a consideration, but you should then go on to show how you are aware that this is no longer deemed completely suitable.

Henry, though, must have been in the course of his employment when he made the statement. However, it occurred in the evening, in a pub, after Henry had been drinking. The test to apply is the close-connection test from *Lister v Hesley Hall* [2002] 1 AC 215. This requires the tort to be so closely connected with the employment that it is fair and just to hold the Bank vicariously liable. Henry met Gideon through his employment with the Bank and the tort is allegedly[3] in making a negligent misstatement to a client regarding a financial investment,

[3] Remember you have not yet established that there is a negligence at this stage.

which is what he is employed to give; the fact that Gideon was told to visit the Bank also suggests that the advice was given in his role as an employee. All of this, together with the fact that Henry is known to work late and uses the pub for work, suggests that he could have been in the course of his employment.

On the basis that the Bank could be deemed vicariously liable for Henry's statement, it is important to advise the Bank now as to whether a duty of care was owed to Gideon.[4] Generally, there is reluctance to find duties for economic losses. Partly this is because, as Lord Reid observed in **Hedley Byrne v Heller** [1964] AC 465, people will often express definite opinions in informal settings, even though recognising that people may be influenced by them, but they do so without the same level of care as if in a professional setting. As words can spread far and be relied upon by people of whom the maker has no knowledge, it can lead to indeterminate liability to an indeterminate class. Therefore the House of Lords held a duty could, in principle, exist but more was needed than for normal negligent injuries. There would need to be an assumption of responsibility by Henry towards Gideon, and then reasonable reliance by Gideon on the statement.

[4] Even if you conclude that the Bank would not be vicariously liable, you need to remember that the main issue of the question is whether a duty of care is owed for economic loss. Therefore, you would still need to go into this but use an opening phrase such as 'On the basis that the Bank was . . .'.

A duty can occur outside of contractual and fiduciary relationships (**Hedley Byrne**) as the assumption with the reliance is deemed to create a special relationship which overcomes the law's reservations. The Bank should be advised, though, that Lord Reid in **Hedley Byrne** suggested that a special relationship could only arise in a business situation owing to the reasons stated above. Therefore, while the social nature of the incident may still warrant being classed as in the course of Henry's employment, it may negate the imposition of a duty of care. The Court of Appeal has, though, found a duty in a situation of non-business advice between friends (**Chaudhry v Prabhakar** [1988] 3 All ER 718). In any event the existence of an assumption of responsibility is judged objectively (**Henderson v Merrett Syndicates** [1995] 2 AC 145), but a divergence of opinion exists as to whether it refers to the task or actual legal responsibility.[5] In **White v Jones** [1995] 2 AC 207 Lord Browne-Wilkinson felt it referred to the task. If this is the case, by making the statement Henry could be said to have assumed responsibility. However, this is questioned academically by Murphy (1996), who argues it must refer to assuming legal

[5] Reference to this debate in this part of your advice allows your answer to develop into an academic discussion of the law and shows your awareness of differing academic and judicial opinion about what this element of the test means.

responsibility to the claimant. On this basis Henry arguably fails this requirement. He has indicated that Gideon should visit him tomorrow in the Bank to discuss the investment and also indicates that he has been drinking. These facts could actually also be used to counter any suggestion of even satisfying Lord Browne-Wilkinson's interpretation, as he has not technically given advice.

[6] Insert a reference to causation to show that you are also advising in the wider context of negligence as, if the Bank is to be liable, which is what the question asks you to advise them on, this is a factor which would need to be satisfied.

Gideon obviously relies on the statement, which means that if a duty was found, causation would also be satisfied;[6] however, reliance must be reasonable. The informal context – with Henry leaving a pub, indicating that he has drunk a lot of strong lager,[7] while additionally only saying they will discuss the investment tomorrow – means it can be strongly argued, especially in light of the sums involved,[8] that Gideon's reliance was in fact wholly unreasonable.

[7] Although you have said this a lot, you want to keep driving home the facts which support the view you are expressing. As long as the context is there, this is fine.

[8] In this part of your answer it is all about the application of the facts, so you do not need to write that much here and you do not need any great reference to case law.

Therefore, while it would seem that the requirements for a duty have not been satisfied, it has been held in ***Customs and Excise Commissioners v Barclays Bank plc*** [2007] 1 AC 181 that the absence of an assumption of responsibility does not prevent resort to finding a duty on the basis of the alternative three-fold test. However, while foreseeability is present here and proximity is also arguably satisfied owing to their past relationship, the reasons why Gideon's reliance is not reasonable are also likely to mean that it is not fair, just and reasonable in these circumstances to find a duty towards Gideon.

[9] Although the preceding paragraph may read like a conclusion and the end of your answer, you should just draw both strands of potential liability together and conclude by reiterating that both tests are likely to fail.

In conclusion,[9] it appears that on either basis of establishing a duty for economic loss, Gideon is unlikely to be successful and, therefore, the Bank will not be liable for Henry's advice.

✓ Make your answer stand out

- Advise the Bank on the rationale behind vicarious liability as the doctrine may be used to support why they could end up liable.

- Explain why the law is more reluctant to recognise a duty of care in relation to purely economic losses.

- Relate your discussion of the impact of the statement being apparently made in a social context to the issue of whether Henry is in fact in the course of his employment.

- Include a fuller discussion on whether the other elements of negligence are present to round off your advice to the Bank, if the Bank was deemed to owe a duty.

! Don't be tempted to . . .

- Spend too long on the vicarious liability element. Show that you have spotted that there is a potential issue there and that you have an understanding of how the law works, but remember that the main thrust of the question is on economic loss. Although at the same time, make sure you do cover all aspects of it.

- Go off on a long tangent with your discussion of what the phrase 'assumption of responsibility' should mean; remember the question is ultimately about advising the Bank of their liability and requires application of the law to the facts.

📝 Question 8

Cogmire Builders Ltd contracted to renovate a sports complex for Quay Borough Council, who had bought the existing premises after the complex had closed down. Under the terms of the contract the shell of the building is to be built by Cogmire Builders Ltd, but certain specialist electrical work was carried out by Peter & Sons Ltd. All building operations were solely supervised by a firm of consulting architects, Cleveland Consultants, who were employed by Cogmire Builders Ltd at the request of the Council, as they had previously overseen other Council projects and were specialists in this type of work.

On the day the new complex was due to open, a fire broke out which was caused by the negligent electrical work of Peter & Sons Ltd, and the complex remained closed for a further two months.

Several months after the complex finally opened, cracks appeared in the floor of the gym. Investigations showed that the floor was not laid properly and could not take the weight of the machines. The sports complex was closed for several weeks while the gym floor was re-laid and reinforced.

Cogmire Builders Ltd has now gone out of business; advise Quay Borough Council on what action, if any, they may take in common law negligence.

Diagram plan

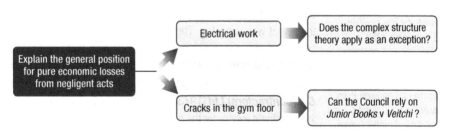

A printable version of this diagram plan is available from **www.pearsoned.co.uk/lawexpressqa**

Answer plan

➜ State the law's position on economic losses arising from negligent acts of construction and advise the Council why this is the case.

➜ Then take each defect separately.

➜ Explain the 'complex structure theory' and whether this may provide the Council with an exception to the general position.

➜ Discuss the applicability of *Junior Books* v *Veitchi* [1983] 1 AC 520 in relation to the cracked floor as an option for claiming the losses from that defect.

➜ In doing so, explore the ex-post rationalisation of *Junior Books* as an application of the *Hedley Byrne* principle and assess whether this helps.

Answer

[1] As the law is quite firm in its reluctance to recognise a duty in such a situation as this, it is perhaps even more beneficial to highlight early on how you are going to go about arguing your case so the marker knows.

[2] It is important that near the start of your advice to the Council you explain not only what the legal position is, but also demonstrate that you understand why their situation falls within that position. This sentence shows the marker that you have fully understood the context of the question and grasped the basic principles.

[3] By then going into the rationale for this position and explaining it to the Council, you will reinforce the impression that you fully understand the framework for this area and early on in your answer have obtained a good foundation of marks before you have really got into the question.

The issue here is whether the Council has any redress for the economic losses which they have incurred through the negligent construction of the new complex. This area of negligence is one which is tightly restricted on policy grounds, meaning there is little scope for a duty of care to be established. However, there are some limited exceptions and the Council will be advised of two which may be applicable to their case: namely, the 'complex structure theory' for the electrics and the case of *Junior Books* in relation to the gym floor.[1]

The Council should be advised that the general position is that where someone negligently performs an act, they will not be liable for any losses which result that are of a purely economic nature. However, economic losses that are consequential to property damage or physical injury can be claimed if a duty was owed and its breach caused such damage or injury. While it may seem that the fire damage and the floor cracks are property damage, they should be advised that the courts see situations such as this as simply a case of purchasing something which is of less quality and, thus, value, than what was expected. Therefore, the actual loss is the financial cost of bringing the premises up to the standard that was expected (***Murphy v Brentwood DC*** [1991] 1 AC 398).[2] The rationale for this position[3] was explored in ***Spartan Steel & Alloys Ltd v Martin & Co. (Contractors) Ltd*** [1973] 1 QB 27 and includes the prospect of indeterminate liability for the defendant, the fact that the nature of the risk was such that precautions could be taken, e.g. insurance, and the need to avoid undermining contract law. Allowing a tortious claim for a defective product would create a transferable non-contractual warranty. It would also duplicate contract law which provides remedies where a product is not of satisfactory quality or fit for purpose.

In relation to the fire damage, if the Council directly contracted with Peter & Sons, a claim under the contract would arise. If not, the Council may still have an exception to the general position under the 'complex structure theory', which would allow a claim against the electricians. The theory suggests that the different elements of a building can be viewed as distinct items of property and thus if one part damages another part, there would be sufficient appropriate property damage on which to base a claim for economic loss. In the Council's case this would mean that the electrical work is distinguished from the rest of the complex which it damaged through its negligent installation.[4] However, the theory, first mooted in *D & F Estates v Church Commissioners for England* [1989] AC 177 as a basis for explaining *Anns v Merton LBC* [1978] AC 728, is not an adopted legal principle. The theory received a closer evaluation in *Murphy,* and notwithstanding academic criticism it received some judicial support for its application in limited circumstances. Lords Keith, Jauncey and Bridge[5] stated that the complex part in question would need to have been installed by a sub-contractor. Here, the Council should be advised that if the electricians were sub-contracted by Cogmire Builders, they would appear to have a claim. This is supported by the fact that all three gave an example of when the theory could apply – negligently fitted electrical wiring which caused a fire.

If a duty is held to exist, as we are told the electrical work by Peter & Sons was negligently fitted and this caused the fire to break out,[6] it appears that the Council would have a claim against them in negligence for the economic losses suffered. The only possible defence they may have is an exclusion clause;[7] however, in view of the danger to life, this is likely to be unreasonable under the Unfair Contract Terms Act 1977.

In relation to the gym floor, as Cogmire Builders have gone out of business, any potential claim, in contract or tort, would be futile.[8] This leaves only the consultants as possible defendants. This is complicated by the absence of a contract between them and the Council: they were contracted by the builders. As above, the loss is purely economic, but the Council may have recourse to the case of *Junior Books* in any claim.

[4] After explaining the outline of the theory, illustrate how it transfers to the facts to show the marker what you are thinking before you go on to discuss the merits of the theory in full.

[5] By including the comments of all three you show that, while not part of the *ratio* of the case, it did have majority support.

[6] As the facts indicate that this is a given, there is no need to go into depth as to what is required in these aspects of negligence, but for completeness you should use the facts as stated in the question to support the proposition that a negligence claim can be supported.

[7] Although there is nothing to suggest this is the case on the facts, you should consider it, as, just because one is not expressly mentioned, it could well be the case and so your advice would be incomplete without assessing the implications of one being present.

[8] This is obviously a practical point but important in the context of giving advice on what action may be taken. Demonstrate that you have picked up on the fact and understand the implication.

In that case, a specialist sub-contractor, specifically chosen by the claimant to be employed by the main contractor, was successfully sued when their work, defective flooring, turned out to have been negligently performed. There is a slight factual similarity, therefore, between both instances. This is important as *Junior Books* has been subsequently heavily criticised and seems now confined to its own facts (*Muirhead v Industrial Tank Specialities* [1986] QB 507). In the case, Lord Roskill outlined several factors which created a sufficient degree of proximity between the parties. These included being nominated and specialists in the role they were contracted for. Further, the sub-contractors were solely responsible for the contracted task and knew exactly what was required. As such, they knew that their skill and experience were being relied upon by the claimants. While slightly different, the Council should be advised that there is some correlation here. The consultants were specialists in overseeing this sort of work and hand-picked by the Council for their skill and experience. As such, they were solely responsible for overseeing the construction and would have appreciated this and that their expertise was being relied upon by the Council.

The Council should be warned, though, that while the case has not been overruled, it has been criticised at every opportunity by the House of Lords and, therefore, basing a claim on this authority may not be the best course. As the case has been subsequently rationalised on the basis of the *Hedley Byrne* principle of assumption of responsibility, any claim should perhaps be framed on this basis. This requires the Council to demonstrate that Cleveland Consultants, in performing their service, assumed responsibility towards the Council who reasonably relied upon their service. This appears supported on the factors mentioned above in relation to *Junior Books*; however, in *Henderson v Merrett Syndicates* [1995] 2 AC 145 this explanation of *Junior Books* was doubted. Therefore, any claim for the losses from the cracked floor may prove futile, no matter how it is framed, for the absence of a duty.

In conclusion, owing to the nature of the losses suffered by the Council, their chances of any actions being successful are remote. However, it may be possible to successfully sue the electricians in relation to the cost of restoring the complex following the fire, but the losses from repairing the gym floor will be harder to recoup.

✓ Make your answer stand out

- Advise the Council as to their position regarding any consequential economic losses and explore further why these are more justifiably recovered.
- Include some explanation about the merits of the rationale for restricting recovery in this area – would it really undermine contract law?
- Include some comparative analysis with other jurisdictions which have not followed *Murphy* v *Brentwood DC* [1991] 1 AC 398.
- Read O'Sullivan, J. (2007) Suing in tort where no contract claim will lie: a bird's eye view. *Professional Negligence*, 23(3): 165–92 and Hedley, S. (1995) Negligence – pure economic loss – goodbye privity, hello contorts. *Cambridge Law Journal*, 54(1): 27–30 for some academic opinion on this area of law and the cases which you will refer to in your answer.

! Don't be tempted to . . .

- Stray into examining in depth the merits of recoverability for economic losses; remember the question is about whether the Council can establish a duty owed to them by either party.
- Focus heavily on the history of recovery in this area and the merits of *Anns* v *Merton LBC* [1978] AC 728, as it has been overruled, and as this is a problem question you need to focus on what the law is and how it might be applied.
- Miss out reference to the other aspects of negligence. They are needed briefly for completeness.

@ Try it yourself

Now take a look at the question below and attempt to answer it. You can check your response against the answer guidance available on the companion website (**www.pearsoned.co.uk/lawexpressqa**).

Following a gas explosion, the local Fire Brigade Unit were called to the scene. Bert, the driver of the fire engine, made sure he had the siren on and the lights flashing, but his sole concern was to get to the scene as quickly as possible and so, naturally, he was driving very fast. This meant that he was not paying as much attention to the road as he would normally.

Ernie, an elderly man with a slight limp, was crossing the road as Bert's engine came around the corner. Although he saw the fire engine, he misjudged the speed and thought he would have time to cross the road. He was wrong, and in the collision he suffered multiple injuries, including the permanent loss of movement in his leg that had previously caused him to limp.

Advise Ernie as to his injuries.

www.pearsoned.co.uk/lawexpressqa

Go online to access more revision support including additional essay and problem questions with diagram plans, you be the marker questions, and download all diagrams from the book.

Product liability

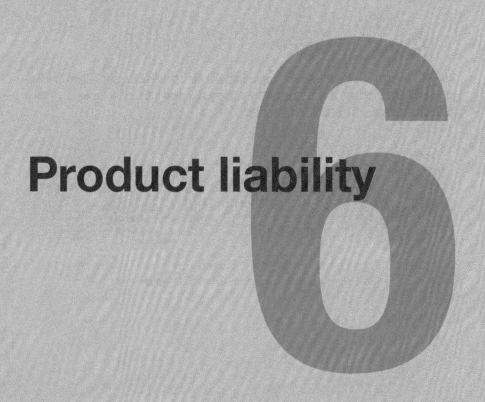

How this topic may come up in exams

This topic is centred primarily on the Consumer Protection Act 1987; however, the Act did not abolish the common law negligence action. Therefore, you also need to be aware of the narrow rule in *Donoghue* v *Stevenson* and how this applies to manufacturers of defective products. The existence of both actions means that a comparative essay is likely, alongside issues of why the Act was needed. However, the differences between the two actions mean that both will have to be discussed in problem questions in order to assess which claim may be best.

Before you begin

Acquaint yourself with the following components and key issues of this topic; and familiarise yourself with how you would structurally progress through them all, if necessary, when attempting to answer a question on this topic.

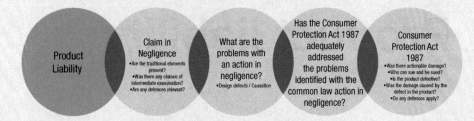

Product Liability

Claim in Negligence
• Are the traditional elements present?
• Was there any chance of intermediate examination?
• Are any defences relevant?

What are the problems with an action in negligence?
• Design defects / Causation

Has the Consumer Protection Act 1987 adequately addressed the problems identified with the common law action in negligence?

Consumer Protection Act 1987
• Was there actionable damage?
• Who can sue and be sued?
• Is the product defective?
• Was the damage caused by the defect in the product?
• Do any defences apply?

A printable version of this diagram is available from **www.pearsoned.co.uk/lawexpressqa**

 Question 1

'The principal and obvious shortcoming of the traditional *Donoghue* v *Stevenson* cause of action is the need to prove fault. Though perhaps this should not be overplayed.' Jones *et al.* (2014) *Clerk & Lindsell on Torts,* 21st edition. London: Sweet & Maxwell. 11–45

Evaluate the merit of both forms of negligent liability for defective products and whether the statutory form has provided needed improvement.

Answer plan

➡ Discuss the level of protection provided by the traditional cause of action under *Donoghue* v *Stevenson.*

➡ Consider whether there is merit in saying the protection offered had shortcomings.

➡ Outline the basis for Parliament intervening in this area by enacting the Consumer Protection Act 1987.

➡ Explain the requirements for liability under the statute, highlighting the difference to the common law.

➡ Consider whether the Act's provisions have improved the situation.

Diagram plan

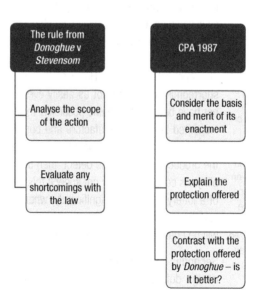

Answer

The issue to assess is whether the traditional action for protecting consumers from defective products was satisfactory or whether its shortcomings necessitated the passing of the Consumer Protection Act 1987. If this is so and the shortcomings at common law can be overplayed, then the Act can be said to be unnecessary. It is argued though that, while the Act was passed as part of a wider EU-driven process of consumer protection within the Internal Market,[1] it overcomes shortcomings that would otherwise limit consumer protection.

The narrower importance of **Donoghue v Stevenson** [1932] AC 562 is that it created the traditional action for product liability by imposing a duty of care on manufacturers to the ultimate consumer of their products if the product is intended to reach the consumer in the condition it left the manufacturer, with no reasonable chance of inspection by an intermediary. Therefore, if this duty was breached by failing to take reasonable care and this breach caused damage, which was of a foreseeable nature, then the manufacturer was liable unless they had a valid defence.[2]

This means, as the quote highlights, showing fault by the manufacturer is the principal shortcoming. While this is a hurdle, particularly as evidence of compliance with set standards may go against negligence, as *Clerk & Lindsell* states, it is not insurmountable. The more crucial obstacle is the need to prove causation, which is also a feature of a strict liability regime. However, the traditional action has further shortcomings that are not as easily overplayed.[3] First, there must not have been a reasonable possibility for the product to have been inspected between manufacture and purchase by the consumer. If someone in the supply or manufacturing chain could have inspected the product and found the defect, then the manufacturer avoids liability. As consumers may not know if this is the situation, something of a lottery is created. Significantly, where the goods are imported, and the importer has not had the chance to inspect them, any claim will be against an overseas-based manufacturer.

Secondly, **Donoghue** concerned product manufacture and not design defects. Often the design creates the defect rather than

[4] Demonstrate your awareness of the principles of tort, and your understanding of this tort, by showing how the justification for the new basis of liability is rooted in the fundamental principles of tort.

[5] Use this opportunity to show off your deeper knowledge of tort and its underlying principles in order to support why the idea of a strict liability regime had merit. By relating its implementation to tort principles, you strengthen the argument that it is justifiable.

[6] The point here is to show that you are aware of the imperative to pass the statute due to the influence of EU law while also tying in your knowledge of current affairs and how the current political situation could influence this area of tort. It will also allow you to set up your answer, if you prefer the Act's protection, to argue that it should be retained even if the EU compliance justification is lost.

[7] Although you are now talking about the Act, make sure you show that you know how the two actions relate to each other, as both still exist.

[8] Your aim here is to show that you are considering not only whether the position under the Act is an improvement, but will stay an improvement in light of forthcoming political changes.

the absence of reasonable care when making the product. Further, where a design defect exists there is a greater potential for harm as all of the products are affected, not just a batch. The importance of causation in negligence deepens this problem, as a claimant must show that the design defect is capable of causing the harm in question, and then did cause that harm. This difficulty is clearly evidenced in relation to medicinal drugs and the Thalidomide cases. In negligence, claimants do not benefit from hindsight (*Roe v Minister of Health* [1954] 2 QB 66) and must show that at the time of the product's circulation the manufacturer acted unreasonably.

Consequently, the idea of a strict liability regime emerged which is consistent with the principles of loss distribution, deterrence and economic efficiency.[4] The manufacturer is best placed to insure the risk and can then pass this cost on to consumers. To ensure lower prices, greater care would be taken to ensure premiums do not rise.[5] The idea also reflects the viewpoint that it is fair to impose the risk on the manufacturer as they created the product for profit. The EU took the initiative, however, with Product Liability Directive 85/374/EEC aiming to harmonise the level of protection across all Member States by implementing a strict liability regime. Therefore, even without the shortcomings of the traditional approach in *Donoghue* there was a need to enact the statute, although this could be reviewed post-Brexit if the statutory regime is deemed less adequate.[6]

Notwithstanding its shortcomings, Parliament retained the traditional action.[7] The Act's central aim is to impose liability without fault on the producer of a defective product (s. 2(1)). Section 1(2) defines 'product' broadly, namely as any 'goods or electricity', including a component of a larger product, such as the fan within a laptop. Under the Act, the product's producer also includes the person who imported the product into the EU which overcomes a significant shortcoming of the traditional action by making it easier for consumers than having to sue a manufacturer from overseas, although this advantage may be lost in a post-Brexit Britain.[8] Generally, however, suppliers avoid liability for the defect unless the conditions of section 2(3) are satisfied.

[9] By starting this part of your answer like this, it means that you are relating your discussion back to the statement and shows that you are now dealing with the underlying premise within the statement.

[10] There are a number of cases that you could use here. It does not matter which you do use, so long as you include one which illustrates the point that the courts were interpreting 'defect' in a way that was akin to looking for fault. This forms the basis of whether, despite the Directive, the Act was worthwhile or just reiterating the common law position.

[11] Until recently *A* was the clearest authority on the meaning of defectiveness; however, the more recent case of *Wilkes* casts doubt on the decision. You therefore need to ensure that you consider this case in your answer.

Provided the Act does impose a strict liability regime it can be justified.[9] However, the Act's wording and early cases suggested liability was not so strict. Section 3 defines 'defect' as being where 'the safety of the product is not such as persons are generally entitled to expect'. Under section 3(2) all circumstances should be taken into account when determining the level of safety that the public can expect. These include the product's marketing and whether any instructions or warnings regarding its use were provided. Further consideration is to be given to how the product may reasonably be expected to be used and the time when the product was supplied. The issue is that, while the Act seeks strict liability, determining whether the product was defective allows for the consideration of fault, and so negligence reappears by the back door. This was seen in *Worsley v Tambrands Ltd* [2000] PIQR 95 where a warning placed on the product regarding a small risk of toxic shock syndrome meant that liability was avoided.[10] The courts' assessment of a warning's sufficiency can be said to amount to whether the manufacturer has been at fault. This negates the Act's purpose and supports the suggestion that it was not needed as it does not solve the difficulties of negligence, since establishing a lack of care would still be required, and then that this caused the resultant injury. The use of fault-based reasoning was criticised in *Abouzaid v Mothercare (UK) Ltd* [2000] All ER D 2436, with whether the defect had come to Mothercare's attention deemed irrelevant. The lack of negligence was held to not prevent liability under the Act. The emphasis on strict liability was followed in *A v National Blood Authority* [2001] 3 All ER 289, where consideration of the care taken by the manufacturer was excluded; what should be assessed is all relevant circumstances, not all circumstances. However more recently in *Wilkes v DePuy International* [2018] 2 WLR 531, Hickenbottom J indicated that 'avoidability' does not necessarily fall outside the scope of determining defectiveness, thus introducing a greater level of flexibility and potentially opening the doorway to fault-based analysis of defectiveness.[11]

In conclusion, the Act provides increased consumer protection to that which exists under *Donoghue* despite the greater degree of flexibility introduced by *Wilkes.* Even if the obvious shortcoming can be overplayed, and the action under the Act shares the difficulty of proving causation, the broader shortcomings of *Donoghue* necessitate the statutory regime. Notwithstanding any difficulties arising from the Act and its subsequent interpretation, a strict liability regime is a welcome addition to the law on product liability and should be retained even when not needed to comply with EU directives.

✓ Make your answer stand out

■ Discuss briefly the limited scope of liability in this area prior to *Donoghue* v *Stevenson* [1932] AC 562.

■ Read Stapleton, J. (1994b) *Product Liability.* London: Butterworths. This will allow you to incorporate material regarding the theoretical basis for strict liability in this area and why this approach was adopted in the EU in light of American experiences. You can then question the merits of strict liability.

■ Refer to journal articles on *A* v *National Blood Authority* [2001] 3 All ER 289 and *Wilkes* v *DePuy International* [2018] 2 WLR 531 as, if *A* is wrong to adopt such a strict line in relation to 'defect' and Wilkes has introduced too much flexiblity, then we arguably do have a system that considers fault. You can then consider whether there is still enough distinction between the claims to warrant the existence of both actions. For example, look at Hodges, C. (2001) Compensating patients: case comment on *A* v *National Blood Authority* [2001] 3 All ER 289. *Law Quarterly Review,* 117: 528; and Howells, G. and Mildred, M. (2002) Infected blood: defect and discoverability a first exposition of the EC Product Liability Directive. *Modern Law Review,* 65: 95.

■ Evaluate in more detail whether any improvements could be lost post-Brexit and how.

! Don't be tempted to . . .

■ Try to cover all of the provisions of the Act. Remember that the main aspect of the question focuses on whether the Act improves the situation by overcoming the difficulties of the common law.

■ Describe in detail the full requirements of negligence. Explain what they are, but focus on the problems they caused.

■ Gloss over the influence of European law in this area. Ultimately that was the reason for passing the Act and, so, on a question regarding whether the Act was necessary, it is quite a fundamental point. Similarly, do not gloss over Brexit as if the EU was the driver for the Act that need may soon disappear.

■ Allow your answer to become a politics essay if you do consider the implications of Brexit.

◤ Question 2

WM Electronics have developed and released a new type of phone charger, the 'Safety Charge'. The phone charger has a safety feature that causes it to switch off when it recognises that a phone has reached full charge. The charger should then only switch back on once the user presses a button on the plug. It is marketed as being particularly useful for people who prefer to charge their phone overnight. The 'Safety Charge' is manufactured in China and has been sold there for around 6 months. It is also imported into the UK by a number of phone retailers, including Phone Warehouse; however, the product only launched in the UK 2 weeks ago.

Carlos frequently has to charge his old phone as the battery does not hold its charge well. He has become increasingly concerned about how hot his charger and phone get when charging his phone, but cannot afford to buy a new phone and isn't eligible for an early upgrade on his contract. Carlos goes into Phone Warehouse in order to discuss his options with the sales assistant and she recommends that he purchase the 'Safety Charge' to tide him over until the end of his phone contract.

The 'Safety Charge' has a fault whereby the product begins to charge again once the phone drops below 100 per cent, despite the fact that the user hasn't pressed the button on the plug. The fault was identified through complaints from users of the 'Safety Charge' in China. WM Electronics recalled the products already in circulation in China; however, as the product had only just launched in the UK and there was a large amount of stock waiting to be sold, WM Electronics sent stickers to the retailers warning users to avoid using the charger for prolonged period of time. One of these stickers did feature on the bottom of the box for the 'Safety Charge' that Carlos purchased, next to a label that identified WM Electronics as the manufacturers of the phone charger.

Carlos plugged his phone in to charge overnight as he usually did. As his phone does not hold its charge, the 'Safety Charge' continued to charge all night. The charger over-heated and caused a small fire, damaging his bedside table, lamp and an antique watch his father had given to him for his twenty-first birthday. The phone charger and his phone were both destroyed in the fire.

Advise Carlos as to any actions that he may take, and against whom, for the losses that he has suffered.

Answer plan

→ Outline the purpose and scope of the Consumer Protection Act 1987.

→ Consider whether the Act provides redress for the type of property which has been damaged by the product.

→ State what role Phone Warehouse and WM Electronics will have in proceedings.

➜ Evaluate the criteria for establishing liability and identify whether there was a defect with the 'Safety Charge'.

➜ Discuss the possible application of any defences.

➜ Consider an alternative claim by Carlos under the rule in *Donoghue v Stevenson* [1932] AC 562.

Diagram plan

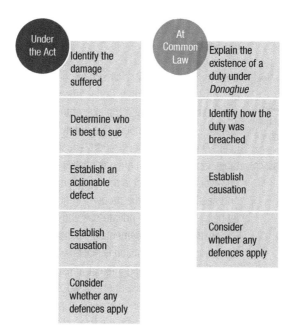

A printable version of this diagram plan is available from **www.pearsoned.co.uk/lawexpressqa**

Answer

Carlos requires advice in respect of his ability to recover for the damage that he sustained to his property as a consequence of the fire, and from whom he can recover his losses. This will require providing Carlos with advice in respect of an action under the Consumer Protection Act 1987 and the common law of negligence.[1] Carlos should be advised that the Consumer Protection Act 1987 was passed by Parliament to give effect to the Consumer Protection Directive. The aim was to better protect consumers from defective products

[1] You could legitimately consider the common law claim in negligence first. If you take this approach, you should adapt the structure of your introduction accordingly.

[2] You should provide some context to the legislation so that you are able to suitably advise Carlos about the different regimes applicable to each of the claims.

by resolving some of the problems that had existed in the common law claims for negligence.[2] Strict liability is imposed on a variety of individuals for producing or supplying products which cause damage due to their defective nature (s. 2(1)). There is no requirement of any fault on the part of the defendant; this can be contrasted with the position in the common law claim in negligence, which often leaves claimants uncompensated. It will be argued that while Carlos will be unable to obtain compensation for the damage to the phone charger, the other property damage sustained will be recoverable under one or both actions.

[3] You should always consider this issue first as if the property is not recoverable under the Act, it will not be possible to bring an action under the Act. Consequently, consideration of other issues in relation to a claim under the Act will be irrelevant.

Considering a potential claim under the Act, the first issue that must be considered is whether Carlos has suffered any actionable damage.[3] Under section 5(2) the loss of the phone charger is not recoverable. This would amount to a purely economic loss to the product itself. Damage to other property, such as Carlos's phone, bedside table, lamp and watch are potentially recoverable under section 5(1); however, this is subject to the limitations contained within section 5(3) and section 5(4). As the property in question can both be described as being intended for private use and is intended for private use by Carlos, then the requirements of section 5(3) are satisfied. In relation to section 5(4) a restriction is placed on property damage so that the total damage, excluding interest, must exceed £275. Consequently, if the total damage does not exceed £275 then Carlos will need to rely upon the common law claim in negligence in order to recover for his losses. If, however, the total damage does exceed £275, then an action may be brought under the Act for the loss that he has sustained.

[4] Here you are demonstrating that you have an appreciation of the practical implications that may be relevant to Carlos. Although you will ultimately advise Carlos that an action against WM Electronics may be inevitable, you are showing that you understand the wider issues.

The next matter is who is liable for the damage that Carlos has sustained. As WM Electronics have designed and manufactured the phone charger, they will be considered to be the producers of the product for the purpose of section 1(2). However, as WM Electronics are based in China, it may be more expedient and practical to sue Phone Warehouse as the importer and/or supplier of the product.[4] Phone Warehouse will only be considered the importer of the product under section 2(2)(c) if they have imported the product into a Member State from a place outside the Member States in the course of business. It is not clear from the facts whether Phone Warehouse were themselves the importer of the phone chargers, or if this was

⁵ Although this is potentially a possibility, a firmer conclusion cannot be drawn, due to the lack of facts in support of a conclusion either way.

⁶ You should explain why the courts have taken such an approach and comment on the justification for it. This is particularly so considering that some authorities have attempted to incorporate a degree of fault into an assessment of defectiveness.

⁷ You should try to remember as many of the key points from the legislation and paraphrase them in your answer. This will then provide you with a framework for your application.

done by another company. Depending on whether or not this was the case, Phone Warehouse may or may not be a suitable defendant in an action brought by Carlos under section 2(2)(c).⁵ What is clear from the facts is that Phone Warehouse would be considered to be a supplier of the product under s. 2(3). However, as the packaging of the phone charger identifies WM Electronics as the manufacturer of the product, a requirement for imposing liability on Phone Warehouse as the supplier is missing. Therefore, any action that Carlos brings would need to be brought against either WM Electronics or the importer of the product, whoever this may be.

Under section 3(1) of the Act, a defect in the phone charger must be established. The section makes it clear that a product is defective if the 'safety of the product is not such as persons are generally entitled to expect', taking into account all the circumstances. Carlos should be made aware that although the Act dispenses with any need to prove fault on the part of the defendant, the burden will still rest with him to prove that the phone charger is defective. 'Such as persons generally are entitled to expect' is an objective assessment rather than one which is taken from the subjective perspective of either the claimant or the defendant (*A v National Blood Authority* [2001] 3 All ER 289; *Wilkes v DePuy International Ltd* [2016] EWHC 3096). Although this creates a certain amount of flexibility, it should be noted that what is considered defective remains a stringent requirement, which is in keeping with the strict liability ethos of the Act.⁶ According to section 3(2) the courts will take into consideration the manner in which, and purpose for which the product has been marketed, the get-up of the product, any warnings or instructions as to use, what reasonably is expected to be done with or in relation to the product, and the time at which the product is supplied.⁷ Persons generally would expect that a phone charger could be plugged in to charge a phone overnight. The overheating and fire risk that WM Electronics and Phone Warehouse were aware of as a consequence of the complaints made in China would imply that the product would be considered defective. This is particularly the case given that the product was marketed under the name 'Safety Charge' and directed towards persons who charge their phones overnight, which implies a higher expectation in terms of safety as compared with a regular phone charger. However, the inclusion of a warning on the packaging of the phone charger may mean that the courts consider that

8 Use your wider research
to offer some evaluation in
respect of the issue that you
are addressing.

the product is not defective. Where the danger is a known one, it is argued in *Clerk and Lindsell* (2018)[8] that the standard will bear some similarity to that in negligence, despite the strict liability approach of the Act, as the courts will need to consider the adequacy of the warning provided by WM Electronics. The vagueness of the warning label may be insufficient to alter expectations about safety and, as such, the product is likely to be considered defective.

In the event that the phone charger is considered to be defective despite the warning on the box, it is clear that this defect caused the damage sustained by Carlos. It is also clear that none of the defences contained in section 4 are applicable. However, under section 6(4) contributory negligence can still apply under the Act. The warning specifies that the phone charger should not be used for a prolonged period of time; however, Carlos left his phone on to charge overnight, which is arguably a prolonged period. While not capable of absolving WM Electronics of liability, they may be successful in arguing that Carlos's failure to heed the warning on the box, contributed to the damage that he sustained. If successful, the amount of any compensation payable to Carlos would be reduced based upon what was considered 'just and equitable' in the circumstances.[9]

9 Make sure that you convey to the marker that you understand that it is only a partial defence, as this shows that you fully understand the nature of the defence.

10 Include this to show that you are aware of the distinction between the two actions and to demonstrate why you are discussing the common law claim, even though it seems likely that Carlos would be successful in a claim under the Act.

Although the Act sought to better protect consumers, the statutory regime under the Act operates in a complimentary manner to common law negligence, which can still be utilised by a claimant. There is no value threshold and therefore if Carlos's property is valued at less than £275, then the common law claim will be the only claim available.[10] Carlos should be advised that the loss of the phone charger will be regarded as pure economic loss and, as such, will not be recoverable (***Murphy v Brentwood DC*** [1991] 1 AC 398) as is the case under the Act.

Carlos must show that he was owed a duty of care in relation to the product which is straightforward to establish. The *ratio* of ***Donoghue v Stevenson*** [1932] AC 562 is that a manufacturer of a product owes a duty of care to the ultimate consumer of the product. Consequently, WM Electronics will owe a duty of care to take reasonable care in the manufacture of the phone charger to ensure that they would be reasonably safe for their intended use.

The issue here is whether or not WM Electronics have taken reasonable care. The courts have been willing to infer a lack of reasonable care from the presence of a defect (***Grant v Australian Knitting***

Mills Ltd [1936] AC 85). The fact that WM Electronics were aware of the fault in the product is a strong indication of a lack of care on their part. WM Electronics did, however, provide a warning which may discharge their duty of care, but this is dependent upon the sufficiency of their warning. The warning must be such as to enable the user to be reasonably safe (*Vacwell* v *BDH* [1971] 1 QB 88). Informing the user to avoid 'prolonged use' is likely to be considered too vague for this purpose and, as such, a breach will arise.

[11] On the facts there appears to be no real issue in respect of causation and therefore you should sum these points up briefly in a single paragraph. Some questions may require more extensive consideration of causation issues and you may want to divide your answer into a paragraph on causation in fact and a paragraph on causation in law.

Carlos will need to demonstrate that the breach caused the damage sustained. There is no indication that the phone charger would have gone through any intermediate examination between manufacture and purchase and the fire damage was damage of a foreseeable type which would occur from the fault in the product.[11] Consequently, causation can be established. As explained above, the partial defence of contributory negligence may also apply in respect of the common law claim.[12]

[12] You have already addressed this point above so there is no need to repeat this in full.

In conclusion, Carlos is likely to have a claim under the Act for the damage sustained, provided that his property damage exceeds £275. Alternatively, Carlos is likely to have a claim at common law in negligence if this is not the case. Carlos should be aware, however, that the value of the phone charger will not be recoverable under either claim as this would amount to pure economic loss.

✓ Make your answer stand out

- Explain the rationale and merit for imposing strict liability on producers of defective products.
- Explore the problems which exist with each action and make a deeper comparison of the merits of Carlos bringing an action under each.
- Enhance your understanding of the actions by furthering your reading on them beyond your textbooks. Consider reading *Clerk and Lindsell on Torts*.
- Read Hodges, C. (2001) Compensating patients: case comment on *A* v *National Blood Authority* [2001] 2 All ER 289. *Law Quarterly Review*, 117: 528 in order to obtain some academic criticism of the judicial interpretation taken to the meaning of 'defect' under section 3.
- Read Nolan, D. (2018) Strict product liability for design defects, *Law Quarterly Review* 134:176 to explore the effect of the recent case of *Wilkes v DePuy International Ltd* [2016] EWHC 3096 on the meaning of 'defectiveness'.

! **Don't be tempted to . . .**

- Spend more time on the negligence action at the expense of the provisions of the Act. Remember that this is ultimately a question on product liability and you are likely to have a question elsewhere solely dedicated to common law negligence. If you treat the product liability problem question as an opportunity to repeat your answer from that other negligence question, you risk losing out on marks for not fully appreciating the scope of this question. You will also fail to show the full range of your knowledge.

- Try to show that you have more knowledge than you need by reciting parts of the Act which are not relevant, such as the range of defences within section 4. If you cover these in depth, it will instead show that you have not read the question properly and do not fully understand those provisions.

- Get tied up in the requirements of causation and remoteness unless the facts indicate that they warrant particular discussion. You must mention them, but the weight of discussion should reflect the extent that they are an issue on the facts of the question.

 Question 3

Piper and Galbraith plc is a pharmaceutical company and has recently produced a new drug, Fiagera, which is marketed as preventing anxiety attacks. The drug was subjected to trials in the UK in line with industry standards and approved by the national regulator.

Approval, though, was subject to the drug's packaging highlighting that it should not be used by people suffering from epilepsy. However, research in Canada indicated that an ingredient of the drug could cause kidney damage if it was taken for a sustained period. This was published in the *Journal of Canadian Medicine,* which is also available globally.

Manisha had regularly suffered anxiety attacks during her first two years at university. As a result, she visited Dr Legg who, having never seen Manisha before, prescribed her Fiagera without knowing that she suffered from epilepsy. After taking the drug for four weeks, Manisha went into epileptic shock. However, while she was in hospital it was also discovered that Manisha had suffered damage to her kidneys.

Advise Manisha on whether she could succeed in a claim against Piper and Galbraith for her injuries.

Diagram plan

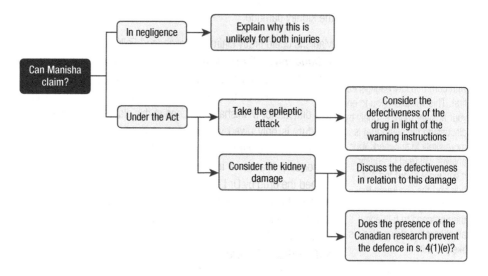

A printable version of this diagram plan is available from **www.pearsoned.co.uk/lawexpressqa**

Answer plan

➡ Start with whether Manisha could claim successfully in negligence for her injuries.

➡ Discuss the implications of the drug being prescribed by Dr Legg and whether this was a reasonable chance to inspect the product.

➡ Advise Manisha on how she could alternatively claim under the Consumer Protection Act 1987.

➡ Deal with the epilepsy injury first and consider whether the drug was defective in this regard.

➡ Discuss separately the kidney damage and whether the drug was defective in relation to that injury.

➡ Consider the possible defence under section 4(1)(e) and the issue of the state of scientific knowledge at the time of the drug's circulation.

Answer

The issue to advise Manisha about is whether she can successfully sue Piper and Galbraith (P&G) for the epileptic attack and the kidney damage following her taking Fiagera. There are two options available to her: one in negligence and another under the Consumer Protection Act 1987. It is argued that Manisha may succeed under the Act for the kidney damage.

[1] Owing to the facts of the question and the difficulties of bringing such a claim, deal with common law negligence first. This will allow you to end your answer more strongly by discussing the claim that is more likely to succeed. Your answer will read strangely if you write about the Act first and the argument that Manisha may succeed and then proceed to talk about an alternative claim which is likely to fail.

[2] While you have not been asked to advise Manisha regarding Dr Legg, by highlighting this you demonstrate your wider knowledge and understanding of negligence, so it is beneficial but do keep it brief.

[3] Use a sentence such as this, explaining why the Act has come about to link the two sections of your answer. You will show that you are aware of the Act's aim as a response to the difficulties mentioned, as well as developing a nice flow for your structure.

[4] While perhaps not seemingly directly in issue, highlight your awareness of this briefly to show your depth on the subject. This places your discussion of the Act in context.

Manisha could firstly claim in negligence.[1] Following the specific rule in **Donoghue v Stevenson** [1932] AC 562, a manufacturer owes a duty to take reasonable care when manufacturing a product, to ensure it is safe when used by the ultimate consumer. However, it would be very difficult for Manisha to succeed in this claim. Under **Donoghue** the duty is only owed when the product is intended to reach the consumer in the same state as it left the manufacturer, without any reasonable chance of intermediary inspection. Manisha was pre-scribed the drug by Dr Legg and so arguably there was a reasonable chance of inspection by him. Dr Legg should have enquired whether Manisha suffered epilepsy and thus not prescribed it to her in light of the warning. An analogy could be drawn here with **Evans v Triplex Safety Glass Co. Ltd** [1963] 1 All ER 283, where the windscreen was fitted by another party. Manisha should be advised that Dr Legg's failure to ask whether she suffered from epilepsy may mean that she would have a claim in negligence against him under **Bolam v Friern Hospital Management Committee** [1957] 1 WLR 582.[2] Even in relation to the kidney damage, Manisha is likely to have problems in negligence owing to the need to prove that, even if P&G failed to take reasonable care in producing the drug, this breach of duty caused her injuries. There could be various reasons for the kidney damage, such as Manisha's lifestyle or whether she was taking any other med-icines. This task is made harder by the fact that this is a design defect rather than a manufacturing defect and the courts have been more ready to infer negligence in the latter (**Grant v Australian Knitting Mills Ltd** [1936] AC 85). Therefore, Manisha is unlikely to succeed in negligence against P&G.

However, in view of the difficulties with a fault-based system of liability for defective products, a strict liability regime has been implemented in addition.[3] The Act implemented Directive 85/374/EEC, which sought to introduce strict liability for defective products as a means of ensuring a level of harmonisation for consumers within the Internal Market.[4] It is clear from section 1(2) and section 45 that the drug will be a product for the purposes of the Act. The fact that Fiagera is made up of different ingredients will not matter as section 1(2) states that a product also includes the component parts within an overall product. It is also clear that P&G will be the producer for the purposes of the Act as they have manufactured the drug (s. 1(2)).

The damage must be actionable under the Act which this is, as under section 5(1) damage means personal injury, which Manisha has clearly suffered. The question is whether the product was defective. Section 3 defines 'defect' as where the 'safety of the product is not such as persons generally are entitled to expect'. Guidance is given in section 3(2) which significantly states[5] that account should be taken of how the product is marketed and the instructions given. We are told that Fiagera was approved and marketed as not being suitable for epileptics. This causes a problem for Manisha as the first injury she suffers is that of an epileptic attack. In view of the marketing and that in section 3(2)(b) provision is made for what may reasonably be expected in terms of the product's use, Fiagera is unlikely to be defective. This is a prescription drug and so it is reasonable for P&G to expect that the drug would not be used by epileptics, especially as a warning was given against this. Therefore, Manisha is unlikely to succeed in a claim for the attack.

However, Manisha has also suffered kidney damage and the likelihood of this was not shown on the product.[6] Therefore, Manisha needs to be advised as to whether Fiagera was defective in relation to this injury. The issue in relation to this is that under section 3(2)(c) the courts should take account of the time at which the product was put into circulation. At this time, the trials had not shown that it could cause kidney damage. There was evidence from Canada that this would be the case. Further, this information was available globally and so, as a pharmaceutical company, it is arguable that P&G should have known of this. This is supported by the strict approach endorsed in **A.** The public would expect Fiagera to be safe, especially as it had undergone a trial. Therefore, the drug could be said to be defective. Manisha's problem, though, is that even if defective it must, on normal causation principles, be shown to have caused the kidney damage. Therefore, it must be shown that 'but for' the taking of Fiagera Manisha would not have suffered kidney damage.[7] It is difficult to say whether this was the case and a lot will rest on the conclusiveness of the Canadian research.

[5] When discussing this guidance, focus on the aspects which are most relevant to the facts of the question and ensure that you apply them to the facts. This will keep your answer structured and relevant. If you just spell out all of the points, your answer will become descriptive and not read as well.

[6] As the drug is more likely to be defective in relation to the kidney damage, you should deal with this separately from the epilepsy. This will aid your structure by making it clear that you have identified two separate issues.

[7] If you covered causation in more depth previously when dealing with the action at common law, then you can just refer back to it here. Make sure you do not repeat yourself.

If the drug is deemed defective and causation shown, Manisha should be advised that the Act does contain defences. The most significant is within section 4(1)(e). This concerns development risks. The producer's knowledge must not be such that a producer of the same product might be expected to have discovered the defect while the product was under his control.[8] Therefore, there is some overlap with whether the drug was defective. The question is whether a reasonable producer of the same product would have known that the defect existed at the time. While criticised as diluting the strictness of liability under the Act, it was approved in **Commission v UK** [1997] 3 CMLR 923.

[8] You could learn the section in full and quote that, but as it is quite long it may be better to paraphrase it. This will also show that you understand what the section means, as you can write it in your own words.

However, even if generously interpreted, it is unlikely P&G would satisfy this as, arguably, a reasonable producer would keep up to date with the latest scientific research.[9] Further, the journal was published before Fiagera was marketed and as it is a global publication it was accessible, which is what is necessary (**Commission v UK**).

[9] By highlighting that the claim is likely to succeed even on a generous view, it strengthens the argument that the defence will fail.

Therefore, Manisha will be successful in claiming for the kidney damage under the Act provided she can satisfy the issue of causation, which may not be easy, as shown in **X v Schering Health Care Ltd** [2002] EWHC 1420. The drug is unlikely to be deemed defective in relation to the epilepsy.

✔ **Make your answer stand out**

- Explore the debate further around section 4(1)(e) and the corresponding part of the Directive and the extent to which the section is compatible.

- Explain in more depth the distinction made in *A* v *National Blood Authority* [2001] 3 All ER 289 between standard and non-standard products.

- Consider the merits of strict liability over fault-based negligence. In furtherance of this, look at Hodges, C. (2001) Compensating patients: case comment on *A* v *National Blood Authority* [2001] 2 All ER 289. *Law Quarterly Review,* 117: 528; and Howells, G. and Mildred, M. (2002) Infected blood: defect and discoverability, a first exposition of the EC Product Liability Directive, *Modern Law Review,* 65: 95.

- Discuss the prospect of P&G being jointly liable with the national regulator that approved the drug.

Don't be tempted to . . .

■ Ignore either of the possible claims in favour of solely talking about the other in depth. As the question does not set any limits, you need to discuss both. Even if you do not do so because you feel that claim is futile, it may look as though you did not realise there is a chance of the claim. At the very least raise it to dismiss the possibility of success.

■ Get into a discussion of loss of a chance and *Gregg* v *Scott* [2005] 2 AC 176 with regards to any chance of the kidney damage occurring.

■ Merge your discussion on both injuries, as arguably the outcome will be different and so you may find you compromise the clarity of your argument.

■ Set out all of the defences within section 4 unless you can make the case for them being relevant; otherwise you will use up valuable time without gaining any real benefit.

@ Try it yourself

Now take a look at the question below and attempt to answer it. You can check your response against the answer guidance available on the companion website (**www. pearsoned.co.uk/lawexpressqa**).

Sue is a professional beauty therapist and has run her own salon for 20 years. One day she was offered an alternative supply of fake tan lotion from a producer, Ray Tans Ltd. She bought them as these were considerably cheaper than her current stock, even though she would not have usually done so as she had heard some negative comments about one of the ingredients. The next day, Sue applied the lotion on Gail who had wanted a tan for a cocktail party she was going to that night. Due to the ingredient that Sue had been wary of, Gail quickly developed a burning sensation all over which developed into a severe rash. Gail was unable to attend the party that night which had cost her £80 for the ticket and a further £400 for a new outfit.

Advise Gail about her options.

www.pearsoned.co.uk/lawexpressqa

 Go online to access more revision support including additional essay and problem questions with diagram plans, you be the marker questions, and download all diagrams from the book.

Vicarious liability

7

How this topic may come up in exams

Vicarious liability is an important topic as there could be an element of it in a problem question on any other topic, with varying degrees of emphasis. However, it can also be examined on its own. Where this is the case, it is more likely to be an essay with questions focusing on the justification for imposing liability on a third party who did not commit the tort. Therefore, as well as knowing the mechanics of how the doctrine works, you will need an in-depth knowledge of the policy and theoretical reasons for and against it.

■ Before you begin

Acquaint yourself with the following components and key issues of this topic; and familiarise yourself with how you would structurally progress through them all, if necessary, when attempting to answer a question on this topic.

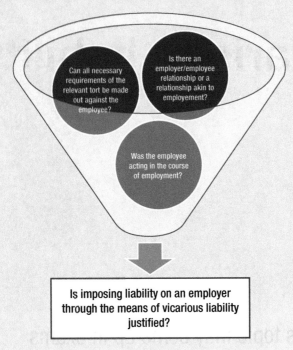

Is imposing liability on an employer through the means of vicarious liability justified?

A printable version of this diagram is available from **www.pearsoned.co.uk/lawexpressqa**

 Question 1

'The law of vicarious liability is on the move.' *Per* Lord Phillips in *Various Claimants* v *Catholic Welfare Society* [2012] UKSC 56 at [19]

Critically evaluate how the law of vicarious liability has developed in recent years and whether its expansion has merit.

Diagram plan

A printable version of this diagram plan is available from **www.pearsoned.co.uk/lawexpressqa**

Answer plan

→ Explain how the law works and assess the traditional justifications for its operation.

→ Discuss the traditional requirements for the doctrine to operate on employers.

→ Consider how the law has been 'on the move'.

→ Evaluate the merits of the law's development and whether it is still compatible with its original rationale.

[1] Use aspects of the quote to support your proposition as to what you feel the question is asking you to address and prove you have understood what is being asked as opposed to having had a lucky guess.

Answer

The issue to address here is the manner in which vicarious liability is 'on the move'[1] and whether its recent expansion is justifiable. The traditional requirements of the law were interwoven with its policy

[2] Your aim here is to introduce briefly why the issue that you are asked to address arises and needs addressing. You want to indicate that you are aware of the underlying issues and what has caused them; you can then build on these in the main body of your answer. This helps to reinforce that you understand the area of law as well as the question.

[3] It is worth showing that you appreciate the true nature of this topic and it is particularly important to demonstrate that you know it is not a tort itself.

[4] Corrective justice is a fundamental principle of tort, so it is always good to incorporate reference to it in an answer to highlight your appreciation of it. Here, as the question explores the justification for the doctrine of vicarious liability, the aim is to start to contrast its compatibility with this fundamental principle.

[5] Start with this point as it relates back to the criticism raised in the previous paragraph and so helps your answer flow. You can then also link it to other tortious principles to show how the doctrine is compatible with the wider underlying theory of tortious liability. Additionally, by evaluating the theoretical justification for the doctrine first, you can establish whether any issues are at this level or simply ones of application by the courts.

justifications. Therefore, any change in its scope to address new issues raises questions as to whether those policy justifications are still met. If not, the validity of the law can justifiably be called into question.[2] However, it is argued that the current application is a logical extension of the traditional position, which is flexible, and still correlates to the doctrine's original justifications.

Vicarious liability is a doctrine[3] which has historically shifted liability from an individual tortfeasor to their employer, even in the absence of direct fault or breach of duty by the latter. Accordingly, the burden of strict liability is placed on businesses with the potential for negative economic consequences, and arguably contrary to principles of corrective justice due to the lack of obvious fault on their part.[4]

However, the doctrine has several justifications. While seemingly at odds with corrective justice, it actually supports it by ensuring that an injured claimant obtains compensation as the business, through insurance policies, will be better placed to pay than the individual employee tortfeasor.[5] As such, its operation also gives effect to the principles of loss distribution, economic efficiency and deterrence. The more that compensation is paid out, the higher the costs of operating that business activity are, even if only through increased insurance premiums. Higher costs will be passed to their customers

[6] Discuss the practical impact of the doctrine, as it is against this which its justification must ultimately be judged. If it causes firms to go out of business, the doctrine could be argued as being objectionable on policy grounds.

[7] Staring your discussion of the requirements in this way allows you to relate them to the justifications which you have just considered. This will help enable you to determine where any problems lie and perhaps more strongly support the doctrine by showing that its application correlates to its rationale.

[8] You need to set up a discussion on the merits of this development, but in a way which identifies what the issue is in light of what you have mentioned previously.

[9] Whatever you feel the justifications are, you ought to introduce them with wording such as this to tie these concluding remarks back to your introduction and the issue that you have raised at the start of this paragraph.

[10] This requirement has not really 'moved' in some time, but in discussing what vicarious liability is, you need to highlight what the requirement entails for completeness. This allows you though to then evaluate whether it does need be moved on as well, despite what the courts have recently said in response to criticism of it.

which increases the price of their goods/services, reducing their market competitiveness.[6] Therefore, competiveness and profitability rely on the activity not causing injuries. The social justification for this is that employers have put in motion an activity for their benefit and so should carry the risk of liability if that activity causes damage (**Rose v Plenty** [1976] 1 WLR 141).

While justified theoretically, the law's rationale means liability is not automatically imposed, and two requirements need satisfying.[7] First, the tortfeasor is an employee, and secondly, they are acting in the course of their employment. Originally, the employment status of the tortfeasor was based on the level of control exerted over them, but as employment practices changed alongside technological developments, an economic reality test was applied which requires an assessment of factors which could illustrate an employment relationship alongside control (**Market Investigations Ltd v Minister of Social Security** [1969] 2 QB 173).

However, the first requirement has moved on following a series of cases whereby the relationship between the organisation in question and the individual tortfeasor could not realistically be described as one of employment, regardless of how that is assessed. This raises questions about the doctrine's validity as the initial justifications for it would seem inapplicable.[8] Now, the doctrine can apply to any relationship provided that the tort was committed as a result of activity taken by the tortfeasor on behalf of the defendant enterprise and which is likely to be part of its business; and the defendant enterprise created the risk of the tort by engaging the tortfeasor to undertake that activity.

The inherent vagueness of the position was acknowledged in **Cox v Ministry of Justice** [2016] UKSC 10, but this was accepted as being necessary to reflect the wide range of situations to which it will need to be applied. Overall, these requirements maintain the law's compatibility with its original justifications[9] of economic efficiency and deterrence, and the above statement of principle in **Rose v Plenty.**

The doctrine's second requirement was also developed[10] in **Lister v Hesley Hall** [2002] 1 AC 215. Now, a 'close-connection' test assesses whether the tort was so closely connected with the function the tortfeasor was entrusted to conduct so as to make it fair and just to shift liability to the enterprise in question. This has

[11] In *Lister* no test of uniform language was adopted, so it is important that you identify which judge you are referring to as this can help show that you are aware of that fact.

[12] Generally, you should avoid listing several cases that all say the same thing: save time and space by just picking the best authority to support your point. Think quality not quantity. However, here the situation is different. The aim is to demonstrate the significance of the problem with the test by showing the repetition of the same critical point from the highest level of the judiciary.

[13] If this requirement is at odds with part of the law's justification then it is hard to defend, which leads you into a discussion of whether the law should have been moved on in *Mohamud*.

[14] It could be easy to overlook Lord Dyson and just focus on Lord Toulson who gave the leading opinion with which everyone else agreed. However, Lord Dyson, in his short individual opinion, covers this point in more detail. Using him also shows you have a fuller level of knowledge of the case.

[15] As above, have the courage to express your own view and consider whether the issues that are suggested as being detrimental are in fact so, even if they do not feature in any judicial comments. This allows you to really evaluate the merits of the arguments relating to the

resulted in questionable applications of the doctrine, particularly in cases where the conduct was illegal and prohibited. In *Lister* the employee warden had sexually abused children in his employer's care. Liability was imposed because as Lord Steyn[11] highlighted, the tort was 'inextricably interwoven' with his duties. The warden had the function of discharging his employer's duty of care owed to the children, which he clearly failed to do.

That the test is also inherently imprecise has been acknowledged repeatedly in the Supreme Court with Lord Nicholls in *Dubai Aluminium Co. Ltd v Salaam & Others* [2003] 1 AC 366 accepting it offers no clear guidance on the degree of connection that is necessary, which Lord Phillips agreed with in *Various Claimants v Catholic Child Welfare Society* [2012] UKSC 56.[12] Operational vagueness raises questions as to the doctrine's rationale, with Longmore LJ in *Maga v Birmingham Roman Catholic Archdiocese Trustees* [2010] EWCA Civ 256 querying whether the aim is simply to ensure someone can pay and encourage more vigilance from employers. Enterprises may have difficulty in securing sufficient insurance though to pay compensation when they do not know what acts may need covering. Even if obtained, the premiums may be too prohibitive, thus reducing their competitiveness and their financial health: all for an act which was not of their doing and even expressly prohibited. This is hard to defend and negates this aspect of the law's rationale.[13] Accordingly, the Supreme Court was invited to abolish the test in *Mohamud v WM Morrison Supermarkets plc* [2016] UKSC 11.

The invitation was rejected as the test only imposes liability where it is just to do so. While giving the doctrine further ambiguity, as Lord Dyson noted,[14] it allows further flexibility and application to new situations, with the imprecision being common to many aspects of tort. As the test had been repeatedly applied, any replacement test would need to be clearly better. Further, as any uncertainty could instead be viewed positively,[15] enterprises must ensure they undertake appropriate and regular checks so those they engage are competent. While all wrongful acts may be unforeseeable, organisations have a degree of control on events by engaging the individual. It is surely good commercial practice to perform adequate risk assessments.

Significantly, Lord Dyson in *Mohamud* also held that while the law needed to be 'on the move' in relation to the type of relationship doctrine's justification. What you need to do is show that they build on the views that you have already expressed and supported with authority so that the reader can see they provide the authority for your original view. This is why using words such as 'further' and 'additionally' at the start of the point matter; they make the link back to the previous point.

[16] Arguably by this point you have addressed this aspect of the law and the question sufficiently, but by briefly including this final point from Lord Dyson's opinion you can round off your answer by tying it back to the quote and highlighting the distinction between the two elements of the doctrine.

[17] This is worded in this way, particularly the use of 'corrected', to link back to the idea of corrective justice and to reiterate the law's compatibility with fundamental principles of tort.

required in order to respond to changes in the modern world, there was no such societal change which necessitated this second element of the law to be 'on the move'.[16]

In conclusion, aspects of the doctrine have been 'on the move' in order to ensure that the law remains relevant in light of the world in which it now operates. This development has been a logical progression to its traditional operation and without it the law would arguably be unjustifiable, as claimants could lose out due to technical distinctions between types of working practices, undermining the foundation principles of tort. The current approach provides flexibility to ensure liability is imposed on those whom it is just to be burdened by it and ensure tortious acts are corrected through compensatory payments,[17] spreading losses to those who are most able to bear them.

✔ **Make your answer stand out**

- Demonstrate your understanding of the underlying general principles of tort so that you can draw on them in support of the argument that you advance. In particular, explain how the new requirements are compliant with traditional principles.
- Ensure that you have read the linked cases of *Cox* v *Ministry of Justice* [2016] UKSC 10 and *Mohamud* v *WM Morrison Supermarket plc* [2016] UKSC 11 which review each requirement of the subject and the development they have had since their inception. They also state the current law on each requirement within the context of the policy justification for each.
- Read Morgan, P. (2013) Vicarious liability on the move. *Law Quarterly Review*, 129: 139 to obtain academic insight on whether the changes to the type of relationship needed should lead to development of the second requirement despite the view expressed in *Mohamud*.

■ Incorporate additional academic opinion into your work in support of your argument and also as something to argue against. Try:

 – Gilliker, P. (2006) The ongoing march of vicarious liability. *Cambridge Law Journal*, 489;

 – Hope, Lord (2013) Tailoring the law on vicarious liability. Law Quarterly Review, 129: 514;

 – Bell, J. (2013) The basis of vicarious liability. *Cambridge Law Journal*, 17.

! Don't be tempted to . . .

■ Simply focus on describing how the law has moved on. You need to consider the validity of the moves.

■ Try to establish a definitive explanation and justification for the doctrine. Simply outline the basic premise and highlight some of the various factors advanced in support of it.

■ Gloss over the need to discuss the requirement for an employment relationship. Even though this has now seemingly been reduced in importance, it is this change which really raises questions about the ongoing justification of the doctrine.

🖎 Question 2

'It is a fact of life, and therefore to be expected by those who carry on businesses, that sometimes their agents may exceed the bounds of their authority or even defy express instructions. It is fair to allocate risk of losses thus arising to the businesses rather than leave those wronged with the sole remedy, of doubtful value, against the individual employee who committed the wrong.' (*Per* Lord Nicholls in *Dubai Aluminium Co. Ltd* v *Salaam & Others* [2003] 1 AC 366 at [22].)

Critically evaluate whether the current test for establishing whether an employee has acted in 'the course of employment' is justifiable, with particular reference to intentional wrongdoing on the part of the employee?

Answer plan

➡ Explain the operation of the doctrine of vicarious liability in the employment context.

➡ Outline the basic requirements for establishing vicarious liability in the employment context, with particular reference to the 'close-connection' test.

➡ Critically examine the merits and criticisms of the doctrine with particular reference to intentional wrongdoing by the employee.

➡ Conclude on whether or not the current regime for establishing vicarious liability in the employment context is justifiable.

Diagram plan

A printable version of this diagram plan is available from **www.pearsoned.co.uk/lawexpressqa**

Answer

Employers can be held liable for the act of employees who commit tortious acts while acting in the course of their employment. This is through an operation of the doctrine of vicarious liability, which transfers liability from the tortfeasor to their employer. The doctrine operates in a strict manner that requires no fault or wrongdoing on the part of the employer in order for liability to be established and an obligation to pay compensation to the injured party imposed. This strict liability approach does not accord with the typical notion of fault-based liability upon which tort law is frequently premised and, as such, numerous justifications have been advanced in order to justify liability that operates in this manner.[1] While vicarious liability can be justified in the context of an employee who has negligently performed his employment duties in the course of furthering the employer's business interests, the position is more difficult to justify in relation to the intentional wrongdoing of an employee. It is argued that although vicarious liability is potentially more difficult to justify as a consequence of recent legal developments, it continues to be appropriate to impose liability on employers for the tortious conduct of their employees.[2]

In order for an employer to be held vicariously liable for the acts of their employees, there must be an employer/employee relationship or a relationship akin to employment between the defendant and the

[1] Ensure you identify the nature of vicarious liability in your introduction of your first paragraph as it provides the context for the remainder of your evaluation.

[2] By stating this in your introductory paragraph you indicate to the marker from the outset where you are going with the remainder of your answer.

[3] You should outline the requirements of employers' vicarious liability towards the beginning of your answer. Although the issue of employee status is one which could be explored in extensive detail, it is not appropriate to do so in response to the question asked of you.

[4] Consider the practical implications of the test as supported by both legal and academic opinion. You can then rely on these when evaluating the law in the context of the overarching justifications.

[5] Up until this point in your answer, you have only really been scene setting. The remainder of the answer will consider the underlying justifications for vicarious liability, which is where you will respond more directly to the question asked of you.

[6] By opening the paragraph in this way, you are demonstrating that you are able to link the closeness of the connection test with the issues raised in the quotation in the question.

[7] Although you could finish this point here, by expanding on the reason why an employer is in a better position to compensate, you enable yourself to expand on your evaluation.

tortfeasor (*Various Claimants* v *Catholic Child Welfare Society* [2012] UKSC 56).[3] Further, the tortfeasor must have committed a tort that is referable to the employment relationship. The test for determining whether this is the case, is the 'close-connection' test as outlined in *Lister* v *Hesley Hall Ltd* [2002] 1 AC 215, which asks whether the acts of the employee are so closely connected to his employment that it would be fair and just to hold the employer vicariously liable.

The test appears more expansive than the pre-*Lister* position and provides the courts with a greater degree of latitude in determining whether or not vicarious liability should be imposed. Giliker (2006; 2010) has consistently argued that the lack of definitive formulation of the test is causing problems for lower courts,[4] which is reflected in the opinion of Lord Nicholls in *Dubai Aluminium Co. Ltd* v *Salaam and Others* [2003] 1 AC 366. Giliker further suggests that *Lister* has allowed the doctrine to be applied in inappropriate areas. This is arguably the case in situations where there is intentional wrongdoing on the part of the tortfeasor, such as the sexual abuse in *Lister* and the assault in *Mohamud* v *WM Morrison Supermarkets plc* [2016] UKSC 11, which previously would have been unlikely to have fallen within the scope of the doctrine. However, given the opportunity in *Mohamud,* the courts rejected abolition of the close-connection test, as it was deemed sufficient for the purpose that it should be utilised for.[5]

Ensuring that the claimants received adequate compensation was clearly a matter that was influential on the approach taken in *Lister* and its importance is reiterated by Lord Nicholls in *Salaam.* The post-*Lister* expansion to employer's vicarious liability is obviously favourable to the claimant and more readily ensures that compensation is available to them.[6] However, there is also scope for suggesting that the longstanding justifications for vicarious liability are being undermined.

Vicarious liability has been justified as a method of ensuring distributive justice, by facilitating the payment of compensation by the party who is in the better position to bear the loss. In the employment context, it is the employer that has the 'purse worth opening' (Williams: 1956) as compared with the potentially impecunious employee.[7] This is due to the fact that the employer can be expected to insure against the risk of liability and, as a consequence, the loss is more widely distributed. It will be the insurer and not the employer that will pay the sum of the compensation and the employer can potentially absorb any costs that arise as a consequence of successful litigation, by passing them on to consumers. However, a lack of legal certainty arising from the flexibility inherent in the close-connection test and an extension of vicarious liability to cover an employee's intentional wrongdoing,[8] may mean that employers are potentially unable to adequately insure themselves to mitigate against the possibility of litigation. This may arise due to a lack of foresight about conduct which would fall within or outside of the course of employment. In the absence of adequate insurance, it is submitted that the doctrine would operate harshly[9] on employers.

Notwithstanding this potential harshness, vicarious liability can be further justified upon the basis that damage to the claimant has arisen in pursuance of the employer's course of business, from which they derive a benefit. As Fleming (1998) suggests, an employer who employs another to pursue his own interests, should be placed under a corresponding liability for losses that arise in the course of such an enterprise. This is echoed by Lord Nicholls in **Salaam** and while readily justifying the imposition of liability on an employer, whose employee merely carries out their employment duties in a negligent manner, it is more difficult to extend to intentional wrongdoing.[10] In **Lister** for example, the sexual abuse could not be considered as the employee carrying out an authorised act in an unauthorised manner. The conduct was clearly prohibited by the employer, illegal in nature and was completely contradictory to the pursuance of the employer's business interests.[11] However, the employment relationship was considered more than just the backdrop to the tortious conduct; Lord Steyn highlighted that the tortfeasor's abuse of the children was 'inextricably interwoven' with his duties as a warden. As Lord Hobhouse explained, a relationship between the claimant and the employer which imposed duties on the latter had been assumed. By entrusting performance of that duty to the warden, it created a sufficient connection to make it fair and just to impose liability. Explaining the approach taken by the court in this manner allows the decision to be reconciled with the justification outlined above; however, it is harder to do so in cases such as **Mohamud.**

A further justification for imposing vicarious liability on an employer is that it brings with it a deterrent factor. The possibility of litigation

[8] This relates back to the points that you have previously made.

[9] 'Harsh' is not the same as 'unjustifiable'. Ensure that you utilise precise language to convey the tenor of your argument.

[10] Do not neglect to consider intentional wrongdoing in your answer. If you do, you will not be adequately addressing the question asked.

[11] Relate your analysis of the case back to the justification that you are evaluating to provide further support for the argument you are making. However, be sure to take a balanced approach to your evaluation where it is appropriate to do so.

incentivises the employer to ensure that they employ competent staff and adopt safe working practices. To this end, vicarious liability reinforces an employers' primary common law duties, which stands to benefit not only the employees, but also persons external to an employer's business such as consumers. This justification appears to have been enhanced as a consequence of the post-*Lister* regime. With liability being less predictable and more far-reaching, this may have the effect of raising standards within the work place in anticipation of litigation.

Although the current regime for imposing vicarious liability on an employer and, in particular, the close-connection test advanced in *Lister* have been much criticised, it has been argued that it remains justifiable on the grounds of distributive justice, enterprise risk and deterrence. The more expansive approach to liability endorsed in *Lister* and subsequent cases, can be perceived as operating particularly harshly on employers, especially where the tortious conduct in question arises from the employee's intentional wrongdoing. However, there does appear sufficient merit in the imposition of liability in this way, particularly when regard is given to ensuring that the claimant is adequately compensated.

✓ Make your answer stand out

- Consider some of the arguments used in the Canadian case of *Bazley* v *Curry* (1999) 174 DLR (4th) 45, SC (from which the House of Lords took the test) to show a broader understanding of its merits in applying to situations such as *Lister* v *Hesley Hall* [2002] 1 AC 215.
- Draw on *Mohamud* v *WM Morrison Supermarkets plc* [2016] UKSC to obtain recent quotes in favour of the test and why it should be retained, but also question the validity of that decision.
- Consider wider academic opinion on employers' vicarious liability. Do not be afraid to consider older sources that explore the justifications for vicarious liability; however, ensure that you read and utilise these with the current tests for vicarious liability in mind.

! Don't be tempted to . . .

- Broaden your answer to deal in detail with the wider aspects of vicarious liability; a descriptive account of the law relating to employee status, for example, will not enable you to adequately respond to the question.
- Simply describe the justifications for vicarious liability. You need to relate your consideration of the justifications back to the question that it is asked of you.

🖎 Question 3

Brett is an uninsured plumber who gets his work from Brogan Construction. Brett is always instructed on what is required for the job and how it should be carried out by the Brogan foreman, although he must supply all his own tools, including a van to get to each job; he can bring his own labourers to a job, but he must pay them out of his wages. Brogan pays Brett a daily rate for any jobs, but he receives no other benefits.

Recently, owing to a shortage of plumbing work on offer, Brogan arranged for Brett to do some work with Hacker Heating Ltd in return for a fee. The job involved fitting a new boiler in a residential property, owned by Ted. However, owing to a part turning up late, Brett rushed the installation as it was already past his normal finish time with Brogan Construction, he had a hangover from the night before and wanted to get to bed. The boiler subsequently exploded, killing Ted.

It has been accepted that the boiler was installed negligently and that this caused the explosion; however, Brett has argued that as an employee he should not be held personally liable, while Hacker Heating Ltd argue he was certainly not their employee.

Advise Brogan Construction on whether they could be held vicariously liable for Ted's death.

Diagram plan

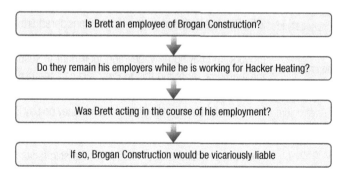

A printable version of this diagram plan is available from **www.pearsoned.co.uk/lawexpressqa**

Answer plan

➡ Explain what the doctrine of vicarious liability is and why it is important to this situation.

➡ Establish whether Brett can be considered an employee of Brogan Construction.

➡ Discuss whether Brett is in the course of his employment.

➡ Evaluate the implications of the work being for Hacker Heating Ltd.

Answer

[1] Although it is not going to need discussing as the doctrine can apply to all torts, it is worth confirming that you are aware of what tort Brogan Construction could be vicariously liable for.

[2] As you have to advise on their potential liability, you will be referring to them a lot, so abbreviate the name.

[3] This means that straightaway you have identified the key aspect of the topic to be addressed without straying into irrelevant material.

[4] BC would naturally argue they did not do anything wrong so why should they be liable. Therefore, in a question such as this explain why the issue of liability even arises to illustrate that you understand the theory behind the doctrine.

[5] You need to state enough to show that you understand the basis for the doctrine, while not deviating from a structure which the question warrants.

[6] The point here is to show that you know what the purpose of the requirement of employee status is, but you need to remember to frame your explanation in the context of giving advice to a lay party, i.e. BC.

There is no issue that compensation for Ted's death is due under the tort of negligence;[1] the matter to be resolved is simply whether Brogan Construction (BC)[2] will have to pay this under the doctrine of vicarious liability. This rests on whether Brett is actually an employee of BC.[3] It is argued that while they may have some liability, they should be able to successfully argue that Hacker Heating (HH) should be the predominant contributor of any compensation.

BC should be advised that the reason they face potential liability is that the doctrine operates to shift losses so that they are borne by those who are most appropriate to do so.[4] As employers have set in motion matters for their benefit, it is deemed acceptable for them to run the risk of their employee's malfeasance and compensate any injuries caused through the work.[5]

This explanation forms the basis of the requirements which need to be met for an employer to be liable. The first is naturally that the tortfeasor is an employee. If they are not, there is no justification behind the transferring of liability.[6] Traditionally, this is determined by applying the control test (***Short v J & W Henderson Ltd*** (1946) SC (HL) 24). This is significant as the factors considered are the employer's power to select who does the work, their right to control the method of work, the paying of wages and their right to suspend or dismiss the individual. Applying this to Brett, we can see that BC do choose what work he does and dictate how it is performed. While we do not know the details regarding the last point, they do pay Brett his wages. Therefore, in all, Brett would seem to be their employee.

However, the control test is no longer the sole factor to determine a person's employee status. Reflecting changes in working practices and technological developments, it was felt that simply looking at the level of control was not appropriate. Instead a range of economic factors are also considered – the economic reality test (***Market Investigations Ltd v Minister of Social Security*** [1969] 2 QB 173). This requires, among other factors, an assessment of who provides the equipment and whether the person can hire helpers. On these factors, Brett seems more of an independent contractor, as we are told he brings his own equipment and pays labourers from his own wages; contractors are also quite common in this field. If Brett is a

[7] While the issue may be unclear, you do need to offer some advice on Brett's status; otherwise you are not really answering the question, which is to advise BC. Highlight what you feel is the key factor which may swing a decision to support your opinion.

[8] Reflect the fact that it is uncertain by framing the opening sentence like this. Even if you do not feel Brett is an employee, you still need to continue to this section on the transfer issue as clearly this is a key part of the question; if you just stop with the previous section, there will be significant aspects of the question and topic which you will not have demonstrated any knowledge of.

[9] This is why it makes more sense to refer to *Mersey Docks* first and not just focus on *Viasystems* which comes next. If dual vicarious liability is possible on the facts, it would mitigate BC's otherwise potential full liability.

contractor, the doctrine would not apply and BC would avoid liability, but there are other economic factors which suggest Brett is an employee. Although not told definitively the facts regarding these, it seems Brett has no management responsibility and other than wages has no opportunity of profiting from the sound management of his task. Therefore, while it is possible Brett is not an employee, taken as a whole, particularly the element of control exerted over his work, it is quite likely that he is.[7]

On the basis that Brett is an employee,[8] the next issue to advise BC on is the fact that at the time of the tort Brett was working for HH. Under *Mersey Docks & Harbour Board v Coggins & Griffith (Liverpool) Ltd* [1947] AC 1, the permanent employer of the employee remains liable even after lending them to another firm. From the case, the decisive factors will be whether BC still pays Brett's wages and can still dismiss him, as well as how long Brett was sent to HH and how complex any machinery to be used is. In relation to the latter two points, Brett was only there to install a boiler and this was within his usual work for BC. As HH paid BC a fee for Brett's services, it is unlikely that they paid him as well; in view of the short duration and nature of the job BC should be advised that the facts suggest that they would remain liable for Brett's work.[9]

However, BC could benefit from *Viasystems (Tyneside) Ltd v Thermal Transfers (Northern) Ltd* [2006] QB 510 where the Court of Appeal held dual vicarious liability could exist in a situation such as this. Liability could be joint or several, with the contributions to be made by each side being determined by the Civil Liability (Contribution) Act 1978. While the court agreed dual liability was permissible, the judges gave differing reasoning. The judgment of Rix LJ was subsequently endorsed by the Supreme Court in *Various Claimants v Catholic Child Welfare Society* [2012] UKSC 56. A sufficient level of integration of the tortfeasor into the second enterprise would be needed. Brett would need to be so much of part of both businesses that it is just to hold both liable. From what we are told, Brett seems to have only been temporarily transferred to HH to perform the job of installing the one boiler. The facts suggest that after this job was finished, that day, he would return to BC. As such, there is not much in the way of integration into HH's organisation due to the very short nature of the transfer; while they may have had some control over how he worked while there, it does not appear he was working under their direction and with their equipment. As such, this is akin to the sort of situation that Rix LJ felt would not warrant dual liability, even if HH had some control over Brett's work. At most, BC may be able to obtain a contribution to the compensation payable to Ted's estate if they can show that there was sufficient integration of Brett into HH; they would not fully avoid liability though if all other requirements are satisfied.

[10] Do not forget this aspect of vicarious liability, as without it the previous discussion is irrelevant. While it seems apparent it will be satisfied, you do still need to touch on it to firmly show that you do in fact know it and can apply it.

Brett would still have needed to act in the course of his employment.[10] Clearly, as a plumber engaged to install a boiler, the negligent act was within his employment. The installation took place after Brett's normal finishing time, but while the tortious act must be performed within the authorised employment time, it is clear that Brett extended his day in order to finish the job and so will be classed as still within his employer's time (*Ruddiman & Co.* v *Smith* (1889) 60 LT 708). The fact that Brett would not be authorised to install a boiler negligently will also not suffice as the test is simply whether there is a sufficiently close connection between the tortious act and his employment to make it fair and just for the doctrine to operate (*Lister* v *Hesley Hall Ltd* [2002] 1 AC 215). This seems clearly satisfied on the facts.

Therefore, the potential vicarious liability of BC will turn on, firstly, whether Brett is deemed to be an employee of theirs. Even if he is, there is a small prospect of arguing that there should be dual liability with HH if sufficient integration can be shown, but this appears unlikely on the facts.

✓ **Make your answer stand out**

■ As there are not as many concrete facts to definitively apply in this question, draw on facts from similar cases involving borrowed employees, starting with *Viasystems (Tyneside) Ltd* v *Thermal Transfers (Northern) Ltd* [2006] QB 510, and judicial reasoning from those cases to support the arguments that you do advance.

■ Explain, using the judgment of May LJ in *Viasystems (Tyneside) Ltd* v *Thermal Transfers (Northern) Ltd* [2006] QB 510, why dual vicarious liability had not been used previously and consider the merits of allowing it. You can further draw on academic literature in this regard.

■ Question whether the Supreme Court has been right to favour the approach of Rix LJ to May LJ when it comes to what is required in this situation.

! Don't be tempted to . . .

- Make a definitive statement of fact as to Brett's employment, as the facts are not definitively conclusive; do assert a reasoned opinion though, about whether he is likely to be an employee.
- Explain the justification for vicarious liability simply on the common basis of insurance and the employer being better able to pay compensation, as this was viewed as not a principled justification in *Cox* v *Ministry of Justice* [2016] UKSC 10.
- Get into a full discussion about the 'close-connection' test. You will need to reference this, but remember the focus of the question is on the employee part of vicarious liability.
- Set out a full account of the tort of negligence, as the presence of the essential requirements are not an issue in the question. The issue is vicarious liability.

@ Try it yourself

Now take a look at the question below and attempt to answer it. You can check your response against the answer guidance available on the companion website (**www.pearsoned.co.uk/lawexpressqa**).

'The scope of vicarious liability depends upon the answers to two questions. First, what sort of relationship has to exist between an individual and a defendant before the defendant can be made vicariously liable in tort for the conduct of that individual?' *Per* Lord Toulson JSC in *Cox* v *Minsistry of Justice* [2016] UKSC 10; [2016] AC 660, [2].

Evaluate the approach taken by the courts in determining whether a relationship between a tortfeasor and another person is sufficient for the doctrine of vicarious liability to operate and shift liability to the latter.

www.pearsoned.co.uk/lawexpressqa

 Go online to access more revision support including additional essay and problem questions with diagram plans, you be the marker questions, and download all diagrams from the book.

Employers' liability

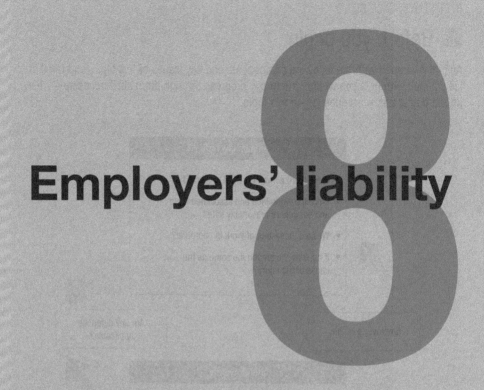

How this topic may come up in exams

Although the tort in question is negligence, it is again a specific application covering injuries caused by the claimant's colleagues, equipment or the system of work imposed by the employer. Naturally, there is an overlap with vicarious liability, but this area is theoretically distinct as liability is primary in nature, rather than secondary; the employer is deemed to have personally committed the wrong. Problem questions are more common than essays, but you should check carefully how this area is dealt with on your course in relation to vicarious liability and the extent that breach of statutory duty is covered alongside the common law duties.

Before you begin

Acquaint yourself with the following components and key issues of this topic; and familiarise yourself with how you would structurally progress through them all, if necessary, when attempting to answer a question on this topic.

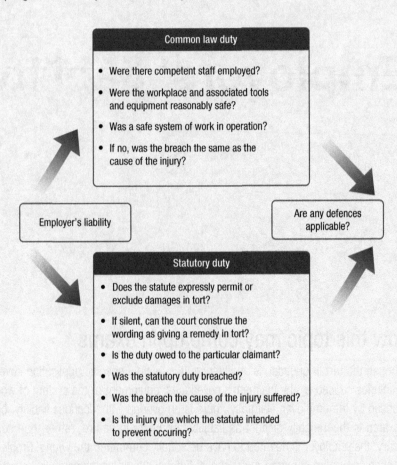

Common law duty

- Were there competent staff employed?

- Were the workplace and associated tools and equipment reasonably safe?

- Was a safe system of work in operation?

- If no, was the breach the same as the cause of the injury?

Employer's liability

Are any defences applicable?

Statutory duty

- Does the statute expressly permit or exclude damages in tort?

- If silent, can the court construe the wording as giving a remedy in tort?

- Is the duty owed to the particular claimant?

- Was the statutory duty breached?

- Was the breach the cause of the injury suffered?

- Is the injury one which the statute intended to prevent occuring?

A printable version of this diagram is available from **www.pearsoned.co.uk/lawexpressqa**

❓ Question 1

Samantha Avery is the managing director of Easy-Clean Cleaning Ltd, a cleaning company who provide both domestic and commercial cleaning services. The company has experienced the following incidents.

Lucille and Janet work on one of the commercial cleaning teams. Each of the teams is provided with a van, which is used to transport the cleaning trolleys and equipment between cleaning jobs. Each trolley includes all of the cleaning materials and safety equipment that should be used. They are restocked once a week at the main depot.

After feedback from their customers, the company decided to change the floor cleaner they use. A new floor cleaner was added to the trolleys as well as the safety masks that should be used because of the fumes that the cleaner emitted. No masks were required with the floor cleaner previously used and no additional instructions were provided to each team, other than those that were on the bottle. Lucille, who is responsible for cleaning the floor, did not use the masks provided and suffered from headaches after using the floor cleaner.

In the same week the main depot also forgot to restock the rubber gloves that should be used when using the cleaning chemicals. Janet, who does not tend to use the gloves when cleaning, has contracted dermatitis on her hands, which has meant that she is unable to work.

Kai works on one of the domestic cleaning teams with Beryl. Kai is known to be a bit of a jack-the-lad and only took the cleaning job as Samantha is his aunt and he needed the money to fund his nights out at the weekend. Kai is always messing around while at work and Beryl has made several complaints about him to Samantha. Although Samantha has had a word with Kai about this, Kai has not changed his behaviour. While on a cleaning job, Kai decides to swap the bottles over that Beryl was using to clean one of the bathrooms. Unbeknownst to her, she uses a very strong bleach which causes burns to her hands and arms.

Advise Samantha on the company's potential liability for the incidents.

Diagram plan

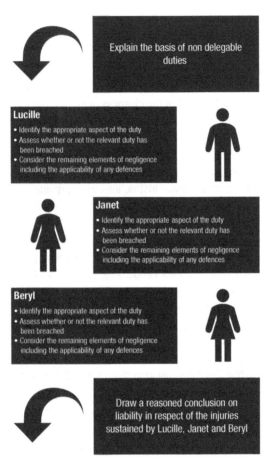

A printable version of this diagram plan is available from **www.pearsoned.co.uk/lawexpressqa**

Answer plan

→ Analyse the rationale for non-delegable duties and how they operate.

→ Explain that Lucille was owed a duty by the company to adopt a safe system of work and what that duty entails.

→ Consider whether the failures on the part of the main depot constitute a breach of duty.

→ Confirm that any breach could be said to have caused the injuries and that they were not too remote.

→ Discuss the possibility of the company successfully relying on a defence.

➜ Discuss the duty to provide adequate material and equipment in relation to Janet and then work through the same process used in relation to Lucille.

➜ Discuss the duty to employ competent staff in relation to Beryl and then work through the same process used in relation to Lucille.

Answer

[1] By discussing this in your introduction, you are able to demonstrate that you have correctly identified what specific issue of tort the question is addressing and that you have not mistakenly confused the question as one on vicarious liability.

[2] By identifying the aspects of the non-delegable duties that are at issue, you indicate to the marker where your answer is likely to go.

[3] This demonstrates an understanding of how liability operates in practice. The possibility of any compensation payable being covered by her insurance, is likely to be something of concern to Samantha.

[4] A short reference to the law prior to *Wilson and Clyde Coal Co* provides some context; however, you should not get too carried away with this part of your answer. The question is asking you to advise a party and not provide an account of the historical development of the law.

Samantha needs to be advised upon whether her company, Easy-Clean Cleaning Ltd, will be held liable in negligence for the injuries sustained by the parties, even though these were the fault of specific individuals. An employer owes a non-delegable duty of care to their employees and therefore may be held personally liable for harm caused to them.[1] It is argued that the relevant duties of providing a safe system of work, adequate material and equipment and a competent workplace, may have been breached in the instant case and caused the injuries sustained by Lucille, Janet and Beryl.[2] If an action by any of these parties were to be successful, the damages payable would potentially be covered by the company's insurance, as generally speaking employers are obliged to insure against liability in respect of bodily injury or disease to their employees since the Employers' Liability (Compulsory Insurance) Act 1969 came into force.[3]

An absence of insurance and a desire to allow emerging enterprises to flourish unencumbered, meant that historically employers were not burdened with civil liability in the manner by which it currently arises.[4] However, in response to the development of the doctrine of 'common employment', the case of **Wilson and Clyde Coal Co v English** [1938] AC 57 developed a series of non-delegable duties that are imposed upon all employers. The nature of the duty is such that an employer should see that reasonable care is taken for the safety of their employees. This duty is non-delegable in nature and therefore, in relation to any of the alleged breaches, it is not sufficient for Samantha to demonstrate that responsibility was delegated to another person such as those persons who restocked cleaning supplies to discharge. It is the responsibility of the employer to ensure that reasonable care *is* taken and, as a consequence, the company would be held liable even where they were themselves reasonable in delegating the responsibility of performance to another party.

The non-delegable duty of care comprises a number of different aspects, namely the duty to provide a safe place of work, duty to provide a safe system of work, duty to provide adequate plant and equipment and the duty to provide competent staff. Although often considered separately, these duties are in fact manifestations of the same overarching duty on an employer to take care for the reasonable safety of their workforce (*Wilson v Tyneside Window Cleaning Co* [1958] 2 QB 110).

[5] Give some depth to your answer by not only identifying the relevant aspect of the duty but also stating its scope. By explaining how the duty operates you are able to draw on it when applying the duty to the facts.

The first aspect of the duty that is relevant to Samantha is the duty to provide a safe system of work for employees to operate in. A safe system of work extends to the organisation of the work, the procedure to be followed in carrying it out, the sequence of the work, the taking of safety precautions, the number of workers to be employed and what roles they fulfil, and the provision of any necessary supervision (*Speed v Thomas Swift & Co Ltd* [1943] KB 557).[5] Samantha should be advised that in respect of the headaches suffered by Lucille, a breach of duty on the company's part may arise. The company may seek to establish that they provided a safe system of work as they provided additional safety materials, namely the masks, for use with the new floor cleaning chemicals and that the container for the chemicals suggested that masks should be worn. However, Lucille may argue

[6] Remember that you need to consider the arguments that are likely to be advanced by the opposing party in order to fully advise Samantha. Considering the different perspectives of the parties invites evaluation and analysis into your answer.

that the provision of the masks in the trolley alone was insufficient and that, in order to discharge their duty, specific instruction regarding the use of the masks and a warning about the dangers that would arise as a consequence of not utilising them should have been given by the company.[6] Following the decision in *Pape v Cumbria County Council* [1992] 3 All ER 211, it appears that Lucille would be successful in this argument and that a breach of duty be deemed to have arisen. This is particularly so, given that wearing masks constituted a change in the working practices that were utilised prior to the change in floor cleaner.

[7] Make sure that you do not overlook these points. Although they may not be particularly contentious issues, they are still crucial to the success of a claim. An answer that does not address matters such as causation when asked to advise on liability generally is likely to be considered to be incomplete.

This breach of duty to provide a safe system of work was the clear cause of Lucille's injury and there is no issue in respect of the injuries being too remote.[7] This would leave the company liable to pay compensation in the absence of any defence. The company may potentially raise the defence of contributory negligence under the **Law Reform (Contributory Negligence) Act 1945,** which would give them a partial defence and thus reduce the amount of compensation owed to Lucille.

The second aspect of the duty that is relevant to Samantha and her company is the provision of adequate plant and equipment, due to the failure to restock the rubber gloves in her cleaning trolley. 'Equipment' includes any material used by an employee for the purposes of the business (*Knowles* v *Liverpool City Council* [1993] 1 WLR 1428) and thus extends to the gloves. Although there appears to be a *prima facie* breach of duty as the gloves were not provided, an employer may be able to avoid liability in relation to a failure to provide safety equipment if they can establish that even if such equipment had been provided it would not have been used (*McWilliams* v *Sir William Arrol & Co Ltd* [1962] 1 WLR 295). This is essentially an argument based on causation. As Janet does not normally utilise the rubber gloves while cleaning, it appears likely that the company would avoid liability in this instance.

[8] This allows you to show not only that you have knowledge of vicarious liability, but also that you have an understanding of the relationship of the two and when each is applicable.

The third aspect of the duty that is relevant to Samantha and her company is the provision of competent staff. This extends further than just employing people who are competent to do the actual work and extends to situations falling outside the 'course of employment' requirement of vicarious liability (*Hudson* v *Ridge Manufacturing Co.* [1957] 2 QB 348).[8] In *Hudson* an employee was injured when a colleague, who had a reputation for being a practical joker, tripped him up. The colleague had previously been reprimanded in respect of his behaviour; however, owing to the seriousness of his conduct, the courts held that the employer should have done more to deter his behaviour and a breach of duty arose. Likewise in this case, although Samantha had previously spoken to Kai about his behaviour due to the complaints made by Beryl, little more appears to have been done to deter such behaviour and, as such, the company have breached their duty to employ competent staff.

[9] As with Lucille, you should state this clearly and concisely. Do not go through the motions of showing that there are no issues on this point. Save the time that you have for points which are more contentious and that allow you to demonstrate the higher level skills that a marker is looking for.

From the facts there do not appear to be any causation issues in respect of the injuries sustained by Beryl.[9] There also do not appear to be any relevant defences available to the company and, as a consequence, they will be liable to pay compensation to Beryl for the injuries sustained.

In conclusion, Samantha should be advised that duties are imposed on employers to ensure the safety of those who carry out work for them and thus from whom they are benefitting. In regards to the injuries sustained by Lucille and Beryl, it is likely that the company will be found to have fallen below the standard of a reasonably competent employer in this regard. However, in respect of the dermatitis contracted by Janet, issues pertaining to causation will be likely to prevent her from bringing a successful action.

✓ Make your answer stand out

- Demonstrate an appreciation of how this type of claim would operate in practice, particularly as a consequence of the mandatory insurance requirement imposed upon Easy-Clean Cleaning Ltd under the Employers' Liability (Compulsory Insurance) Act 1969.
- Expand slightly more on the difference between liability under this area and vicarious liability. On this point see Lord Sumption's opinion in *Woodland* v *Swimming Teachers Association* [2013] UKSC 66 and also Murphy, J. (2007) The juridical foundations of common law non-delegable duties in Neyers *et al.* (eds) *Emerging Issues in Tort Law.* Oxford: Hart Publishing.
- Draw on the opinion of Lord Sumption JSC in *Woodland* v *Swimming Teachers Association* [2013] UKSC 66 in order to consider in more detail the theoretical justification for imposing such duties on employers and for academic opinion look at Cotter, B. and Bennett, D. (2013) *Munkman on Employer's Liability,* 16th edition. London: LexisNexus.

! Don't be tempted to . . .

- Turn the question into one on the standard negligence duty: it is specifically about the non-delegable duties that an employer has. So the focus needs to be on those duties which are relevant to each situation.
- Go into detail about the non-delegable duties which are not within the focus of the question, as you will merely be describing everything you know and not advising Samantha on the specific issues which she is faced with.
- Focus too much of your answer on non-contentious issues such as causation in respect of Lucille and Beryl's claims. Your time is better spent focusing on contentious issues that invite discussion and evaluation.

❓ Question 2

Fleetwood Mechanics Ltd is a garage providing mechanical repairs for all types of automobile. As such, they are subject to the (fictitious) Automotive Engineering (Protection of Workers) Act 2012, which was passed after a series of accidents involving mechanics. This provides in section 1 a list of safety equipment which must be supplied to mechanics and includes eye goggles. Section 2 also provides that all safety equipment supplied to any workers must comply with British safety standards and have an appropriate safety certificate. Section 3 simply states that a breach of sections 1 and/or 2 will result in a fine. Due to a parliamentary oversight, the Act, and the consequences of a breach, are not mentioned in any other legislation.

However, at the time the legislation was passed the garage was struggling financially, so Otis, the company owner, chose not to purchase goggles with a British safety certificate as these were more expensive. Instead, he purchased some from another country with less rigorous safety standards. One day, Ray, wearing the goggles supplied by Otis, was working on an engine fitting a new mount; however, when taking out the old bolts, one became lodged in the mount. Ray managed to force it loose but, in doing so, the bolt flew up, striking him in the eye. As the goggles Otis had bought were not of sufficient safety strength, the bolt cracked the lens and blinded Ray.

Also that day, Dobie was working near the entrance of the garage sorting out a tyre delivery. However, the way he had stacked the tyres meant he had narrowed the entrance. Booker was driving a car into the garage for a service, but the entrance was now too small and tight to enter so he hit the tyres, which fell onto Dobie, leaving him with broken ribs.

Advise Otis of his company's liability for the injuries to Ray and Dobie.

Diagram plan

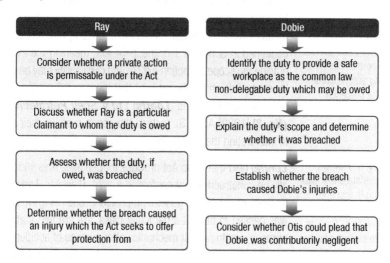

A printable version of this diagram plan is available from **www.pearsoned.co.uk/lawexpressqa**

Answer plan

➡ Consider whether the Act may give rise to damages in tort.

➡ Discuss how this statutory duty was breached and assess causation.

➡ Evaluate whether Otis has also breached his non-delegable duty to Dobie regarding a safe place of work.

➡ Determine whether Dobie has been contributorily negligent for his injuries.

Answer

[1] This indicates that you have identified the area of tort covered by the question.

[2] This shows that you have seen that both aspects apply and in relation to which injury.

[3] While the main point to discuss is the Health and Safety at Work etc. Act 1974, by referring to this legislation you show you are aware it is a recent change in the law.

[4] Make sure you use the facts you have been given to explore all possibilities rather than making assumptions based on the presence or absence of certain information.

[5] Structurally, it is always important to state and explain the general rule first and then explain how there may be exceptions to it. Then, as you go on to state the factors which create the exception, ensure that you apply them to the facts.

Although Otis was not the direct cause of either injury, the issue which arises is whether he will still be liable as their employer[1] for breaching a statutory duty to Ray and a common law duty of care to Dobie.[2]

The first issue is whether a civil remedy is permitted. If so, it is simply a case of establishing whether the elements of negligence are satisfied. Alternatively, the Act may expressly exclude civil liability. Either way, we are not told. Following the Enterprise and Regulatory Reform Act 2013,[3] civil liability for breaches of health and safety duties provided by 'existing statutory provisions' will not arise unless expressly provided for in regulations under the Health and Safety at Work etc. Act 1974, section 47(2A). As there do not appear to be any such regulations providing for civil liability, Otis is seemingly without redress. However, the absence of the 2012 Act from any other legislation means it would not feature in the list of 'existing statutory provisions', contained in Schedule 1 of the 1974 Act, meaning the 2012 Act is outside the scope of section 47(2A) and civil liability may be possible.[4] However, Otis should be advised that there is still no general notion that civil liability arises (*Lonrho Ltd v Shell Petroleum Co. Ltd (No. 2)* [1982] AC 173). Instead the courts exercise their discretion in interpreting the Act to determine the matter.

Lonrho held that if the Act provides for penalties, this should generally be construed as not conferring a right. However, *Lonrho* identified exceptions to this general proposition,[5] one being where the Act was passed to protect a particular class. We are told that the Act's purpose was to protect mechanics after a series of accidents, therefore the exception appears applicable. *X v Bedfordshire County Council* [1995] 2 AC 633 supports this, although it also stated that Parliament must additionally have intended to grant a private right of action on members of the protected class. Where the Act is deemed to have 'social welfare', the intention to create a private right will not exist (*Phelps v Hillingdon LBC* [2001] 2 AC 619). In relation to this

Act, while it is aimed at the welfare of mechanics this is a far narrower class than society at large, as in **Phelps.** Arguably, it is unjust if an Act aiming to prevent injury to a class did not allow injured class members to seek a civil remedy.

[6] This naturally follows on from the preceding sentence, but deal with this aspect in a new paragraph to enhance the clarity of the arguments. Simply use a sentence such as the preceding one to create a flow from one paragraph into the next.

[7] Don't dwell on this point as it is not of primary relevance, but provide an example to illustrate your point.

[8] Be careful not to sound repetitive. You are just building on the general point that you made earlier. You could alternatively deal with this point at the time of first raising the general proposition.

One reason why the Act may do this is if it expressly provides for an alternative remedy, or a better alternative exists elsewhere.[6] The latter could be where the duty is placed on local authorities whereby the claimant would have recourse to administrative law remedies.[7] This is not the case for Otis, and the more significant issue is the fact that section 3 states that a breach will result in a fine. This shows a remedy is within the Act; however, as **Lonrho** states, if the Act is specifically for the protection of a class, a civil action may still arise.[8] A fine is unlikely to go to the injured mechanics unless it goes to a central fund akin to the Motor Insurance Bureau to pay victims. If this is not the case, then the mere imposition of a fine would not mean it is inappropriate to give rise to a civil action, and indeed where the situation relates to workplace safety a more generous approach is adopted (**Ziemniak v ETPM Deep Sea Ltd** [2003] EWCA Civ 636). Notwithstanding these considerations, the process has been criticised for ultimately coming down to the courts making a policy decision on the merits of the case. However, there would not seem to be any policy reasons for denying a claim and, on balance, it is likely that the duty would give rise to a civil action.

If the matter is actionable in tort, several other requirements must be satisfied. However, it is clear that Ray is certainly, as a mechanic, owed the duty, and that this was breached, as we are told that Otis bought cheap goggles that were not compliant with British safety standards. Causation appears satisfied as we are told that the bolt cracked the goggles because they were of insufficient strength. On the basis that a British Standard pair would not have cracked, it is clear that 'but for' failing to supply the right goggles, as the duty requires, the injury would have been avoided. Finally, as the Act specifically mentions supplying goggles, it is clear that eye damage was an injury which the Act sought to protect mechanics from. Otis should be advised that he will not have a defence as, even if the Act is not construed as strict liability, Ray cannot be said to have assumed the risk or contributed to the injury in any way himself as he was wearing what was supplied.

In relation to Dobie, while the Act does not deal with his situation, Otis should be advised that as an employer he also has a series of non-delegable, personal duties towards each of his employees (***Paris v Stepney BC*** [1951] AC 367). These are non-delegable in the sense that responsibility for discharging the duty owed cannot be delegated to someone else.[9] They ensure that the claimant is able to prove an action against someone and thus receive compensation (which is also aided by compulsory insurance under the Employer's Liability (Defective Equipment) Act 1969). The duties were set out in ***Wilson and Clyde Coal Co. v English*** [1938] AC 57 and are to reasonably ensure competent staff, adequate plant and equipment, a safe place of work and a safe system of work.

[10] As previously, create a flow between the paragraphs: separate out this aspect of your question into one paragraph on the nature of the duty and a second on the application of the duty to facts.

[11] On these facts this is highly relevant, so make sure you explain the scope of the duty's application.

The relevant duty here[10] is the provision of a safe workplace, as Dobie was injured after the entrance to the garage was narrowed by the tyre wall. The duty requires the employer to take reasonable care to create a safe environment, and this extends to entrances[11] (***Ashdown v Samuel Williams & Sons Ltd*** [1957] 1 QB 409). From the facts, Booker crashed through the tyres because the entrance was narrowed, which suggests a breach. It is apparent that if the duty was breached it did cause the injury, as the falling tyres broke Dobie's ribs as they hit him. While seeming harsh as the danger was created by Dobie himself, the Law Reform (Contributory Negligence) Act 1945 means a reduction in Dobie's compensation may be possible to reflect any contributory negligence on Dobie's part. By stacking the tyres in the entrance so as to restrict it and then continuing to work behind the stack, Dobie has indeed been negligent.

[12] As you will have already concluded each injury as you dealt with it, you only need a short overall conclusion here to round off your answer.

Therefore, in conclusion, Otis should be advised that he is likely to be found liable for both injuries as he breached his duties owed, although the compensation payable to Dobie could be reduced.[12]

✓ Make your answer stand out

- Consider, briefly, the wider implications and merit of the changes to section 47 of the Health and Safety at Work etc. Act 1974.
- Consider whether the injury to Ray may also be a breach of the common law duty to provide reasonably safe equipment and/or a safe system of work, particularly if you feel the injury may not be actionable in tort under the Act.

- Discuss in a bit more depth why Ray could not be said to have voluntarily assumed the risk of injury.
- Give some explanatory comment about the policy behind the non-delegable duties in order to justify Otis being found liable for Dobie's injury, notwithstanding the probable application of the contributory negligence defence. Explore reading materials beyond your usual textbook for this purpose.
- Include a bit more on the difference between liability under this area and vicarious liability.

! Don't be tempted to . . .

- Turn the question into one on standard negligence, or vicarious liability: it is specifically about employer's liability for breach of statutory duty and one specific non-delegable duty.
- Go into detail about the non-delegable duties which are not within the focus of the question, as this will make your answer come across as a description of everything you know and you are not advising Otis on the specific issues.

🖎 Question 3

'The statutory right has its origin in the statute, but the particular remedy of an action for damages is given by the common law in order to make effective, for the benefit of the injured plaintiff, his right to the performance by the defendant of the defendant's statutory duty. It is an effective sanction.' (*Per* Lord Upjohn in *London Passenger Transport Board* v *Upson* [1949] AC 155, 168.)

Discuss the approach taken by the courts to determine when a tortious remedy will be permitted to redress a breach of a statutory duty when the statute itself does not expressly provide for one.

Diagram plan

A printable version of this diagram plan is available from **www.pearsoned.co.uk/lawexpressqa**

Answer plan

➡ Outline the leading case of *Lonrho Ltd* v *Shell Petroleum Co. Ltd (No. 2)* [1982] AC 173, explaining its importance.

➡ Discuss the general rule from the case.

➡ Analyse the exceptions that exist to the general rule.

➡ Comment on the merits of the current position.

Answer

[1] By setting out the specific issue in full here, not only do you immediately show your marker that you understand the question, you also save having to repeat it again, such as in paragraph 2, and can simply refer to 'the issue' or 'this issue'.

The issue to analyse is the manner in which the courts will determine when someone will be burdened with tortious liability towards another private individual when they have breached a statutory duty. This involves exploring the rules of statutory interpretation used by the courts as the approach taken in interpreting a statute and the factors the court considers when doing so is vital to any outcome.[1] These rules are important because quite often statutes are not clear on the matter and do not expressly provide for a common law remedy. However, as Lord Upjohn suggests, it is common law damages which provide the most effective sanction for a claimant injured by a breach of a statutory duty. While the courts have consistently held this to be a matter of construction, it is argued that the actual decision in each case is, in fact, influenced by policy considerations.

[2] Include this point in your outline of the facts, as the presence of the criminal sanctions was a factor which influenced the court's decision. Mentioning it now will tie in with your discussion of this factor later.

[3] Do not go into the exact details of the case. Remember: your aim here is just to set out the fact that this is the leading case and introduce the starting point for the court's approach.

The leading case which sets out the framework of how the courts will approach this issue is **Lonrho Ltd v Shell Petroleum Co. Ltd (No. 2)** [1982] AC 173. The case concerned losses suffered by Lonrho arising from compliance with a sanctions regime created by the Southern Rhodesia Act 1965. The subsequent legislative orders made it a criminal offence to supply oil to Rhodesia and outlined the punishment for non-compliance.[2] However, as Lonrho's competitors did not comply with the order, Lonrho lost out financially. The question was whether, in the absence of an express provision of a civil remedy, the legislation could be construed as providing one.[3] Lord Diplock, giving the opinion for the House, noted it had been held since **Cutler v Wandsworth Stadium Ltd** [1949] AC 398 that the matter was one of construction of the legislation. His Lordship then proceeded to set out the process for undertaking such construction.

The starting point is always what the legislation states; however, the problem is that Parliament regularly fails to expressly cover the issue when drafting legislation. Consequently, the courts have developed a general rule whereby if the Act creates an obligation and specifies how it will be enforced, the obligation cannot be enforced in any other way. Therefore, where criminal sanctions are provided in the legislation, a tortious sanction cannot also be applied to enforce the duty. The rationale for this is that Parliament has clearly considered the issue of enforcement and remedies for a breach and, while not expressly ruling out a tortious action, has expressly opted for another form of enforcement.[4] The same is also true where a breach of the statutory duty will give rise to remedies in administrative law.[5] For example, where the duty under the legislation is placed on a public authority, an action in judicial review will exist. The courts have preferred this action rather than subjecting the public authority to a tortious action which would reduce the funds available for the operation of that authority; at the very least, operational costs will rise through insurance premiums to cover any potential actions against it in tort. This threat of litigation can stifle the operational performance of the authority and so is considered to be against public policy. However, this approach perhaps needs reconsidering in light of the restrictions now placed on judicial review applications.[6]

However, **Lonrho** provided for two exceptions to the general position. The first is where the statute is passed to protect a specified limited class, as opposed to the public generally. In determining this, it is important to consider the purpose of the statute as just because a specified class is referred to, it does not automatically follow that protecting them was Parliament's intention. **Cutler** is a good example:[7] the Betting and Lotteries Act 1934 provided that bookmakers must be given space at dog tracks. However, it was held that the purpose of the Act was not to protect the livelihood of bookmakers, but simply to regulate proceedings at dog tracks. Therefore, as explained in *X v Bedfordshire County Council* [1995] 2 AC 633, for the exception to apply it must be shown that the statute imposed a duty on someone for the protection of a limited class and that Parliament intended to give members of that class a tort action for a breach of the duty.

[4] It is important to explain the reasoning behind this. Use this reasoning as the basis of your analysis of whether it is right for the courts to deny a party the chance of obtaining compensation.

[5] Include a discussion of this, as not all statutes will provide for criminal sanctions and so it is a different factor within the debate. This also allows you to get into the treatment of public authorities and discuss whether they should be protected from tort actions because of the possibility of administrative law remedies.

[6] Don't be afraid to demonstrate your knowledge of other branches of law when there is a link to the area being discussed, provided you keep it to the context of the discussion you are having. This will show that you have a broader level of knowledge of the issue and the arguments.

[7] Using an example at this point demonstrates your knowledge of that case but also strengthens your explanation of how the exception operates and what is required for it.

The second exception is where the statute creates a right to be enjoyed by the general public. While seemingly contrary to the first exception, it is essential that one of the public then suffers 'particular, direct and substantial' damage (*per* Brett J in ***Benjamin v Storr*** (1874) LR 9 CP 400), which is different from the public generally. However, where these are welfare statutes implementing social policy, the duty is naturally going to be placed on a public authority. This brings into play the considerations discussed above regarding whether another branch of the law already provides a more suitable remedy, such as administrative law.[8] The right conferred under the duty is part of a wider public policy and not simply a private matter between the authority and the individual, and this is why there is a strong requirement to show damage beyond that suffered by others before the individual tortious right will arise. In ***O'Rourke v Camden LBC*** [1998] AC 188, Lord Hoffmann also noted that the wide discretion given to authorities under such social welfare legislation means that Parliament would have been aware there could be errors of judgment and thus unlikely to see these lead to tortious liability.

[8] By stating that the previous material applies here, you will not need to repeat that part of your answer. The marker will already have read your points on the matter. This allows you to then focus on additional points which relate directly to this exception.

Therefore, while there is a clear general rule, uncertainty is created by the presence of exceptions. This uncertainty arises because there is no set formula to when a case will be deemed to be within an exception and the heavy influence of public policy factors. This is why the likes of Williams (1960) dismissed the process undertaken as a fiction of looking for something which is not there. While this has helped employees in industrial situations, it could be said to have been unfair on the employer by increasing costs and creating an artificial liability.[9] Parliament has responded with section 69 of the Enterprise and Regulatory Reform Act 2013, which removes all civil liability for breaches of all health and safety duties. Regardless of the particular merits of that decision, the approach is in line with reform proposals by the Law Commission; namely, that a presumption of a civil right will exist unless the contrary is clearly expressed in the statute. This is a better overall approach.[10] Parliament would at least be required to fully contemplate the implications of any proposed statutory duty, following a debate on the merits of permitting civil liability, and clearly

[9] It is beneficial to highlight this, particularly if you adopt the argument that this answer does. If you have time before you start your conclusion, you could use this point as the basis of a penultimate paragraph and explore the positive impact that policy can have in more detail.

[10] Obviously, if you are criticising how something works, you should offer an opinion on how it can be rectified. This is particularly important if there are published proposals for reform, as otherwise it may indicate your lack of knowledge.

decide what the consequences of a breach should be. This would create certainty and reduce the financial burdens of litigation and insurance, particularly in light of the growing number of regulatory statutes which create duties on parties.

✓ Make your answer stand out

- Read academic articles such as that by Williams, G. (1960) The effect of penal legislation in the law of tort. *Modern Law Review,* 23: 233 to obtain some depth to the criticisms of the current process.

- Look at Law Commission (1969) Report No. 21, *The Interpretation of Statutes,* to be able to provide a fuller explanation of what the Commission proposed and contrast this with the counter-arguments by Buckley, R. A. (1984) Liability in tort for breach of statutory duty, *Law Quarterly Review,* 100: 204.

- Explore further how policy can be seen as the basis for finding a civil action and whether this is fair. Consider where the abolition of civil liability for breaches of health and safety statutory duties by section 69 of the Enterprise and Regulatory Reform Act 2013 leaves the scope of this tort.

! Don't be tempted to . . .

- Spend too long on the facts of *Lonrho*; you need to set up the issue you are discussing.

- Similarly, when considering the impact of the new parliamentary approach to civil liability for breaches of health and safety duties, do not get tied down in a detailed examination of the merits of that decision. Stick to the overall approach that the courts should adopt if Parliament's intention is unclear.

- List a series of case examples where a tort action was found to exist or not. Focus on the rules for dealing with the issue and what factors are considered. Just draw on case examples where necessary to support your argument. An excessive amount of fact from cases will have a negative impact on your structure.

- Go into detail regarding what else the court must consider after determining whether the Act in question permits a civil action in tort. The question is focused on the issue of construction of the statutory wording.

Try it yourself

Now take a look at the question below and attempt to answer it. You can check your response against the answer guidance available on the companion website (**www.pearsoned.co.uk/ lawexpressqa**).

Hendrix Cleaning Ltd is a commercial cleaning operation that contracts with other businesses to clean their premises. As such, they are subject to the (Fictitious) Commercial Cleaners (Regulation of Equipment) Act 2009 that was passed after a rise in dermatological conditions amongst cleaners. The Act states in section 2 a list of substances that must not be used in cleaning products. Section 3 also provides that all safety equipment for cleaners must comply with EU health and safety standards, and be certified as such. Section 4 states that a breach of any preceding section will result in a fine.

However, due to the ongoing economic downturn, Hendrix Cleaning Ltd had lost a lot of its business and so needed to cut costs. The first method of doing so was by importing rubber gloves from China as these were 80 per cent cheaper than the company's British supplier. The other method was to start using a new imported cleaning detergent. This included Cillitox that was far stronger and also needed lower quantities than the company's regular detergent. However, Cillitox was on the list of prohibited products due to its highly corrosive nature if used in large amounts.

One day, Eric, was on a job for Hendrix Cleaning Ltd using the imported gloves. However, when confronted by the mess he had to clean, Eric used more cleaning solution, thinking it would get the job done quicker. This meant that Eric had used far more Cillitox than was safe and when he put his hands in his bucket of water the gloves, which were thinner than EU safety standards, were instantly corroded and left Eric with severe burns to his hands and arms.

Advise Eric whether he would succeed in any claim against the company for their breach of the Act.

www.pearsoned.co.uk/lawexpressqa

 Go online to access more revision support including additional essay and problem questions with diagram plans, you be the marker questions, and download all diagrams from the book.

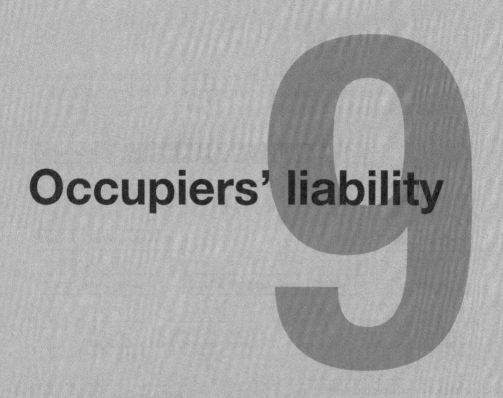

Occupiers' liability

How this topic may come up in exams

This topic is an extension of the tort of negligence. However, it has its own self-contained statutory framework governing when a duty will arise, and so you need to be careful to recognise whether a problem question is concerned with normal negligence or occupiers' liability. In the question, look for premises that are controlled by one of the parties. Although the situations where the duty of care arises differ, some aspects are the same, notably causation and remoteness. The Acts do not have many sections, but what is needed is located in specific subsections so ensure you know these. Problem questions are more common than essays. However, when the question is an essay, it tends to focus on whether the legislation is necessary and/or whether it achieves the right balance between the parties in terms of burden and protection.

Before you begin

Acquaint yourself with the following components and key issues of this topic; and familiarise yourself with how you would structurally progress through them all, if necessary, when attempting to answer a question on this topic.

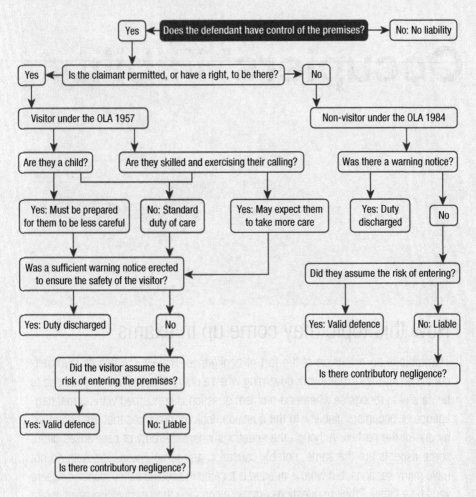

A printable version of this diagram is available from **www.pearsoned.co.uk/lawexpressqa**

❓ Question 1

Urban Property Developers Ltd (UPD Ltd) recently purchased an abandoned warehouse with the intention of renovating the property and converting it into luxury apartments. UPD Ltd hired a number of different contractors in order to complete the renovation works.

Unfortunately, while working on the bathroom of one of the upstairs apartments, Neal, a plumber employed by Mitchell and Sons plumbers, caused a huge water leak. The water flooded the upstairs apartment and began to seep through the ceiling of the floor below. Neal rang UPD Ltd to notify them of the issue and suggested that they close the site down until he was able to rectify the water leak; however, UPD Ltd ignored this advice.

Dimitry, an electrician who was contracted by UPD Ltd to complete the electrical work on the property, slipped on a puddle of water in the hallway that had been caused by the leak from the floor above. There were no warning signs alerting Dimitry to the presence of the water. The fall caused injuries to Dimitry's back and wrist. He also shattered the screen on his mobile phone, which he had been carrying in his hand at the time of the fall.

Advise Dimitry in respect of any claim that he may have against UPD Ltd.

Diagram plan

| Establish all preliminary issues required for a claim under the Occupiers' Liability Act 1957 *Dangerous premises, occupier, visitor status* | Establish the nature and extent of the Duty of Care *Consider the impact of Dimitry being an independent contractor* | Identify whether there has been a breach of duty *Consider the effect of Neal's actions on whether UPD Ltd have discharged their duty of care* | Establish a causal link between the alleged breach and actionable injury | Consider whether any defences are available to UPD Ltd |

A printable version of this diagram plan is available from **www.pearsoned.co.uk/lawexpressqa**

Answer plan

➡ Identify the status of Dimitry and which Act applies to him.

➡ State what the extent of the duty of care is under the Occupiers' Liability Act 1957.

➡ Consider whether this is modified owing to the fact that Dimitry is entering the property as person in exercise of his calling.

➡ Evaluate the significance of the danger being created by an independent contractor.

➡ Consider whether UPD Ltd may have any other defences to Dimitry's claim.

Answer

[1] You do not need to wait to show that you have identified which Act is most relevant to the facts of the question.

[2] This point is often missed by students when answering questions on occupiers' liability. By identifying this in your introduction, you demonstrate that you understand the nature and scope of the legislation.

[3] Show that you know what the key issues in the Act are in relation to the question asked of you.

[4] While the points raised in this paragraph may seem obvious, they are crucial aspects of any claim. It is important that Dimitry identifies UPD Ltd as the appropriate defendant in his claim.

Dimitry requires advice in respect of any liability that may arise under the Occupiers' Liability Act 1957[1] in respect of the injuries that he sustained to his back and wrist, and for the property damage to his phone. The Act imposes liability on the controllers of premises for injuries sustained as a consequence of the state of the premises, or things done or omitted to be done on the premises (s. 1(3)).[2] Liability arises in much the same way as it does in a typical negligence claim, albeit within a statutory framework. It will be argued that UPD Ltd owe and have breached their duty of care towards Dimitry and that they will not be able to rely on the work of independent contractors Mitchell and Sons plumbers to discharge their duty of care.[3]

There are a number of preliminary issues that need to be addressed in respect of any claim that Dimitry may make. Liability under the Act is only imposed on 'occupiers' of 'premises'. A 'premises' according to s. 1(3) extends to 'any fixed or moveable structure, including any vessel, vehicle or aircraft' and, as such, the warehouse clearly constitutes a relevant premises. While not defined in the Act, an occupier has been held to mean any person who has such a degree of control over the premises that they should realise that a want of care on their part may lead to injury to those coming onto their premises (**Wheat v E Lacon Co Ltd** [1966] AC 552). As UPD Ltd own the warehouse and are carrying out construction work on it, they clearly have control over the premises.[4]

In order for Dimitry to be owed a duty of care under the Act, he would need to be classed as a 'visitor' as defined in s. 1(2). The term 'visitor' encompasses persons who are legally permitted to enter a premises by either express or implied permission. As Dimitry is contracted to work for UPD Ltd, he would have express permission to enter the premises for that purpose. Although an occupier is entitled to limit permission to be on a premises (***The Calgarth*** [1927] P 93), no such limitation is evident in Dimitry's case at the time at which he enters the premises.[5] Consequently, Dimitry will be owed the 'common duty of care' under s. 2(1) of the Act.

As UPD Ltd is likely to owe Dimitry a duty of care, the extent of that duty must be examined in order to ascertain whether there has been a breach of duty on their part. Under s. 2(2) the duty of care is to take such care as is reasonable in the circumstances to ensure that Dimitry is safe in using the premises for the purpose for which he is permitted to be there, i.e. to undertake the electrical works as per his contract with UPD Ltd. It is important to note that it is the visitor that must be safe and not necessarily the premises itself. As Dimitry was simply walking across a hallway, there is nothing to indicate that he was utilising the premises in an unusual or unpermitted manner.[6] As the hallway was unsafe for this purpose due to the water on the floor, UPD Ltd appear to have breached their duty towards him.

UPD Ltd may seek to argue that as Dimitry has entered the premises in exercise of his calling as an electrician, he would be expected to safeguard himself against such risks. While s. 1(3)(b) does make provisions for the degree of care expected where a person enters a property in exercise of their calling, a person in so entering is only expected to appreciate and guard against any special risks ordinarily incidental to it, so far as the occupier leaves him free to do so. Although Dimitry was entering the premises as an electrician, the risk of slipping on water on the floor is not a risk incidental to his work and, as such, UPD Ltd can properly be expected to offer some protection against it (***Woollins v British Celanese*** (1966) 1 KIR 438). As no safeguards such as a sufficient warning sign[7] to alert Dimitry to the presence of the water were in place (see s. 2(4)(a)) there does appear to be a breach of the relevant duty.

UPD Ltd may also seek to rely on the fact that the water spillage was caused by Neal as an independent contractor, employed by Mitchell and Sons plumbers, in order to avoid liability. Under section 2(4)(b) the occupier is not to be treated as answerable, without more on their part, for a danger where it is caused by the faulty construction

8 Show your understanding of the subsection by paraphrasing the wording. To aid your structure you can then break it down into individual components and apply them to UPD Ltd.

work of an independent contractor, provided it was reasonable to entrust the work to the contractor and the occupier took reasonable steps to ensure that the contractor was both competent and had completed the work properly.[8] Where the work, here the plumbing work, requires special skill and equipment that the occupier does not possess, then it will be reasonable to engage the services of the independent contractor (*Maguire v Sefton MBC* [2006] EWCA Civ 560). This would seem to be applicable in this situation, due to the nature of the work carried out by Mitchell and Sons plumbers. However, it is incumbent upon the occupier to exercise reasonable care to check that the work has been carried out properly. In *Alexander v Freshwater Properties Ltd* [2012] EWCA Civ 1048 the occupier was still held to have breached their duty of care, owing to the fact that they were made aware of a danger created by an independent contractor and did nothing about it. The same conclusion is likely to be drawn in the instant case, given that Neal notified UPD Ltd that a water leak had occurred and recommended that they closed the site until the issue could be rectified. UPD Ltd chose to ignore the recommendation from Neal and consequently it is likely that UPD Ltd will be held to have failed to discharge their duty of care towards Dimitry.[9]

9 Using a case such as *Alexander* provides authority for the argument that you are making.

In order to bring a successful action against UPD Ltd, Dimitry will need to establish a sufficient causal connection between the breach of duty on the part of UPD Ltd and an actionable injury. Liability under the Act extends to both personal injury and property damage (s. 1(3)(b)). Therefore, Dimitry will be able to recover for the injuries to his back and wrist, and the damage to his mobile phone, provided that no issues in respect of causation arise. There do not appear to be any issues in respect of causation or remoteness in this case.[10] Although a number of defences are potentially available to an occupier, none are applicable to UPD Ltd in these circumstances.

10 As this is still a form of negligence, do not forget to touch on these issues in order to adequately advise Dimitry.

In conclusion, Dimitry is likely to be able to bring a successful claim against UPD Ltd. UPD Ltd failed to discharge the common duty of care owed to Dimitry as a visitor on the premises. As the injuries sustained by Dimitry arose as a consequence of this failure and UPD Ltd are unable to avail themselves of a defence, Dimitry will be likely to recover compensation for the injuries that he sustained.

✓ **Make your answer stand out**

- Highlight the possibility of a claim against UPD Ltd in common law negligence.
- Use the facts of the question as much as possible to build and support your argument.
- Extend your reading beyond the usual textbooks and look at texts such as Jones, M., Dugdale, A. and Simpson, M. (eds.) (2014) *Clerk & Lindsell on Torts,* 21st edition. London: Sweet & Maxwell in order to substantiate the points that you make. It is also an excellent source for finding further case law that is nor normally touched upon in a textbook.

! **Don't be tempted to . . .**

- Discuss section 2(3)(a) and the issue of the duty owed to children; it is not relevant to the specific issue here and you would be indicating that you have not fully understood the question.
- Spend unnecessary time considering the Occupiers' Liability Act 1984. Although you may want to mention the Act briefly for the sake of completeness, this question clearly pertains to the Occupiers' Liability Act 1957.

? Question 2

Noel is a saxophone player who has a licence to practise in the hall of the pub which his friend Paul owns and runs. Recently, Noel has had his 10-year-old brother, Liam, stay with him and so he had to bring Liam with him one night. The entrance to the pub has a large notice stating that no children are allowed inside due to renovation work, although they are usually allowed in. Noel saw the sign and thought that it would be all right as it would be quiet and he would keep an eye on Liam. As they entered, Noel said hello to Paul, who greeted Noel in return, but, not having seen Liam as he was busy, said nothing about his presence.

During Noel's practice, the fire alarm sounded and Paul shouted for everyone to leave immediately. Noel quickly got his things together before heading for the exit at the end of the corridor. However, Paul, who had been carrying out some refurbishment work in the corridor when the alarm went off, had left some tools on the corridor floor. Noel did not notice and slipped on a screwdriver, severely injuring his back to the extent that he could not get up. As the alarm was still going off, Liam panicked and ran for the door to get help, but Paul had locked it to stop people going back inside until it was time. Remembering a fire exit in the hall, Liam ran to that exit, but as he got to the door fell through some rotten floorboards and ruptured his ankle ligaments.

Advise Paul about the two injuries.

Diagram plan

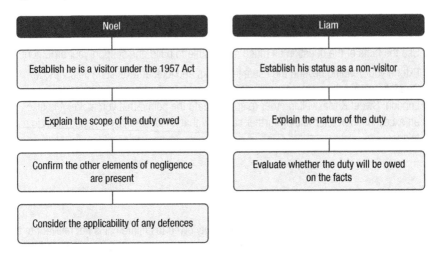

A printable version of this diagram plan is available from **www.pearsoned.co.uk/lawexpressqa**

Answer plan

→ Take Noel first, and establish whether he is a visitor under the 1957 Act.

→ Explain the extent of the duty under the Act.

→ Assess Paul's liability and the applicability of any defences.

→ Highlight how Liam is a non-visitor under the 1984 Act.

→ Consider the scope of the Act and whether Paul will owe Liam a duty under it.

Answer

[1] Abbreviate the name of the statutes to save yourself time, but make sure you shorten them to something which still distinguishes the two Acts.

[2] This sentence indicates to your examiner that you have identified the specific area of tort which the question is concerned with straightaway, particularly as the question does not highlight this for you.

The issue to be determined is whether Paul will be liable to Noel and Liam for the injuries that they have suffered while on his premises. He will need advice as to potential claims under both the Occupiers' Liability Act 1957 (the 1957 Act)[1] regarding lawful visitors to premises, and the Occupiers' Liability Act 1984 (the 1984 Act) which governs injuries to non-visitors.[2] Which Act applies is important, as the law provides far greater protection for visitors. It will be argued that, despite being told to leave, Noel is still likely to have been owed a duty as a visitor and be successful in a claim, while Liam will be a non-visitor and is less likely to be successful.

First, it should be established that Paul will face any action as the occupier of the premises. While 'occupier' is not defined in either statute, it was stated in **Wheat v E. Lacon Co. Ltd** [1966] AC 552 that occupiers are those with such control over the premises that they should realise that want of care on their part may lead to injury to those coming to the premises; as the owner of the pub, Paul would have such control.[3]

[3] Make sure that you use the facts of the question to illustrate, and support, your argument as to the position of the parties.

In advising Paul about Noel's injuries first, it must be confirmed whether Noel was a 'visitor' for the purposes of the 1957 Act. This term is also not defined in the Act; however, section 1(2) does provide that it covers the common law terms of 'invitee' and 'licensee'. Therefore, anyone who is lawfully on the premises will be a visitor. As Paul had given Noel permission to use the hall, Noel will satisfy the definition of a visitor. This is significant for Paul as any duty owed under the 1957 Act is more rigorous and increases his chances of being liable for Noel's injuries.[4]

[4] When you have reached a definite position such as this, make sure you explain what the significance of that position is. This will show that you have fully understood the legal principles and the consequences of them, rather than just luckily applying some law that you have learned, and reached the right answer.

The extent of the duty Paul will owe to Noel as Paul's visitor is provided by section 2(2),[5] and it is to ensure that he takes such care in all the circumstances so that Noel is safe while using the premises for the purposes for which he is allowed. Significantly, this indicates that the duty only extends to ensuring safety during permitted activities. However, Noel suffered his injury after remaining on the premises after he had been told to leave because of the fire alarm. Therefore, Noel was not technically permitted to be there at that time. However, Paul should be advised that people are given a reasonable time to vacate premises after having their permission withdrawn (**Cornish v Stubbs** (1870) LR 5 CP 334). As this was a fire alarm, Noel should have left straightaway, but depending on exactly how long he took, if the timeframe was deemed reasonable, a duty under the 1957 Act will be owed. Further, the facts suggest that Paul breached his duty by leaving obstacles on the corridor floor, which then clearly caused the injury.[6]

[5] While you should always give your authority for statements of law, it is particularly important in a statute-based tort that you constantly refer to which part of the Act deals with the point in question in order to demonstrate your knowledge and give strength to your answer.

[6] Remember that while the main focus of the question is whether a duty is owed under the Act, to be liable all of the other aspects of negligence need to be satisfied. Therefore, briefly highlight their presence on the facts by using the language of the elements to complete your account of what has happened.

The fact that the alarm was going off may negate any argument that Noel was negligent himself when leaving, in not having seen any hazards. We are not told of any warning signs either, other than the notice saying children were not permitted due to the renovation work. Paul should be advised that, under the 1957 Act, to discharge a duty a notice must specify the danger and be sufficient to keep the visitor reasonably safe (s. 2(5)). It is unlikely that any sign would be so worded as to keep a visitor reasonably safe from trip hazards of the kind which Noel suffered, especially as this is the main walkway. Further, Paul should be advised that the notice is to be judged in all circumstances. As there was a fire alarm going off, this may count against the sufficiency of any notice, as naturally Noel was looking to just vacate the premises as soon as possible.[7] Arguably, the duty would be heightened as it was incumbent upon Paul to ensure that people could leave safely. It would also probably rule out any other defence from the Act, such as voluntary assumption of risk, applying against Noel as he was naturally trying to leave the building as requested.

Regarding Liam, it is clear that as children were not permitted due to the renovation work his situation can only fall within the 1984 Act, so he will be assessed as a non-visitor. Although nothing was said when Liam entered, any argument based on an implied licence will fail as Paul had not noticed him enter.[8] Paul should note that the 1984 Act provides that a duty will be owed to non-visitors for the risk of injury by way of the dangerous state of the premises or by things done on them or omitted to be done (s. 1(1)). The danger here was the broken floorboards by the fire exit.

Paul should be advised that, for him to owe a duty under section 1(3) of the 1984 Act, he would need to be aware[9] of the state of the floorboards, which as the owner he must be, as the area by a fire exit is open and therefore noticeable. Paul would also be the person responsible for checking that the premises, including fire exits, are secure. Further, their location also means it is a danger from which it is reasonable to expect Paul to offer protection, as it will be how people try to leave in an emergency.[10] However, the duty is determined by the reference to the likely presence of the actual non-visitor in the vicinity of the danger at the time and place of the danger to him (*Ratcliffe v McConnell* [1999] 1 WLR 670). Therefore it will be difficult for Liam to establish that Paul had reasonable grounds to know that Liam was in the vicinity at that time. As children were not permitted and he did not see Liam enter the pub with Noel, who he would know to be in the vicinity of the danger, it is hard to see how Paul would have known that a child would be in the vicinity at the time Liam was injured. As such, it is unlikely that Liam satisfies the requirements to be owed a duty in this case.

[7] As this indicates you are not dealing with a normal situation, use it to evaluate the factual situation in a bit more depth rather than just quickly reaching a conclusion on the issue.

[8] From the facts we are told that Paul did not see Liam, so use this to support how there is no chance of Liam being able to argue that he was a visitor.

[9] Although paragraph (a) and paragraph (b) within the subsection discuss reasonable belief as an alternative to actually knowing, as the latter is actually the case in the scenario, do not feel the need to explain the full extent of the paragraph.

[10] While this is paragraph (c) of section 1(3) state it first as it is more likely to be satisfied than paragraph (b). This will give your answer a more logical structure as you will not be discussing an uncertain element which is more likely to be unsatisfied, and then going on to the next requirement and saying how that one is satisfied.

In conclusion, Paul should be advised that Noel is likely to have a successful claim under the 1957 Act as he left hazards in the main walkway from the hall to the exit and knew that Noel would be using that route. Paul may have more success against any claim by Liam, as he would not have had grounds to believe Liam was on the premises, and so not owed him a duty of care.

✓ Make your answer stand out

- Highlight how, even if unsuccessful under the occupiers' liability legislation, the pair may still have a claim against Paul in common law negligence, especially Liam.
- Consider the 1984 Act in relation to Noel if you conclude that his claim under the 1957 Act may be unsuccessful.
- Provide some context to the 1984 Act and some depth on how it differs from the 1957 Act.
- Explore the extent of the duty that would be owed by Paul if Liam does satisfy section 1(3) of the 1984 Act, and use *Donoghue* v *Folkestone Properties Ltd* [2003] EWCA Civ 231 to explain the relationship between section 1(3) and (4) of the 1984 Act.

! Don't be tempted to . . .

- Go into depth on the common law definitions of the terms, as they are not really issues in the question.
- Show your full range of knowledge by being too descriptive about both Acts and outlining provisions which are not relevant to the issues.

📝 Question 3

'The working paper evoked a very wide and diverse response. A few of those commenting considered that no reform of the law was desirable, and among the majority who did consider that was desirable, there was again a wide spectrum of views as to the desired result and the best means of achieving it.' Law Commission, *Liability for Damage or Injury to Trespassers and Related Questions of Occupiers' Liability* (Law Com No. 75, 1976)

Evaluate the need for, and the success of, legislative intervention in the field of liability for occupiers of premises.

Diagram plan

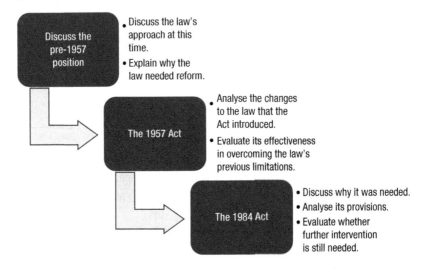

A printable version of this diagram plan is available from **www.pearsoned.co.uk/lawexpressqa**

Answer plan

→ Set out the scope of the common law before the Occupiers' Liability Act 1957 was passed and identify any shortcomings that existed.

→ Evaluate the provisions of the 1957 Act and how the courts have approached applying them.

→ Consider the degree to which the 1957 Act achieved its purpose and the extent to which the Occupiers' Liability Act 1984 was needed to remedy the law.

→ Evaluate the protection offered by the 1984 Act and whether it has dealt with any deficiencies in the law arising from the 1957 Act.

→ Conclude by assessing the level of protection given by the law in its current state and whether additional intervention is necessary.

[1] It is important that you mention this in your introduction as the quote does not expressly mention the first statute. However, properly understood, the rationale for the second intervention by Parliament is inherently linked with the objective behind the first intervention. As such, you need to address each intervention in the appropriate context and relate them. By explaining that you appreciate this, you will let your marker know that you understand what is expected by the question.

[2] Obviously there was a distinction before the 1957 Act so you need to make clear that you are talking about the current position of the law whether you agree with the state of the law or not.

[3] The point which you should be trying to convey here is the need for the legislative reform and why the common law was, therefore, unsatisfactory. This will set up your discussion of the 1957 Act.

[4] For the purposes of fully answering the question, it is important that you highlight what the Act was trying to do. This is because this will influence your concluding arguments on the state of the law, namely that both Acts sought, on policy grounds, to build in a distinction between the levels of protection offered. Therefore, there is no need for further legislation on that basis.

Answer

The issue to consider is the necessity for Parliament to intervene in the area of occupiers' liability in light of the protection initially offered by the common law. This requires exploring the need for Parliament's first intervention in 1957[1] as arguably the 1984 intervention was needed to redress issues which were not dealt with by the 1957 Act. As such, it is argued that both interventions were needed. While there remains unequal protection between types of people entering the land, the current[2] distinction is justifiable. As such, intervention taken as a whole has been successful, meaning no further legislation is needed.

Before 1957, the common law offered a protection through imposing a duty of care to those entering the land. The scope of this varied depending on the classification given to the injured individual and was determined by their reason for being on the premises and ranged from those present under a contract with the occupier through to trespassers. In between were invitees and licensees, those with an invitation or permission from the occupier to enter. While similar, a distinction was made based on the invitee's common interest with the occupier for being on the premises resulting in greater protection. This was overly, and unnecessarily, complex with litigation focusing on determining the relevant status. The artificial nature of the distinctions led a Law Commission Report of 1954 to call for its abolition.[3] The report led to the 1957 Act, which had the primary purpose of simplifying the law, and creating certainty as to how and when a duty would arise.[4] Section 1(2) replicated the meaning of 'occupier' from the common law, namely the person who has sufficient control over the premises so that they ought to realise that a failure of care on their part may lead to injury to another (***Wheat v E. Lacon Co. Ltd*** [1966] AC 552). While defined in the same way, the duty owed was the same for all lawful visitors. Consequently, the difficulty of determining a person's status and their level of protection was generally removed. However, consequently, trespassers at common law still lacked protection unless any injury resulted from deliberate intentional acts of the occupier or acts which were done with reckless disregard for the trespassers'

5 Naturally, building from
the previous comments, you
then need to explain what
the policy reason is for the
distinction which the 1957
Act left.

6 It is important that you
evaluate the merits of what
the Act set out to do and its
consequences; otherwise,
you risk just having a
description of it. Mentioning
this here allows you to set
the foundations for your
discussion around the need
for the 1984 Act.

7 This is why *Jolley* is a good
case to give as an example
here, as opposed to other
famous cases such as *Phipps
v Rochester Corp* [1955]
1 QB 450 and *Glasgow
Corporation* v *Muir* [1943] AC
448. It allows you to evaluate
whether this was just a pre-
1984 issue.

8 A concluding remark such
as this is needed if you are
building to a conclusion that
no further reform is needed.
Without it, you have left an
unanswered question mark
over the adequateness of
the law.

presence (**Addie v Dumbreck** [1929] AC 358). No protection was given from negligent acts, as the view was taken that trespassers came onto the premises at their own risk.[5]

While the 1957 Act successfully simplified the law by equalising the protection for all lawful visitors, it did create a new debate regarding when someone was lawfully on the premises, especially in relation to children.[6] Following **Jolley v Sutton LBC** [2000] 1 WLR 1082 a duty may be owed to a child if the premises contain an allurement, which could equate to granting implied permission to enter. In **Jolley** a rotting boat on the premises was deemed an attractive plaything for children and was easily accessible to them. The year of the case demonstrates that this was not simply an issue prior to Parliament's second intervention and is linked to the long-standing distinction between lawful and non-lawful visitors.[7] The issue is complicated by the diverse range of people who could fall within the meaning of trespasser. However, the case demonstrates that the courts can deal with this complication fairly.[8]

The duty owed is to take such care as is reasonable in the circumstances to ensure that the visitor is reasonably safe using the premises for the purpose for which they are permitted to be there (s. 2(2)). Therefore, acting inconsistently with the permission given, results in the Act's protection being lost. The occupier is also permitted to alter their duty through contract, albeit subject now to the Unfair Contract Terms Act 1977. Some allowance is still made for the type of visitor with section 2(3)(b), providing the occupier can expect those on the premises exercising their trade to guard against its inherent risks. Conversely, children must be expected to exercise less care than adults (s. 2(3)(a)). Although seemingly justifiable, in light of the readiness to find implied licences for children, a greater burden is created towards people who arguably should not be on their premises, particularly unsupervised.[9]

This matter came to a head in **British Railway Board v Herrington** [1972] AC 877 where a duty was found towards a boy injured trespassing over a railway line between two dilapidated fences.[10] While decided unanimously, the judicial opinions lacked clarity on when this duty would arise and its extent. This naturally caused significant uncertainty and detriment for landowners, who now faced liability for people not allowed on their land. As a result, the Law Commission produced another report in 1976, which led to Parliament's second intervention in 1984.

The 1984 Act sought to achieve a better balance between not excessively burdening occupiers in respect of trespassers, while imposing liability in circumstances when they could fairly be deemed at fault for injuries suffered on their premises.[11] Section 1(1) imposes a duty to non-visitors in respect of injuries suffered while on the premises by reason of a danger arising from things done or omitted to be done on the premises. In only imposing a duty in these circumstances, the 1984 Act clearly offers less protection than the 1957 Act.

Before a duty is imposed though, the requirements of section 1(3) must be satisfied.[12] The occupier is aware of the danger or has reasonable grounds to believe it exists; he knows or has reasonable grounds to believe the other, regardless of lawful authority, is in the vicinity of the danger, or may come within it and the risk is one which, in the circumstances, it is reasonable to expect him to protect the other from. If satisfied, the duty is to take such care as is reasonable in the circumstances to see that injury from that danger does not occur. There is no duty for injury by other means, reflecting Parliament's intention to distinguish the protection given to non-visitors in contrast to visitors.

---

[9] This links the discussion back to the previous mention of this aspect of the issue and so gives it more strength. Of more importance though is that commenting on this here allows your answer to flow nicely and directly into why the 1984 Act came about. To maintain a good structure, you need to ensure that you do not just simply move on to describing what the 1984 Act does; set up your discussion with some context. Therefore, while the provisions of the 1957 Act could be dealt with before the paragraph evaluating its success, you would need to take extra care to ensure you maintain a good flow through the answer which still raises all of the issues here. Your answer would need to be structured differently in its entirety to this one.

[10] This fact was important to the decision as it warranted some fault being placed on the defendant, so it is equally important that you highlight it.

[11] By explaining the point of the Act, you highlight your understanding of both Acts as the intention was never to offer the same protection as the 1957 Act due to policy considerations.

[12] Put these in a separate paragraph so that the analysis and evaluation that you offered previously does not get lost in the detail.

[13] Start your conclusion with a definitive statement as to the overall merit of the sentiment expressed in the quote within the question, and then proceed to summarise why you have reached that view.

[14] There are arguably two reasons for possible reform, one that the different treatment is unwarranted; or, secondly, that the law remains unclear and ambiguous. This shows that you are aware of and have considered both. Also by referring to the lack of appeal cases, which would generally deal with the second issue, you demonstrate your knowledge of the current state of the law and judicial thinking.

Therefore, Parliamentary intervention was necessary due to the unsatisfactory state of the common law.[13] However, by failing to deal with all the categories of individuals that existed at common law in 1957, Parliament simply created new problems which necessitated the second intervention in 1984. This was surely foreseeable and the intervention would have been more successful if the law had been reformed in its entirety in 1957. The situation has now been rectified and although there is unequal protection between visitors and non-visitors, the differing policy objectives behind each statute justify the distinction, so there is no need for a further intervention to level the playing field. Further, the lack of reported appeal cases suggests that the judiciary have also reached a clear and settled understanding as to the purpose and application of each statute.[14] Therefore, ultimately, Parliament's interventions have been successful when taken together.

✓ **Make your answer stand out**

- If you conclude the interventions have not been successful, consider what reforms are needed to rectify the situation.

- Consider the impact of the Compensation Act 2006 on this area of law and whether that suggests that Parliament was not happy with the prior situation.

- Read the Law Reform Committee (1954) *Third Report: Occupiers' Liability to Invitees, Licensees and Trespassers* and the Law Commission Report (1976) *Report on Liability for Damage or Injury to Trespassers and Related Questions of Occupiers' Liability* to gain a full insight of the primary reasons for each statute.

- Read *British Railway Board* v *Herrington* [1972] AC 877 and formulate your own views as to the extent, if any, it created problems in the law in relation to trespassers.

- Supplement your arguments with academic opinion and judicial comments on the legislation, looking at cases such as *Tomlinson* v *Congleton Borough Council* [2004] 1 AC 46.

! Don't be tempted to . . .

- Ignore the 1957 Act even though the quote in the question is from the report that considered the need for Parliamentary intervention by way of the 1984 Act. An omission in this respect would suggest that you lack understanding regarding the relationship between the two statutes and the full background of the later Act.

- Extensively discuss the different provisions of each statute. The question is focused on you evaluating the need for each Act and the extent that, overall, they provide adequate protection. Focus on a comparative evaluation of each rather than a description of each.

- Go into detail on the full elements of negligence, particularly when setting out how liability occurred at common law.

@ Try it yourself

Now take a look at the question below and attempt to answer it. You can check your response against the answer guidance available on the companion website (**www.pearsoned.co.uk/lawexpressqa**).

The Hertfordshire Arms is a public house owned by Rodney. He is quite relaxed about who enters and how they look so long as they do not get too drunk and abusive. Derrick was drinking in the pub one afternoon and eventually came to be quite drunk. Derrick started shouting as he spoke and swore repeatedly, even though he was told not to. Eventually, he got so drunk that he completely forgot about the smoking ban and lit a cigarette. Rodney, incensed at this stage, came over and demanded he get out and pointed to the nearest exit. Derrick did as he was told; however, the exit that he was sent towards had several steps to it and a hand rail. The hand rail was, in fact, faulty and Rodney was just about to start fixing it when he came over to tell Derrick to leave. As Derrick put his hand on the rail it broke from the wall and Derrick fell down the stairs, breaking his ankle.

Advise Rodney of his liability, if any, to Derrick.

www.pearsoned.co.uk/lawexpressqa

Go online to access more revision support including additional essay and problem questions with diagram plans, you be the marker questions, and download all diagrams from the book.

Trespass to land

10

How this topic may come up in exams

Trespass to land is a rather small and uncomplicated area and, as such, means that essay questions are rare. However, you could be asked about the need for the tort and the role it plays in the wider context of protecting interests in land. As for problem questions, it is common to find an element of trespass to land combined with other torts such as trespass to the person, occupiers' liability or nuisance. Always check your question to see whether there is an aspect of someone entering another's land without permission or acting in a manner which is inconsistent with their permission.

■ Before you begin

Acquaint yourself with the following components and key issues of this topic; and familiar-ise yourself with how you would structurally progress through them all, if necessary, when attempting to answer a question on this topic.

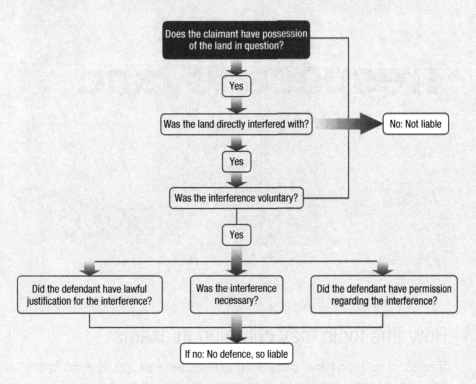

A printable version of this diagram is available from **www.pearsoned.co.uk/lawexpressqa**

🛈 Question 1

John recently purchased a horse-riding school near the village of Old Whittaker. John lives on site in a small cottage and stables his horses there. As a keen competitor, John decided to convert the riding school into a showground, offering equine competitions to riders in the local area. He also intended to hold one national show per year to boost the opportunities available to high-level competitors in the sport. All riders and horses who come on to the site must have a valid entry into one of the competitions. Non-competitors must purchase a ticket for a nominal fee of £2 per competition. Visitors/competitors are made aware of this on the competition entry forms and on a sign at the entrance of the property.

Conditions of entry into the showground stipulate that dogs must be kept on a lead at all times and that horse manure must be removed by the horse owner or moved to the designated muckheap at the end of the car parking area. While walking around the car park prior to a show-jumping competition, John noticed that Michael's Jack Russell dog was running around the car park and that he had scraped the horse droppings from his lorry onto the car park floor. John confronted Michael about this and demanded that he leave. Michael responded by saying, 'give over old man, I am competing after the next horse. I will go after I have won.'

Ellen's horse was particularly fresh when she arrived at the competition. She normally rides her horses out on a hack prior to competing, in order to calm them down and therefore decided to ride out on John's farmland. She has been allowed to do this at other showgrounds so thought it would be OK but missed a sign on the way into a field that stated 'Crow scarers in use, riders should use alternative fields.' Ellen entered the field when the bird scarer went off, emitting a loud bang. Her horses spooked causing Ellen to fall into a fence, breaking one of the top rails.

In preparation for the national competition, John had a large sign made that he erected in front of a hedge that runs from the driveway into his neighbour Robert's property, up to the entrance into the showground. John made sure that the posts for the sign were fixed into the ground on his property; however, approximately one foot of the sign encroached into Robert's property. Robert asked John to move the sign along on several occasions as he wanted to prune his hedge and could not access the part of the hedge where the sign stood in front of it. However, John dismissed him, saying that 'the competition will be over this weekend, surely you can wait.'

Advise John in respect of any actions that he can take/can be taken against him.

Diagram plan

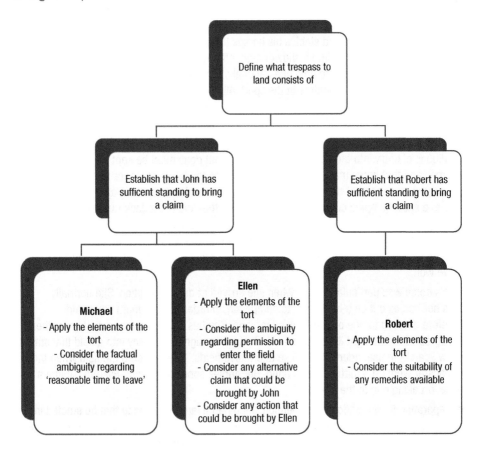

A printable version of this diagram plan is available from **www.pearsoned.co.uk/lawexpressqa**

Answer plan

➜ Define what is meant by trespass to land.

➜ Establish that John and Robert have possession of their respective land so that each may bring a claim.

➜ Examine each incident of trespass complained of in turn as to whether it was voluntarily directed at the land.

➜ Consider any possible justification for each interference.

➜ Advise John on what remedy he should seek in relation to the different actions directed at his land.

Answer

John will be advised in respect of various aspects of trespass to land and any potential remedies that are available to either himself or Robert in respect of this tort. Trespass to land as defined in *Clerk and Lindsell* on Torts (Jones *et al.*, 2014)[1] consists of the unjustifiable intrusion by one person upon land in the possession of another. John should be advised that the slightest crossing of a boundary is sufficient, and the tort is actionable without proof of damage. This is important as not all of the incidents have resulted in any physical damage. It will be argued that John may potentially have an actionable claim against Michael and Ellen, but that he could also face claims from Robert in trespass and Ellen under the occupiers' liability legislation.[2]

The first matter that must be determined is whether or not John has sufficient standing to bring an action in trespass.[3] Trespass is actionable by an individual who is in actual occupation of the land. Mere physical presence on the land is insufficient; however, there is no requirement that the claimant has a legal estate in the land. As John owns and lives on site in a cottage at the showground, he has the necessary possession to be able to bring an action. Likewise, it also appears as though John's neighbour, Robert, has sufficient standing to bring an action against John in respect of the competition sign.

Turning to the incident with Michael first, John should be advised that, as required, there is an immediate, direct and intentional interference with his land. As Michael is a competitor in a show-jumping competition at the showground, it appears as though there has been a justifiable interference, as he has a contractual licence to be on the property. However, John should be advised that the extent of Michael's licence to be on the property can be limited by conditions attached to the grant of that licence. In the instant case, the conditions of entry stipulated that dogs must be kept on a lead at all times and that horse manure be removed by owners or moved to the designated muck heap. As Michael has contravened these conditions by allowing his dog to run freely around the car park and by scraping his horse droppings from his lorry onto the car park floor, Michael's presence, although in a permitted area, has clearly exceeded the limits of his permission to be on the property. As such, this will

[1] You will not be expected to include a full reference in an examination; however, you should try to include some information about the source that you are relying upon. In a coursework you should follow the referencing style outlined in your assessment brief.

[2] This sets the tone for the remainder of your answer. In order to be able to include a sentence such as this in your introduction, you need to have a clear plan of where your answer is going before you start writing.

[3] Clearly if this were not to be the case, there wouldn't be much of a question. Although this issue seems quite obvious, it is still a crucial requirement of any claim and therefore should be addressed in your answer.

[4] Although not asked to advise on breach of contract, this demonstrates a wider appreciation of how different areas of the law interact and can arise out of the same factual situation.

[5] There is some ambiguity in the facts in respect of what Michael does after his conversation with John. You should therefore explore the various possibilities and discuss the impact of these on the likelihood of John bringing a successful action.

[6] Although the question asks you to advise John, it is important to identify arguments that could be made by the opposing party in order to fully advise him.

[7] This demonstrates an awareness of the different remedies available and the suitability of those remedies in various different situations.

[8] Although the question clearly focuses on trespass, the wording of the question provides you with the scope to explore other torts and demonstrate that you understand that a variety of different tortious claims can arise from the same set of circumstances.

constitute a trespass. John should be advised that his revocation of Michael's licence to be on the property will not constitute a breach of contract due to the conditions attached;[4] however, he should be aware that Michael should be permitted a reasonable time to leave (*Cornish v Stubbs* (1870) LR 5 CP 334). There will be no action against Michael, if he left the showground within a reasonable time. However, as Michael indicated that he was going to ride his horse in the competition prior to vacating the property, if he did, this could be construed as an unreasonably long time to leave and, as such, a successful action may be brought against Michael.[5]

Turning to Ellen, it appears as though her presence on the showground generally is justifiable as she appears to be a competitor and, as such, has a licence to be on the property. However, like Michael, she may have exceeded the limits of her licence by entering the field with the bird scarers while riding her horse. Ambiguity arises as a consequence of the use of the word 'should' on the sign. If the sign is construed as merely advisory in nature, then Ellen's presence in the field may be construed as a justifiable interference. If, however, the sign is to be construed as prohibiting entry into the field by persons riding, then Ellen will have exceeded the limits of her licence by entering the field and, as a consequence, trespassed. A lack of permission could have been made clearer, and Ellen may attempt to argue that she did not intend to trespass as she didn't see the sign.[6] However, it is the act of entry which must be intended as opposed to the act of trespassing and, as such, this argument would be irrelevant (*Conway v George Wimpey & Co Ltd* [1951] 2 KB 266). Consequently, in the event that the sign is construed as a limiting permission to enter the field, Ellen's intentional entry into the field will be considered trespass. As John has suffered injury to his property as a consequence of Ellen falling into the fence, the most appropriate remedy would be damages. Injunctive relief would serve little purpose in this instance.[7]

As John suffered actual damage to his property as a result of Ellen falling into the fence, he may have an alternative claim in negligence. This would be of particular importance if the sign were not construed as limiting her permission to enter the field. However, John should be made aware that if Ellen suffered injury as a consequence of her fall, that she may have a possible claim against him under the occupiers' liability legislation. This would be the case, even if she were considered to be a trespasser.[8]

John should be advised that an action may also be brought against him, although in this instance by Robert, and in respect of trespass as a consequence of the sign that he erected at the front of his property. In dealing with this dispute, it is important to note that it is irrelevant that John did not enter Robert's property when erecting the sign, as the fact that he did not enter the property himself does not preclude an action in trespass (**Smith v Stone** [1647] Style 65). The intentional crossing of the boundary on to Robert's land by the sign that John erected could be interpreted as direct harm and thus trespass. The case of **Kelson v Imperial Tobacco Co** [1957] 2 QB 334 involved a sign overhanging the claimant's land by eight inches and trespass was made out. Likewise, in **Laiqat v Majid** [2005] EWHC 1305 an extractor fan that protruded over the claimant's land by 75 cm at a height of 4.5 m was also considered to be trespass. John should be aware that one's land extends skyward and that, although no damage has been caused by the sign, this is still likely to constitute a trespass based upon these authorities. Liability reflects the premise that one's own land should be inviolate, especially from intentional acts of interference.[9] If successful, Robert would be entitled to damages even though actual harm did not occur. He may also seek injunctive relief in order to prevent the continuation of the trespass.

[9] As John was dismissive of Robert's complaint about the sign, it is important to offer some explanation about why he faces liability.

In conclusion, it appears as though John may potentially have actionable claims in trespass against Michael and Ellen. However, he should be aware that he is likely to face a successful claim in trespass from Robert and potentially a claim under the occupiers' liability legislation, should Ellen have been injured in her fall.

✓ Make your answer stand out

- Discuss the theoretical basis of trespass to illustrate to John why he would still be liable even if the sign is only protruding by a couple of inches, but counter this by looking at Hudson, A.H. (1960) Nuisance or trespass. *Modern Law Review*, 23: 188 and whether *Kelsen* v *Imperial Tobacco Co.* [1957] 2 QB 334 is compatible with other authorities.
- Explain in detail how Robert might get an injunction if he wanted one.
- Consider the possible claim in negligence against Ellen.
- Show your awareness of the other areas of the law of torts which the situation may give rise to, such as a claim for damages by Ellen under the occupiers' liability legislation, if she suffered any injuries as a consequence of her fall.

! **Don't be tempted to . . .**

- Just assume that John or Robert are eligible to bring an action in trespass or gloss over this requirement, as it is one that needs to be satisfied in order to bring a successful action.

- Ignore the potential claims by Robert and Ellen and just concentrate on what claims John can make, as the question does not restrict you in that way.

- Overlook the subsidiary claims that John could make as, again, while the question is predominantly on trespass to land, it does not completely restrict you to that tort.

Question 2

'This leaves the squeezing out. It is perhaps doubtful whether the cause of action in respect of this arises in nuisance or in trespass: see *Esso Petroleum Co. Ltd. v Southport Corporation* [1956] AC 218, *per* p Devlin J., at p. 225. In my view it makes no difference to the result.' *Per* Piers Ashworth QC in *Home Brewery Co.* v *William Davis & Co. (Loughborough) Ltd* [1987] QB 339, 354E.

Evaluate the nature of the tort of trespass to land in order to determine whether it has a distinctive purpose.

Diagram plan

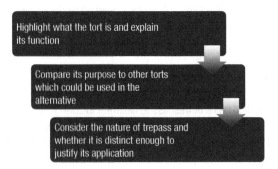

A printable version of this diagram plan is available from **www.pearsoned.co.uk/lawexpressqa**

Answer plan

➔ Define trespass to land and explain its function.

➔ Compare and contrast the tort to potential alternatives.

➔ Analyse the nature of the tort and evaluate whether its nature and scope justifies its existence.

➔ Conclude by considering whether the tort is distinct and fulfils a needed purpose.

Answer

[1] Keep this brief here. This is the introduction so your aim is just to identify the underlying issues of the question that you will address and introduce the points you will develop as you progress your answer.

[2] This may seem like an unnecessary clarification of the definition of *per se*. However, it is quite easy, and common, for students to write Latin phrases that feature often in the textbooks without appreciating what they mean. By clarifying, you demonstrate that you understand the phrase as opposed to having simply remembered reading it.

[3] Although you would not necessarily have to go into detail here as to what is protected, this gives an early indication that you are aware of the scope of the tort.

[4] At each stage of your answer, and especially where you have highlighted similarities with other torts, try to differentiate trespass to show why it can justifiably be said to be distinct. This will also make sure your answer is not purely descriptive.

The issue to determine is whether the tort of trespass has a sufficiently distinctive purpose to warrant its ongoing retention as a tort. If liability for interference with one's land could arise without basing the action in trespass, then it is questionable whether it is needed. Abolishing the tort though would be significant in light of how it operates.[1]

It will be argued that while other torts have similar functions, it is the fact that trespass is actionable *per se*, meaning without proof of actual damage,[2] which makes it distinct and justifies its retention as this reflects the fundamental importance of a person's rights in land.

The tort has much broader scope than the layperson's traditional idea of someone wandering onto their land.[3] *Clerk & Lindsell on Torts* (Jones *et al.*, 2014) define trespass to land as consisting of any unjustifiable intrusion by one person upon land in the possession of another. The tort exists to protect a person's interest in property arising through possession, symbolised through an intention to possess and physical control (*JA Pye (Oxford) Ltd v Graham* [2002] UKHL 22), as opposed to stemming from ownership. What is required is to show a direct and immediate, voluntary interference with that possession. A proprietary interest, while evidence of possession, is not necessary. Therefore, while the purpose of trespass, protecting land from interference, is indeed similar to that of the tort of nuisance, there is a crucial difference in that nuisance requires a proprietary interest in the land (*Hunter v Canary Wharf Ltd* [1997] AC 655) that is being interfered with so the choice of action could matter a great deal depending on the status of the claimant.[4]

The quote from the judgment in *Home Brewery Co. Ltd* suggests, though, that substantially trespass serves no distinct purpose and,

[5] The fact that trespass can be caused through a negligent incursion on to the land, due to it still being voluntary, means that if damage occurs, as in the case with *Network Rail*, the tort of negligence could be relied on instead. As such, it is also worth contrasting it to trespass to assess how distinct the latter is. Mentioning this in this context also allows you to demonstrate quickly the difference that does exist between the two actions.

[6] Although the question does not ask specifically for a comparison to nuisance, it does require you to look at whether trespass is sufficiently distinct from other torts so a comparison is needed to at least one. Focusing primarily on nuisance has merit as there are similarities and, as it is referred to in the statement, by using it you are clearly relating your discussion back to the question.

[7] The aim here is to conclude the point that you raised at the start of the paragraph, while again providing some context to the evaluative discussion you are having by relating it back to the proposition in the question. Nuisance in its current form could not perform the same role as trespass. You can then also build on the point made by flowing straight into the requirements that trespass's purpose requires.

the claimant's status aside, need not be pleaded in order to succeed in a claim. This premise may have merit where actual damage is caused by the interference, but it also demonstrates the distinctiveness and value of trespass, where there is seemingly no actual physical damage, the basis of the action would matter. A lack of physical damage would rule out a claim in negligence even if trespass can be committed negligently[5] (*Network Rail Infrastructure Ltd* v *Cornarken Group Ltd* [2010] EWHC 1852). Interference in nuisance,[6] while again similar in that actual physical damage is not necessary, does differ in that the interference must cause substantial damage to the claimant's interest, reflecting the need for some give and take between neighbours (*Sedleigh-Denfield* v *O'Callaghan* [1940] AC 880).

Therefore, claimants in cases such as *Kelsen* v *Imperial Tobacco Co.* [1957] 2 QB 334, where a sign marginally hung over the boundary line, would be left without redress in the absence of trespass, as the interference was held not sufficient to be an actionable nuisance. The damage in nuisance must also be pleaded and proven which provides an additional evidential obstacle that does not exist in trespass. Therefore, the purpose of each tort differs and is in fact fulfilled in different ways through the need to prove specific elements, which means that how the interference occurs may also influence which tort the action needs to be brought in.[7]

As noted, trespass requires interference with the land which must also be the result of a direct and voluntary act. If it is indirect, then another form of action would be needed, rendering the choice of action important. The interference can take many forms though and can relate

8 What you are going to do in this section is analyse the nature of trespass and justify its existence in theoretical terms and principle rather than just because it is different to other torts. By doing so, you are not just describing the requirements, but also providing a critique of them.

9 Such examples are arguably not needed as you have explained what is required. However, using examples shows that you more fully understand the requirement and the broader range of situations that it applies to which leads into the point you are about to make.

10 As the example you are going on to explain here is a different issue from that which you highlighted earlier in the paragraph, it is fine to draw on another case as you are not simply listing cases on the same point.

11 A sentence along these lines is important in order to tie your answer back to the question and reinforce the impression that you are aware of the full scope of the question.

to the land's surface, subsoil or airspace.[8] Examples include simple entering the land, remaining there after one should leave, and even just placing a stone against a wall (***Gregory v Piper*** (1829) 109 ER 220).[9] This means that there is an extremely low threshold for trespass liability. In ***Gregory,*** arguably, no harm was actually done. This clearly illustrates the distinctiveness of the tort and its value: no actual damage to the land is required. However, there could be said to be damage present in that the protection of a person's interest in property is a fundamental right, as seen in Article 1 of the First Protocol of the European Convention on Human Rights. Trespass's role is simply to protect the interest in possession of the claimant. The right owner should be able to determine who enters the land. If a person voluntarily and directly performs an act which directly interferes with another's land, then surely the law is justified in holding that person liable, even without actual damage resulting. The mere fact that it has been interfered with warrants the imposition of liability. This is particularly the case when the interference is intentional. However, the problem of the low threshold is exacerbated by the fact that the simple act of interference just needs to be voluntary, an intention to actually interfere is not relevant. Clearly, some harshness flows from this, e.g. in ***Conway v George Wimpey & Co. Ltd*** [1951] 2 KB 266[10] liability resulted where the entry followed a completely innocent mistake because the entry onto the land was still intended, but the interference could still be said to be direct.

Therefore, it is clear from the requirements of trespass that its operation and, therefore, applicability to a given situation is unique. It has a distinct scope compared to other torts, which allows it to fill a void in the level of protection afforded by tort which would otherwise exist if the issue was left to actions dealing with indirect interferences such as nuisance or indeed negligence.[11] Further, only one act is required for a claim to arise and, therefore, other torts such as harassment, based on a course of conduct, offer no relief in such a situation.

To conclude, while there are similarities with other torts, the underlying function of trespass to land shows that it is ultimately aimed at providing a different form of redress to torts such as nuisance and negligence. The purpose and operation of the protection is unique and other torts can only satisfactorily replace trespass in circumstances where there is something more akin to actual damage, and so what they are in effect protecting is something different. Therefore, a distinct tort embodied by trespass to land is needed to protect rights in land when the injury is to the right of possession of the land itself. A simple voluntary act leading to the direct interference with that interest is sufficient damage even if the land is not physically affected. If this is not recognised, then all forms of trespass to the person would also need abolishing. However, it is perhaps arguable that in light of the more abstract nature of the damage required, the interference should be intentional to warrant liability being imposed. That would also further reinforce the distinctiveness of trespass to land and bring it in line with trespass to the person.[12]

[12] The purpose of this sentence is to indicate that you are aware how this tort sits with the other forms of trespass and that you are aware of the wider repercussions of simply abolishing the tort.

✓ Make your answer stand out

- Evaluate the justification for trespass as a distinct tort constantly as you progress through your answer, rather than just including a passage at the end of an account of the requirements.
- Read Hudson, A.H. (1960) Nuisance or trespass. *Modern Law Review*, 23: 188 and evaluate the principle from *Kelsen* v *Imperial Tobacco Co.* [1957] 2 QB 334. This will allow you to consider if the distinction between trespass and nuisance could in fact be narrower.
- Look at the history of the overall trespass action in order to comment more fully on whether trespass to land should require intention.
- Consider the broader role that the tort plays in terms of settling disputes about rights over land and its links to preventing breaches of the peace.

! Don't be tempted to . . .

- Simply describe the requirements of the tort; you need to evaluate each as you deal with them.
- Merely discuss nuisance as a comparison to trespass. The fact that trespass can be committed negligently means that an action could be brought in that tort as an alternative and that there are similarities.
- Provide a detailed account of the requirements of any other torts that you discuss. Instead, just ensure that you highlight the role that those torts play, their purpose and whether they could perform the same function as trespass in a more justifiable manner.
- Just agree with the proposition in the question; feel free to disagree with it if that is what you feel.

Try it yourself

Now take a look at the question below and attempt to answer it. You can check your response against the answer guidance available on the companion website (**www.pearsoned.co.uk/lawexpressqa**).

> Miles and Jill have gone to see their local football team play. At the entrance to the stadium there is a large sign which says that offensive language is strictly prohibited and alcohol must not be consumed within sight of the pitch. Once there, they met Martin who, having recently paid for his daughter's wedding, could not afford the entrance fee so he had climbed over a wall to gain entry.
>
> During the game, incensed by a late tackle by an opposition player, Jill flies into a rage and shouts out a string of expletives aimed at the player in question and the referee. At half-time John decided to treat himself to a beer but due to the long queue the second half was about to start so he took it back to his seat to watch the rest of the match.
>
> Advise the parties as to any potential liability for trespass to land following their actions.

www.pearsoned.co.uk/lawexpressqa

 Go online to access more revision support including additional essay and problem questions with diagram plans, you be the marker questions, and download all diagrams from the book.

Nuisance

How this topic may come up in exams

Nuisance problem questions require several different factors to be considered to determine whether a claim has been made out. You will also have to determine whether the nuisance is private or public and whether the nuisance is covered by statute such as environmental protection legislation. In addition, there is the possibility of a question having the potential to explore issues of negligence and the rule in *Rylands* v *Fletcher* as well. There is also a significant human rights impact in this tort, particularly Article 8 of the European Convention on Human Rights, and the implications this has for *Hunter* v *Canary Wharf* and the necessity for a proprietary interest to bring an action, which can form the basis of essay questions.

■ Before you begin

Acquaint yourself with the following components and key issues of this topic; and familiarise yourself with how you would structurally progress through them all, if necessary, when attempting to answer a question on this topic.

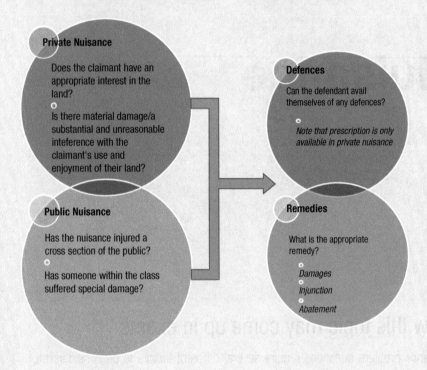

Private Nuisance

Does the claimant have an appropriate interest in the land?

Is there material damage/a substantial and unreasonable inteference with the claimant's use and enjoyment of their land?

Defences

Can the defendant avail themselves of any defences?

Note that prescription is only available in private nuisance

Public Nuisance

Has the nuisance injured a cross section of the public?

Has someone within the class suffered special damage?

Remedies

What is the appropriate remedy?

Damages

Injunction

Abatement

A printable version of this diagram is available from **www.pearsoned.co.uk/lawexpressqa**

❓ Question 1

Nina lives in a semi-detached house in the quiet village of Barbourne and has done so for 7 years. Nina is currently off work on maternity leave as she gave birth to her daughter, Clara, 4 months previously.

Nina's neighbour, Axel, is a musician. He plays in a band most evenings and normally warms up for his gigs by playing his guitar before leaving at around 6 pm. When Axel returns home, he often continues to play his guitar in order to wind down after the gig. He tends to return home at any time between 11 p.m. and 3 a.m. Nina can hear the music through the wall between the two houses. It is interfering with her ability to get Clara to sleep. Nina, in a state of sleep-deprived desperation attempts to speak to Axel; however, he responds by pointing out that his playing had never been a problem before and that Clara's crying was keeping him awake, so they both needed to just put up with each other.

Nina's house backs on to farmland, which is one of the features of her house that she found particularly appealing when she bought it. The farmer had been granted planning permission 5 years ago to erect a barn to house equipment used to process grain that he harvests from his farm. The barn is visible from Nina's garden; however, due to poor weather conditions, the farmer had been unable to successfully grow sufficient crops to make use of grain processing equipment until this year. Due to excellent weather conditions, a bumper crop has been harvested and, as a consequence, the grain processing equipment has been running from 6 a.m. to 10 p.m. for the past 3 weeks. This has caused noise and dust, which has meant that Nina has been unable to use her garden.

Advise Nina in respect of any action that she may be able to bring against Axel and/or the farmer.

Diagram plan

> **Does Nina have sufficient standing to bring an action in private nuisance?**
> *Consider Nina's interest in the property*

Is Axel causing a substantial inteference? *Identify that this is possibly an amenity nuisance*	**Is the farmer causing a substantial inteference?** *Identify that this is possibly an amenity nuisance*
Is the inteference unreasonable? *Assess the seriousness of the inteference in light of its extent/duration and the particular sensitivities of the claimant.*	**Is the inteference unreasonable?** *Assess the seriousness of the inteference in light of its extent/duration. Consider the resonableness of the farmer's use given its social utility and the locality.*
Can Axel rely on any defences?	**Can the farmer rely on any defences?** *Discuss the significance of Nina purchasing the property knowing the farmer's use of the land*
If Nina is able to bring a successful action, what is the appropriate remedy?	**If Nina is able to bring a successful action, what is the appropriate remedy?**

A printable version of this diagram plan is available from **www.pearsoned.co.uk/lawexpressqa**

Answer plan

→ Confirm that Nina is eligible to a claim against Axel and the farmer.

→ Consider whether there is a substantial and unreasonable interference with Nina's use and enjoyment of land due to the noise created by Axel's guitar playing.

→ Consider whether any defences may be available to Axel and, if not, which remedies may be appropriate in the circumstances.

→ Consider whether there is a substantial and unreasonable interference with Nina's use and enjoyment of land, due to the dust and noise created by the grain processing by the farmer.

→ Consider whether any defences may be available to the farmer and, if not, which remedies may be appropriate in the circumstances.

Answer

[1] You should demonstrate
from the beginning of
your answer that you have
identified the nature of the
potential nuisance.

[2] A mere licensee has no
standing to bring an action in
nuisance – the claimant must
have a proprietary interest
in the land. While it may
seem obvious that Nina has a
proprietary interest in the land
due to the fact that she has
lived in the property since she
purchased it 7 years ago, this
requirement has been strictly
applied and so you should
address it at the beginning of
your answer.

[3] As you are advising Nina,
explain to her what the
potential remedies are for the
tort. This also demonstrates
to your marker that you
have an appreciation of the
practical operation of the tort.

[4] Demonstrate that you
understand the central issue
that the tort of nuisance seeks
to address prior to moving
on to the specifics of your
application.

[5] By adding this, you
demonstrate that you
understand how the underlying
principles for the tort will be
considered when applying the
requirements of the tort and
how it differs from other torts
related to land.

The issues raised are whether Nina has an action for private nuisance against Axel and/or the neighbouring farmer, as it appears as though her use and enjoyment of her land is being interfered with due to the activities conducted on their land.[1] As Nina appears to own and occupy her property, she will have enough proprietary interest to enable her to have sufficient standing in order to bring an action against both Axel and the neighbouring farmer[2] (**Hunter v Canary Wharf Ltd** [1997] AC 655). It is important that these disputes are resolved, as a successful action by Nina could result in Axel and/or the farmer being prevented from carrying out the relevant activities.[3] Nina will be advised in respect of any action she may bring against Axel and the neighbouring farmer in turn.

In respect of Axel's guitar playing, this is clearly interfering with Nina's use and enjoyment of her land; however, in order to be actionable Nina will need to demonstrate that the noise caused amounts to a substantial and unreasonable interference. The tort of nuisance aims to strike a fair balance between the competing interests of neighbouring landowners and acknowledges that there must be a certain degree of give and take between the respective parties.[4] Unlike the tort of trespass to land, not every interference will amount to an actionable interference and each case is determined upon its own merits (**Sturges v Bridgman** (1879) 11 Ch D 852).[5]

As the interference that Nina is claiming in respect of has not caused material damage but is based upon her amenity interests, the courts are afforded a degree of latitude in determining the existence of the alleged nuisance. The case law has developed a matrix of factors that will be utilised to determine whether an interference is substantial and unreasonable, with various factors such as locality of the properties in question, the intensity and

[6] Although you should not normally simply list all potential considerations, these are all relevant in determining the existence of a nuisance in respect of Axel and therefore it is appropriate to list them in this way, as it sets the scene for the remainder of your answer.

[7] Although the facts of the question are relatively vague, make use of whatever factual information that you have in order to attempt to draw a reasoned conclusion. Students should be prepared to address ambiguity in a question.

timing of the interference and, where relevant, the sensitivity of the claimant,[6] having to be weighed in the balance. If the scales tip in favour of the claimant, in the absence of an appropriate defence, the claim will be successful.

As Nina lives in a rural property, it is expected that the property would be quieter than if it were located in an urban or industrial area (*Sturges*). However, the rural nature of the property does not automatically mean that the noise emanating from Axel's property constitutes an actionable interference; the courts will need to consider whether or not the noise is substantial and unreasonable enough to constitute a nuisance. The fact that the noise can be heard through the walls would imply that the music is significantly loud and although we do not know the exact duration of the noise, it appears as though the playing takes place on most days of the week and during the night, which implies that the interference is substantial.[7] Axel may suggest that the noise is only an interference due to the fact that Nina is particularly sensitive, as a new mother, to the noise that he is creating. The existence of a nuisance is determined by considering its effect on a reasonable user of land. If Nina were considered to be overly sensitive, then her action in nuisance would not be successful (*Robinson v Kilvert* (1889) 41 Ch D 88 (CA)). However, despite the fact that Nina has a young baby, it is likely that the noise would be considered a nuisance by a reasonable person and thus would not preclude her from bringing a successful action. The interference with her use and enjoyment of the land is a reasonably foreseeable consequence of Axel's actions and, as such, is likely to constitute an actionable interference (*Cambridge Water Co. Ltd v Eastern Counties Leather plc* [1994] 2 AC 264).

[8] Even when it appears as though the potential defences are not relevant, you should not miss out consideration of them altogether. You need to highlight this fact; however, you should not labour the point as it is unlikely to enhance your answer.

It appears as though the interference with Nina's use and enjoyment of her land caused by Axel's guitar playing will be actionable, and in light of the fact that none of the potential defences are available to Axel, an appropriate remedy will be available to her.[8] The principal remedies for private nuisance are damages and/or an injunction. In *Coventry v Lawrence* [2014] UKSC 14, it was acknowledged that a claimant may be entitled to an injunction to restrain the defendant from continuing the nuisance in addition to damages for past nuisance and the burden is on the defendant to satisfy the court as to why an injunction should not be granted. However, the issue should be approached with a greater degree of flexibility as compared with slavishly following the tests set out in *Shelfer v City of London Electric Lighting Co.* [1895] 1 Ch 287. Although damages in lieu of an injunction may be more freely awarded, it is likely that Nina would wish to pursue an injunction in order to prevent Axel from continuing to play his guitar at an unreasonable time.[9] This is likely to be granted in addition to some monetary compensation.

[9] Although *Coventry* indicates that damages may be more freely awarded, this is unlikely to be the remedy that Nina wishes to pursue. You should advise on what is appropriate and realistic in the circumstances.

Turning now to the noise and dust caused by the farmer, this too appears to be an alleged interference with Nina's amenity interest and, as such, the interference must be both substantial and unreasonable. As with Axel, the courts will take a number of different factors into consideration in order to determine this. Although the activities undertaken on the farmer's land are within their natural locality, i.e. the countryside (*Sturges*) and thus more likely to be considered reasonable, this does not prevent the courts from finding that the dust and noise constitute a nuisance (*Thomas v Methyr Tydfil Car Auction Ltd* [2013] EWCA Civ 815). The extent, time and duration of the interference are factors to be taken into consideration, which may render the interference unreasonable even in the rural setting. Although the interference has only arisen in the past 3 weeks between the hours of 6 am and 10 pm, even a temporary interference can be actionable provided that it is sufficiently substantial (*Metropolitan Properties Ltd v Jones* [1939] 2 All ER 202). The fact that the noise and dust is so great that Nina is unable to use her garden, implies that this may be the case; however, this is a matter for the courts to determine based upon the evidence provided.

[10] In order to advise Nina, you should consider the points that are likely to be raised by the defendant. This provides a more balanced account of situation and enables better evaluation and application.

Although the harm caused appears to be a reasonably foreseeable consequence of the defendant's actions (*Cambridge*), the farmer[10] may, nevertheless, suggest that the activity should not constitute an unreasonable interference on the basis that he was granted planning permission to erect the barn for grain processing and/or the activity carries with it a social utility. The Supreme Court in *Coventry* unanimously held that the granting of planning permission cannot, in itself, authorise a nuisance although Lord Sumption and Lord Carnwath did indicate that it could be of some assistance in determining the reasonableness of the defendant's conduct where, for example, the planning permission stipulates matters such as frequency or intensity of noise. Likewise, the social utility of a defendant's activity cannot provide an immunity from suit to the farmer as the courts are reluctant to let private rights, such as those enjoyed by Nina, be extinguished in favour of the general public without some form of statutory authority. Nina should be advised that while these factors do not preclude a finding that the interference from the grain processing constitutes an actionable negligence, these factors may be taken into consideration in determining what remedy should be awarded (***Dennis v Ministry of Defence*** [2003] Env LR 34).[11]

[11] Although it would be tempting to move on to remedies after considering both *Coventry* and *Dennis*, you need to ensure that you consider defences first. If you do not do this, you could be advising on remedies that are ultimately not available to the claimant.

On the basis that the courts find the interference from the grain processing both substantial and unreasonable,[12] defences should be considered. Neither prescription nor statutory authority are relevant in these circumstances. The farmer may seek to argue that Nina purchased the land next to a working farm and therefore came to the nuisance. However, this has consistently been held not to be a defence since ***Bliss v Hall*** (1838) 4 Bing NC183. Therefore, the farmer may potentially face liability.

[12] As it has not been possible to draw a firm conclusion on this matter, you should reflect this in the way in which you start your next paragraph.

In terms of the possible remedy, the courts may be more reluctant to grant Nina an injunction in respect of the interference from the farm, due to the effect the injunction may have on the carrying out of the farmer's business (***Coventry***) and the social utility of the farmer's activities (***Dennis***). This is particularly the case if the grain processing can only be completed within a limited time period. Damages in lieu of an injunction may be more appropriate in these circumstances, which would allow the farmer to continue to pursue his activities.

In conclusion, it appears as though Nina has a potential action in nuisance against both Axel and the farmer. However, this is dependent on whether the courts find that the interferences are substantial and unreasonable, which cannot be conclusively determined without further evidence. If successful, damages and/or an injunction may be an appropriate remedy in an action against Axel; however, damages appear to be the more appropriate and likely remedy in any action brought against the farmer.

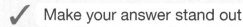 **Make your answer stand out**

- Consider the comments in *Coventry* v *Lawrence* [2014] UKSC 14 regarding the 'defence' of coming to the nuisance and how it could apply where the claimant subsequently alters the use of their land in the knowledge of how the defendant uses their land.
- Explore in more detail, and draw on, the opinions in *Coventry* v *Lawrence* [2014] UKSC 14 in relation to when damages should be granted in place of an injunction.
- Explain in more detail the theoretical basis of the tort and provide a bit more insight as to the balance which lies at the heart of it.
- Read Murphy, J. (2010) *The Law of Nuisance.* Oxford: Oxford University Press, during your revision, and try to incorporate some academic views of how the courts look at the various factors which need to be considered in deciding the matter.

! Don't be tempted to . . .

- Try to explain every factor which could be assessed as part of establishing whether the tort is made out; just focus on those factors which seem most applicable on the facts. Otherwise, you will lose the structure of your answer and could in fact show a lack of understanding, as they are not all relevant to the question.
- Go too deeply into analysing the nature of the tort. While some discussion will push your answer on, and provide context, you need to bear in mind this is a problem question, not an essay.
- Allow your discussion to jump back and forth between the two defendants by sticking rigidly to a structure based upon the requirements of the tort. This is likely to produce a confused answer. Advise Nina in respect of each action in turn, considering only the matters that are relevant to each of them.

📝 Question 2

'There is obviously a powerful case for saying that effect has not been properly given to Article 8.1 if a person with no interest in the home, but who has lived in the home for some time and had his enjoyment of the home interfered with, is at the mercy of the person who owns the home, as the only person who can bring proceedings.' (*Per* Neuberger J in *McKenna* v *British Aluminum Ltd* [2002] En LR 30, [53])

Evaluate the scope of the tort of nuisance and whether the class of people it can help is justifiably limited.

Diagram plan

A printable version of this diagram plan is available from **www.pearsoned.co.uk/lawexpressqa**

Answer plan

➜ Discuss the purpose and nature of the tort.

➜ Explain the reasoning in Hunter v Canary Wharf Ltd and analyse why tort's scope was limited by the court.

➜ Evaluate the feasibility of continuing to insist on the requirement in light of the Human Rights Act 1998.

➜ Consider whether there is a satisfactory way of retaining the essence of the tort which is more compatible with human rights considerations.

Answer

The tort of nuisance protects one's interest in land; however, this function means that its scope is limited to those who own the land (***Hunter v Canary Wharf Ltd*** [1997] AC 655). The issue that this causes is that residents of a property have no redress, even though they would be suffering the same interference as the owner. The issue is heightened since the passing of the Human Rights Act 1998 as the law's compatibility with human rights can be questioned. It will be argued that, while the reasoning in ***Hunter*** is justified, it is not sustainable on human rights grounds and those who reside in the property affected by the alleged nuisance activity should have redress under the tort, or through a new analogous tort.[1]

[1] As you have just indicated that you are going to disagree with the position adopted by the House of Lords, you should offer an insight into what you propose that the law should be.

[2] The question does not specifically call for a discussion of the test for nuisance and how a claim would succeed; however, if you introduce the forms of nuisance in this way you can demonstrate that you know the test without losing focus.

In protecting interests in land from reoccurring substantial and unreasonable interferences, nuisance can take two forms[2] (*St Helen's Smelting Co. v Tipping* (1865) HL Cas 642). First, nuisance can amount to material damage to the land with such claims being relatively straightforward; the land itself is damaged and thus it is logical that the claim should be brought by the owner of the damaged land. The second form is nuisance producing sensible personal discomfort, or amenity interference. The act interferes with the enjoyment of the land, for example producing noise and smells. Therefore, the enjoyment of all those present on the land is affected and not just the owner of the land who actually may not be present.

This issue as to who can rely on the tort came to the fore in *Hunter* where a group of residents claimed nuisance arising from local construction work. Significantly, not all of the residents had a proprietary interest in their respective homes. Their claim initially failed for want of a proprietary interest, but succeeded on appeal with Pill LJ holding that, where an individual occupied the land as their home, they would have a sufficient link to the land to enable them to make the claim.[3]

[3] Obviously, this reasoning was rejected by the majority of the House of Lords, but it is worth stating as a point of reference for your answer later on.

[4] Although here you are advancing the reasons of the majority and why the case was ultimately decided the way it was, you need to subject this reasoning to analysis, and so try to assess the merit of each point you state. You need to look at the flaws directly related to this reasoning before you can get on to advancing the specific arguments *for* the alternate view. If you wait until later, your structure will not be as strong.

This decision was itself appealed and reversed by a majority of the House of Lords who took a traditional view of the tort. Lord Goff observed that parties may seek to negotiate an agreement over the interfering activity. However, if an agreement was needed with everyone who lived in the property, the ease of reaching an agreement and its effectiveness would be reduced. This is a strong point; however, the potential ability to impose implied authorisation on the homeowner to represent non-owning residents means it is not insurmountable,[4] as Lord Cooke highlighted in his dissent.[5] Lord Goff also raised concerns with how to define 'substantial link'. While Pill LJ intended his phrase to cover the owner's immediate family, Lord Goff questioned whether it should include lodgers and au pairs who also live there. His Lordship then questioned why it would not then extend to cover the workplace. To avoid permitting any individual, even a regular visitor, to bring an action, and thus take the tort away from its historical purpose of protecting interests in land, a reference point for determining standing to bring a claim is needed.[6] However, this was again countered by Lord Cooke, who argued it was 'weak' to not lay down a rule which was justifiable in relation to spouses and children just because of a grey area as to where the line is ultimately drawn. While the issue may be one of creating legal certainty as well as giving

[5] This needs to be made clear so that the contradictory views make sense.

[6] You need to make sure you reiterate why this issue matters and is being discussed.

justice to the claimants, this opinion has force in that it could, as Lord Goff observed, be limited quite easily to the immediate family of the homeowner. Other residents could be dealt with on the facts of their case. Lord Cooke further observed that, as employees are the concern of their employers, there was no policy basis for allowing the law to extend to non-resident employees.

[7] A distinction in the approach of Lords Goff and Hoffmann can be made so highlight this to show your broader understanding of the case and to explain why you are setting out the views of another judge who was in the majority.

While agreeing with the outcome, Lord Hoffmann focused on more theoretical matters,[7] basing his opinion on the purpose of the tort being to protect land. He argued it was vital to appreciate that in *Tipping,* while the two forms of nuisance were mentioned, they still amounted to one tort concerned with protecting land from injury. As such, amenity interference is based not on the personal discomfort of an individual, but rather that the utility of the land is diminished and, therefore, the land has suffered injury. The tort exists to protect land from injury, and as such it must be the landowner who sues for its injury. Lord Hoffmann felt that to develop the common law in the manner suggested by Pill LJ would result in the fundamental principles of the tort being distorted.[8]

[8] This is why it is really important that you know the purpose of the tort and can explain it, as this was used to justify the majority's decision. If you do not know the theory behind the tort, then you are less able to fully assess the implications and merit of that decision. The tort's purpose is the bar from which you judge the arguments.

Lord Hoffmann's reasoning is harder to counter and makes the decision in *Hunter* justifiable in light of the tort's purpose. As Lord Hoffmann notes, the land's utility is reflected in the amenity value of the land, and so it is the owner who suffers the damage. However, the consequence is that a non-owning occupier who has their enjoyment of the land diminished is left without redress as the decision denies the existence of any enjoyment of such amenity by anyone bar the owner.

[9] As *Hunter* was decided before the incorporation of the Act, it is important that you then move on to consider, regardless of the merits of Lord Cooke's opinion, whether this now acts as a driver for reforming the position adopted by the majority.

The subsequent coming into force of the Human Rights Act 1998[9] does question the long-term viability of the principle from *Hunter* as the Act incorporates the Article 8 right to respect for privacy and family life. The significance of this is that the Article includes reference to the 'home' and in *Khatun v UK* (1998) 26 EHRR CD 212 this was held to be 'autonomous' and did not require defining domestically. As such, the case arising from the same facts as *Hunter* stated that a proprietary interest was not needed to claim under Article 8. Therefore, anyone whose home is subjected to an actionable nuisance would have a claim. The law must give effect to Article 8 as it develops (*Douglas v Hello Ltd* [2001] 2 WLR 992), and its influence was seen in **McKenna v British Aluminium Ltd** [2002] Env LR 30 where a striking-out application[10] was rejected on the basis that the claimants, who could not sue in nuisance due to **Hunter**, were said to still have an actionable case based on Article 8. Neuberger J, while not offering any further view of the need for a proprietary interest, was mindful that the claim included a tort analogous to nuisance. Creating an analogous action alongside the traditional tort and claims under Article 8 would make the law overly complicated.

[10] As the case was not a full trial and may appear as a lower court at odds with *Hunter*, you need to provide this context.

It is submitted, in conclusion, that **Hunter** will need to be revisited as there is now a clear divergence with human rights jurisprudence. However, if it is deemed too difficult to overcome Lord Hoffmann's objections, an analogous tort based on the interference with the home, actionable by all residents, would need to be developed to give effect to Article 8 and give redress to non-owning occupiers whose enjoyment of the land is diminished. The better option may be to depart from the traditional view of the tort's purpose and operation.[11]

[11] Explain the merit of your position to demonstrate that you have thought out the consequences of such an approach.

✓ Make your answer stand out

- Highlight some of the factors that are considered as part of the test for succeeding in a claim, but in a manner that illustrates how they relate to the tort's function.

- Make sure you have a detailed understanding of the decision in *Hunter v Canary Wharf Ltd* [1997] AC 655 from looking at all of the judicial reasoning, including that in the Court of Appeal, and the thoughts of Neuberger J in *McKenna v British Aluminum Ltd* [2002] En v LR 30, [53].

- Read Geach, N. (2012) The nuisance of the proprietary interest: Lord Cooke's dissent in *Hunter v Canary Wharf Ltd* [1997] AC 655, in Geach and Monaghan (eds.) *Dissenting Judgments in the Law*. London: Wildy, Simmonds & Hill, to garner academic opinion on the issue.

- Consider the implications that the requirement has had on other torts, notably the rule in *Rylands v Fletcher* (1866) LR 1 Ex 265.

- Provide more depth as to how an analogous tort may operate, if developed.

- Offer your own original thoughts about how the matter could be resolved if you think the requirement is no longer sustainable.

! Don't be tempted to . . .

- Turn the question into a simple discussion of the general operation of the tort and what needs to be satisfied in order to succeed. You need to focus more on providing a detailed argument as to the eligibility criteria to properly answer the question.
- Dismiss the opinion of Lord Cooke in *Hunter* v *Canary Wharf Ltd* [1997] AC 655 simply because it was dissenting, as it provides material from which to evaluate the merits of the majority's view. He also gives an insight as to how the law could be developed while being kept within reasonable bounds.

❓ Question 3

Gidsville is an estate which is predominantly residential in nature although there are some businesses. However, to regenerate an area on the edge of the estate, the council recently gave planning permission to Prento Petroleum to build a factory there. The company is a large manufacturer of parts for the oil industry. Having recently won another large contract, Prento Petroleum has had to extend the working day to include shifts up to midnight rather than have the staff work weekends. As a result, the company has employed large numbers of local residents, but the work has generated a vast amount of smoke and particularly noise, which can be heard over the estate. One of the businesses on the estate, Di Rossi's, an Italian restaurant, has witnessed a drop in trade.

Additionally, Spencer, who works on the late shift at the factory, bought a flat opposite Di Rossi's 3 years ago. However, since he started working the late shift 6 months ago he has had problems himself with Di Rossi's deliveries arriving at 10 a.m. and waking him up. When he complained, the owner of Di Rossi's, Morgan, pointed out that the deliveries have been turning up at that time for over 20 years and no one has ever complained.

Advise Morgan about any claim he may have for the loss in trade, and also regarding Spencer's complaints.

Diagram plan

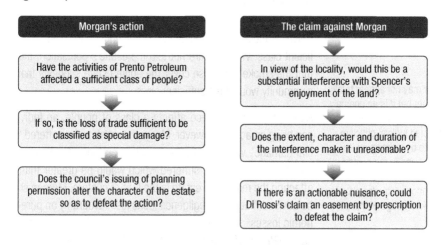

Morgan's action	The claim against Morgan
Have the activities of Prento Petroleum affected a sufficient class of people?	In view of the locality, would this be a substantial interference with Spencer's enjoyment of the land?
If so, is the loss of trade sufficient to be classified as special damage?	Does the extent, character and duration of the interference make it unreasonable?
Does the council's issuing of planning permission alter the character of the estate so as to defeat the action?	If there is an actionable nuisance, could Di Rossi's claim an easement by prescription to defeat the claim?

A printable version of this diagram plan is available from **www.pearsoned.co.uk/lawexpressqa**

Answer plan

➡ Identify whether the estate constitutes a sufficient class of people affected by the activities of Prento Petroleum.

➡ Establish whether Morgan has suffered special damage so as to make an action applicable.

➡ Discuss whether Prento Petroleum can rely on the council's planning permission to defeat any action.

➡ Advise Morgan of the claim he faces by Spencer.

➡ Evaluate whether the interference is substantial.

➡ Consider whether the use of the land by Morgan is reasonable.

➡ Advise as to the merits of a defence, if required, based on prescription.

Answer

[1] Demonstrate at the start that you understand that both forms of nuisance are applicable to the question and which type relates to each claim.

Morgan requires advice on the tort of nuisance, owing to the threat to his business from Prento Petroleum and also claims he may face from Spencer. It will be argued that Morgan is likely to be successful in an action for public nuisance against the factory, while his actions are unlikely to be sufficient for any private nuisance claim against him.[1]

Public nuisance requires an act which 'materially affects the reasonable comfort and convenience of life of a class of Her Majesty's subjects' (*per* Romer LJ in ***Attorney General v PYA Quarries Ltd*** [1957] 2 QB 169). Prento Petroleum creating smoke and noise until midnight would affect the comfort and convenience of the residents. However, the area affected must be large enough to constitute a sufficient class. While we are not told the estate's population, the fact that the smoke and noise cover the entire estate suggests that this community would be a sufficient class.

Although public nuisance affects a class of people, an individual can bring an action. However, Morgan must show he suffered 'special damage', which is greater than that suffered by others within the class. The damage suffered which would be greater than that affecting the rest of the estate is the loss of custom. Morgan should be advised that while negligence looks less favourably on pure economic losses[2] such as this, a loss of business is sufficient for nuisance (***Benjamin v Storr*** (1874) LR 9 CP 400). This particular loss must also be direct and substantial. By analogy with ***Benjamin,*** the facts here suggest that Morgan satisfies the requirements for an action.However, if any of the other businesses have suffered a loss in trade, Morgan's claim would fail as he has suffered no greater loss than others within the class.[3]

The loss suffered is also foreseeable and so no issue of remoteness exists. Therefore, on the basis that Morgan has suffered special damage,[4] Prento Petroleum will argue that the granting of planning permission authorised any resultant nuisance. While statutory authority provides immunity against nuisance, the position is different with regard to mere planning permission (***Wheeler v J.J. Saunders Ltd*** [1996] Ch 19). ***Wheeler*** held that planning authorities have no general power to authorise a nuisance, although they possibly could to the extent that they may alter the character of a neighbourhood through their decisions. Therefore, the question is whether, by granting permission for the factory, the council has altered the estate's character. Regeneration was a factor behind the decision, so this may be the case; however, we are told that this was just for an area on the edge of the estate, not the whole estate. As Gidsville is predominantly a residential area,[5] it is unlikely that the planning permission has sufficiently altered the overall area's character and so the defence will fail. If Morgan is successful, it is unlikely that an injunction[6] would be awarded to prevent the company's actions completely as this would create

[2] This may not appear totally relevant but it is an anomaly with the law which has attracted judicial criticism, and so by mentioning it briefly, and in the context shown, you maintain relevance while also showing your knowledge of this point

[3] As you are giving advice to Morgan and the facts are silent, you must ensure that you explain the situation if this was the unknown factual situation.

[4] As you have ended the previous paragraph with an element of doubt as to the claim, you should start the next part of your discussion in this manner so that it follows on from the previous paragraph.

[5] Make sure that you use the facts of the question to support your argument on this point, as they give a good indication about what the position will be.

[6] Start with the remedy of an injunction, as this is more likely to be the most desired as well as the least likely to succeed. Therefore, you can finish on the stronger consolation point that he would at least receive damages.

unemployment. However, in view of the noise affecting the entire estate, one may be granted to restrict the working times so that work stops earlier. In any event, Morgan would be able to claim damages for his lost trade.

In relation now to the claim against Morgan, the nuisance being claimed is interference with Spencer's use and enjoyment of his land caused by the delivery trucks.[7] The merits of this claim will be weighed, on the facts, against Morgan's right to use his land in a way that he wishes (***Sturgess v Bridgman*** (1879) 11 Ch D 852).[8] As this only affects Spencer, the action would be for private nuisance and so it must be confirmed that, as the owner of the flat, Spencer would have the necessary standing to bring a claim (***Hunter v Canary Wharf Ltd*** [1997] AC 655).

The interference must be substantial in nature. Spencer is not using his land in a particularly sensitive way and so the factor to consider is that of locality. While the whole estate is predominantly residential, we would need to know about this particular part of the estate, as what may be a nuisance in one part may not be in another. Noise from delivery vans in a general residential area would probably be substantial; however, a restaurant is unlikely to exist on a general residential road. Further, the fact that Spencer's property is a flat suggests that this could also be above one of the other shops. If so, then noise from the vans is unlikely to be substantial.

On the basis that this is deemed to be a substantial interference,[9] the next issue is whether the substantial interference is unreasonable. There are several factors on which to advise Morgan, but of most relevance are the duration of the interference, its extent and its character. The character of the interference is obviously noise, although it appears it is only an issue because it wakes Spencer up, which suggests that the interference is not an issue otherwise. From the facts, we are told the vans arrive at 10 a.m., although we are not told whether this is daily or how long they stay. Arguably, this is a reasonable time to deliver when most people would already be awake. Further, as delivery vans usually have several stops, the noise is unlikely to go on for long.[10] The suggestion that Morgan is a reasonable user is supported by the fact that no one else has complained over a long period and even Spencer has not complained until now. Therefore, even if the noise is deemed

[7] Start this section of your answer by identifying exactly the issue that Morgan is faced with.

[8] Show that you know how the tort operates.

[9] Even if you have concluded the previous discussion with a view that it is not substantial, the absence of concrete facts means it could be. However, to maintain consistency in your answer, you will need to phrase the introduction of the next point of discussion in a more tentative manner.

[10] Use your common sense to make an informed argument in order to overcome the absence of concrete facts. It is important that you do not just ignore the issue.

substantial, it is unlikely to be unreasonable unless perhaps the noise is excessively loud and goes on for an excessive period. If overall the nuisance is deemed negligible, it will not be actionable against Morgan.

However, Morgan should be advised that, if the noise is deemed actionable, any claim will probably succeed as he does not appear to have a defence. The only possibility is an easement by prescription. This means that a proprietary interest has been created by long usage (over 20 years). This would be unsuccessful because it is unlikely that noise from delivery vans would constitute an easement, as there is no benefit to the land.[11] Additionally, while the noise has been going on for over 20 years, there was no actionable nuisance during that time as there was no interference with Spencer's land. There would need to be a 20-year period from the time the interference began (**Sturgess v Bridgman**). The interference has only started since Spencer started working the shifts 6 months ago.

[11] While being an issue of land law, it is a significant point in relation to the defence against the tort succeeding, and so you should discuss it, drawing on your knowledge of land law.

In conclusion, Morgan should be able to recuperate his losses caused by Prento Petroleum; in relation to Spencer, it is unlikely that the interference from the vans will be sufficient to warrant a successful action.

✓ Make your answer stand out

- Provide more of an outline of the differences between the two forms of nuisance action.
- If there is deemed to be no special damage, advise Morgan of the possibility of petitioning the Attorney General to bring a relator action on behalf of the whole estate.
- Consider whether the factory may in fact have breached the statutory nuisance provision within section 79 of the Environmental Protection Act 1990.
- Expand your discussion of Morgan's remedies and consider *Andrae* v *Selfridge & Co. Ltd* [1938] Ch 1. Although foreseeable, would it be unreasonable in the circumstances to allow the full extent of his losses?

! Don't be tempted to . . .

■ Litter the second part of the answer with case examples of the factors which are assessed. The important thing is to apply the standard factors to the facts of the scenario. If a case is similar, or if it is a specific authority for a point, then refer to it but otherwise use your time to concentrate on your application.

■ Turn your discussion of Morgan's possible defence into a land law answer with regard to whether this is capable of constituting an easement.

■ Get too bogged down discussing the theoretical differences between the two types of nuisance action at the expense of actually applying the requirements of each to the facts of the question.

@ Try it yourself

Now take a look at the question below and attempt to answer it. You can check your response against the answer guidance available on the companion website (**www.pearsoned.co.uk/ lawexpressqa**).

'Awarding compensation for when a person's enjoyment of their property is interfered with by a neighbour naturally means their neighbour is prevented from going about their lawful business.'

Evaluate the different considerations that the court must balance when deciding whether someone should be prevented from carrying on the activity in question on their own land.

www.pearsoned.co.uk/lawexpressqa

 Go online to access more revision support including additional essay and problem questions with diagram plans, you be the marker questions, and download all diagrams from the book.

The rule in *Rylands v Fletcher*

12

How this topic may come up in exams

While it is a long-standing tort in its own right providing strict liability, the rule is now seen as a sub-species of nuisance dealing with incidents of a one-off escape. As such, while a problem question could consist solely of the tort on its own, you should be aware of the possibility of a nuisance action being present as well, particularly if there is some form of material damage to the land. The development of the tort also means that you could have scope to discuss issues of negligence. Therefore, make sure you are also able to deal with an essay question concerning the future of the tort and its relevance today.

Before you begin

Acquaint yourself with the following components and key issues of this topic; and familiarise yourself with how you would structurally progress through them all, if necessary, when attempting to answer a question on this topic.

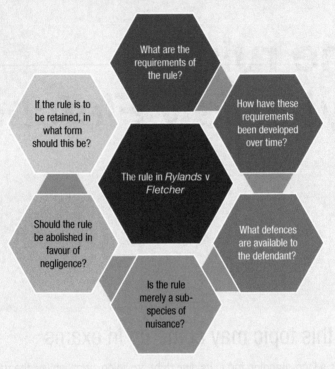

A printable version of this diagram plan is available from **www.pearsoned.co.uk/lawexpressqa**

❓ Question 1

Hydrotricity Ltd is a provider of renewable energy using hydropower. To help meet the consumer demand for green energy, the company sought permission to build two artificial dams on the outskirts of Chemersham as part of a large pumped-storage power generation plant. Permission was given for the proposal under the provisions of the (fictitious) Green Energy Act 2013. This was despite some environmental objections by certain groups on the grounds that it would harm local wildlife, especially migratory fish and the surrounding countryside. The construction of the facility generated significant high-skilled jobs for the area and provided a much needed boost to the local economy. As part of the efforts to win approval for the plan, the local residents of Chemersham would receive discounted energy prices.

However, despite its successful construction, protests about the plant have continued. As part of these protests, Owen, a well-known opponent of the plant, devised a plan to discredit the safety of the plant by engineering a leak from one of the dams. Owen believed that he could control the direction of the resulting flooding, and limit its extent, so as not to cause damage to neighbouring properties. Following several attempts, Owen successfully entered the plant as a maintenance entrance had not been properly secured, and he managed to cause a leak. However, he did so as water was being released back to the lower dam so it escaped with far more force than he anticipated, and more water subsequently escaped.

As a result, Eric, who runs a farm on the neighbouring property, suffered severe flooding to his fields and the loss of the whole of that season's crops.

Advise the company on their chances of successfully defending a claim for the damage suffered by Eric.

Diagram plan

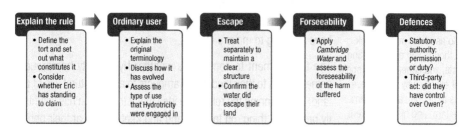

A printable version of this diagram plan is available from **www.pearsoned.co.uk/lawexpressqa**

Answer plan

→ Explain the scope of the rule.

→ Consider whether Eric would be eligible to claim damages under the rule.

➜ Identify the water as the 'thing' which Hydrotricity has brought onto their land and consider whether this is an extraordinary use of the land.

➜ State briefly how there has clearly been an escape of the water.

➜ Evaluate the foreseeability of the harm which would be caused by such an escape.

➜ Discuss the potential defences Hydrotricity may have under statute and due to the escape being caused by a third-party act.

Answer

[1] Show that you know exactly how the tort operates and how it is distinguishable from other torts that concern proprietary interests.

[2] By highlighting this here, you show the person marking your work that you have fully identified all of the relevant issues which need to be discussed.

[3] Before you start to apply the different requirements to the problem, it is worth outlining what the rule consists of. However, paraphrase the rule as stated by Blackburn J to emphasise that you understand the individual parts.

[4] So as to not make it look as though you are assuming facts, you either need to spell out exactly why you believe this to be the case (he runs the farm and his crops were damaged) or use a phrase like this to illustrate you are relying on the facts.

The circumstances surrounding the damage suffered by Eric require advising him on the rule in **Rylands v Fletcher** (1866) LR 1 Ex 265. This tort, while similar to other land torts, offers protection for interests in property which are injured by a one-off occurrence.[1] As such, Eric will be advised as to the elements of the rule and whether the actions of Owen and the statutory permission mean that Hydrotricity has a valid defence.[2]

Hydrotricity should be advised that the applicable tort covers a situation where someone brings something on to their land in furtherance of a non-natural use of their land, which if it escaped would be liable to cause harm. If the 'thing' does escape, then the person is liable for all of the damage which is a consequence of the escape, regardless of their fault in the 'thing' escaping.[3] To bring a claim, Eric must have a proprietary interest in the land affected by the escape of the waste and his property must have been damaged (**Transco plc v Stockport MBC** [2004] 2 AC 1). We are not expressly told this, but it is likely that this is satisfied based on the information we have.[4] On that basis, he would have standing to make a claim.

The first element to consider is whether Hydrotricity has brought something on to their land which amounts to a non-natural use of the land. Underpinning the rule is the idea that if the person has voluntarily brought a 'thing' on to their land and kept it there at their peril – here, the water – liability will arise where the 'thing' is not naturally there or its use is unordinary. Originally, this was held to mean a special use which brought increased danger and not some use which is proper for the general benefit of the community (**Rickards v Lothian** [1913] AC 263). Therefore, **Rickards** is significant as Hydrotricity's use of the land for power generation has brought a significant upturn to the local economy and financial benefits to local

[5] Although part of this has now been doubted, and so will not be applicable, including it in this way allows you to get across some analytical and evaluative comment in your answer, and illustrate your knowledge of the debate.

[6] Be specific here as, for example, Lord Hoffmann did not think that ordinary use was any better than non-natural use. You therefore show more in-depth knowledge.

[7] While it may seem as though this has obviously been satisfied, it still needs to be shown, albeit briefly.

[8] Explaining the rationale for this element allows you to build up the level of evaluation in your answer, especially as it has been seen as being a relatively new requirement.

[9] At the end of applying the elements, you should give a mini-conclusion as to whether the tort is likely to be made out in order to explain why there is a need to discuss defences.

consumers. This could be said, therefore, to benefit the community notwithstanding what has happened to Eric's farm.[5] However, doubt was cast on the latter part of the **Rickards** interpretation in **Cambridge Water Co. Ltd v Eastern Counties Leather plc** [1994] 2 AC 264 where the creation of employment, in itself, was held not sufficient. This was affirmed in **Transco** where Lord Bingham[6] said the focus should be on the increased danger to others from the use, with the question being simply whether the use is extraordinary in light of the time and place that it is done. Ordinary uses, bringing little risk, will be outside the rule. There may be scope to argue that this was an ordinary use in the circumstances, but storing large quantities of water, such as this, does bring increased danger to the neighbouring land if there were an escape. Ultimately, the number of cases which have held that storing water in large quantities on land is an extraordinary/non-natural use, including **Rylands** itself, means that this requirement will be satisfied by Eric.

The next aspect of the rule is that of escape.[7] For a claim to succeed, the 'thing' must cross Hydrotricity's boundary and enter land which is not within their control (**Read v Lyons** [1947] AC 156). This is clearly seen here as we are told that the water leaked out and flooded Eric's farm.

However, the harm caused by the escape must have been a type which was foreseeable. As the rule requires the person to keep the thing at their peril in case it escapes, then, in view of liability being strict, it is just to require that it is foreseeable that damage will be caused.[8] Hydrotricity should be advised that in **Cambridge Water** it was stressed that the tort is not based on negligence and, therefore, even if the company demonstrates that it took all reasonable precautions to prevent the escape, this would not affect the issue of foreseeability of damage if the escape did happen. As the farm is next to the plant, it must have been foreseeable that the farm would suffer flooding if there was an escape of the accumulated water and, therefore, the harm which has occurred – damage to the field and the destruction of the crops – must also be foreseeable. Therefore it appears that, provided the use of the land is deemed an unusual use, the tort has been made out.[9]

Hydrotricity should be advised that, while liability under the rule is strict, there are various defences to a claim. As the construction and

[10] Even if you have determined straightaway that the defence will not help, it is worth including it as the facts raise it. Sometimes a defence may be applicable for discussion even if it will not be successful. The key is to keep it brief and ensure that you include a line demonstrating you know why it does not apply, and therefore, understand its operation.

[11] Ultimately this defence will also be likely to fail so you could discuss the defences in either order. However, where one has more chance of success it is better to end with that as if it does succeed, there is no need to consider the others. In this case, it is probably better to deal with this second as there is at least more of a debate to be had.

[12] These facts are important in determining whether there is any chance that Eric's claim may still succeed and so you need to use them to illustrate why, when it appears the defence is valid, he may still have a chance of success.

[13] Before you end, this is a final opportunity to show your understanding of the relationship between negligence and the rule and whether there is scope for the former to apply in the latter.

operation of the plant was authorised by statute, they would seemingly be able to rely on the defence of statutory authority. However, the defence is only applicable if they were acting under a duty to accumulate the water on their land, and not simply where they have permission to accumulate the water (**Smeaton v Ilford Corporation** [1954] Ch 45). Therefore, this will not aid them.[10]

The defence which Hydrotricity may have more success with[11] is that the escape was due to an act of a third party, whom they had no control over (**Box v Jubb** (1879) 4 Ex D 76). To defeat the claim on the basis that Hydrotricity is not at fault for the escape may seem at odds with the overall purpose of the tort, but there is some justification where it is a completely independent act of a stranger. This appears to be the case here as Owen is completely independent of Hydrotricity and intentionally caused the leak, and thus the flood, and so there should be no liability (**Rickards**). However, Hydrotricity should be advised that the defence, in fact, only applies if the third-party act could not have reasonably been contemplated and guarded against (**Perry v Kendricks Transport Ltd** [1956] 1 WLR 85). Owen was a 'well-known' protestor and had made several efforts to gain entry to the plant,[12] which suggests that the incident should have been in Hydrotricity's mind and efforts should have been made to prevent him gaining entry. Yet what happened was that a door was not properly secured, which allowed him access. This suggests negligence on their part and so the defence would be defeated. Hydrotricity should be advised that, in view of the comments in **Cambridge Water** about the irrelevance to liability of taking reasonable care, and that in **Transco** negligence was again held not to play a part, even if they had not been negligent, they would still probably face liability notwithstanding **Perry**.[13]

In conclusion, Hydrotricity face liability as the facts suggest that this is a non-ordinary use of such land, regardless of what benefits it has brought, and therefore the rule will apply to their activities, which they were not obliged to do. While the escape was caused by Owen, his act was arguably something which Hydrotricity had control over and so any defence on that basis will probably fail.

✓ Make your answer stand out

- Highlight the background to the rule and the reason for its creation.
- Discuss in more depth the problem with the interpretation in *Rickards* v *Lothian* [1913] AC 263 and the significance of the move away from 'non-natural use' made by *Transco plc* v *Stockport MBC* [2004] 2 AC 1, assessing its merit as you do so.
- Consider the validity of distinguishing statutory authority on the grounds of acting with permission as opposed to under a duty.
- Explore the extent that fault, or negligence, has become a part of what is a strict liability tort and whether this is a justifiable development.
- Even though it is a problem question, look to include some of the academic opinion relied on by the judges in their judgments.

❗ Don't be tempted to . . .

- Briefly apply the elements and finish the answer quickly. Make sure that you consider potential practical aspects of the question which may impact on the application of the elements.
- Discuss defences such as act of God or consent, which have no relevance and are not alluded to by the facts, in order to show that you know them and fill out your answer. Use any time and space you have to include more evaluation of the other issues.
- Over-emphasise the relationship with torts such as nuisance.
- Get into a debate regarding the future of the tort.

Question 2

'. . . integration of the rule into the law of private nuisance would involve further confusing an area of law that is already beset by considerable incoherence . . . if the rule were to be subsumed within the law of negligence as in Australia, this would not only create more problems than it solves but also represent a critical loss of legal weaponry to claimants who would naturally fall within the *Rylands* rule'. Murphy, J. (2004) The Merits of *Rylands* v *Fletcher*. *Oxford Journal of Legal Studies* 24(4): 643 at 643–644.

In light of this statement, analyse the nature of the rule in *Rylands* v *Fletcher* and whether there is merit in retaining the rule.

Diagram plan

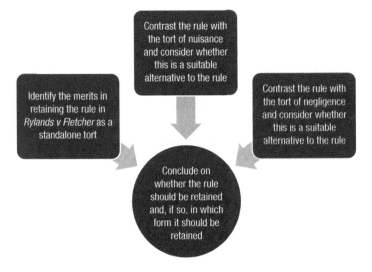

A printable version of this diagram plan is available from **www.pearsoned.co.uk/lawexpressqa**

Answer plan

➜ Explain the rule and its traditional function.

➜ Contrast the rule with the tort of nuisance and evaluate the merits in retaining the rule.

➜ Contrast the rule with the tort of negligence and evaluate the merits in retaining the rule.

➜ Consider whether the rule should be retained and, if so, in what form it should be retained.

Answer

[1] By beginning your answer in this way you highlight immediately that you are aware of the key requirements of the tort. This obviates the need for a step-by-step account of the requirements later in your answer.

The rule in **Rylands v Fletcher** (1866) LR 1 Ex 265, has provided a form of redress to claimants who have suffered damage as a consequence of an escape of a thing, not naturally occurring there and likely to do mischief, from their neighbour's land onto their own.[1] However, recent judicial thinking and the abolition of the rule in other jurisdictions has caused academics to question the ongoing validity of the rule and the merit in retaining it as a cause of action distinct

2 Although the actual question is written in very broad terms, the quotation makes reference to both nuisance and negligence. Therefore, in order to adequately respond to the question, both alternative actions should be explored.

3 There are a wide variety of arguments that can be made in response to this question, therefore it is useful to set out the argument that you will make at the beginning of your answer in general terms. This makes your answer easier to follow for the marker.

4 This paragraph provides not only the rationale for the development of the rule but also some context as to why the validity of the rule has been called into question. It also enables you to introduce some of the key authorities that you will be likely to rely upon in the course of your discussion of the merits of the rule.

5 You should use authority to support the propositions that you make throughout your answer.

from either nuisance or negligence.[2] It will be argued that the tort, properly understood does retain merit as a distinct cause of action. This is particularly so if the tort is retained in the form it was prior to the judicial attempts to subsume it within the tort of private nuisance.[3]

The rule in **Rylands v Fletcher,** like the torts of private nuisance and trespass to land is a method of regulating land usage. It emerged as a consequence of the Industrial Revolution and concerns over the increasing impact that industrial practices were having on society. It affords protection to claimants where there has been an escape of a thing, in the course of a non-natural use of land, onto the claimant's property and that escape causes damage. The tort applies irrespective of any fault on the part of the defendant. Although liability is strict in nature, it is not absolute and certain defences are available to the defendant. Until relatively recently, the tort was considered to be of little importance and was rarely used. Although **Cambridge Water Co. v Eastern Counties Leather Plc** [1994] 2 AC 254 appears to have reawakened interest in the tort, Lord Goff in this case, adopting the analysis of Newark (1994), held that the rule was a subspecies of nuisance that deals with isolated escapes. This view was supported in **Transco plc v Stockport MBC** [2004] 2 AC 1 and as a consequence the validity of the rule in **Rylands v Fletcher** can be questioned.[4]

Although there are clear similarities between the rule and the tort of nuisance, Murphy (2004) asserts that there are relevant distinctions which warrant its retention as a standalone tort. Under the original rule, any person injured by the escape potentially had a cause of action. This was confirmed in **British Celanese Ltd v AH Hunt (Capacitors) Ltd** [1969] 1 WLR 959.[5] This can be contrasted with the position in nuisance, whereby a claimant must have an interest in the land affected in order to bring an action (**Hunter v Canary Wharf Ltd** [1977] AC 655). Similarly under the rule, there is clear authority to suggest that a claimant could recover damages for personal injury sustained as a consequence of the escape (**Miles v Forest Rock Granite Co** (1918) 34 TLR 500; **Hale v Jennings Bros** [1938] 1 All ER 579). By contrast the position is such in nuisance that personal injury is irrecoverable at common law in the absence of negligence. Recoverable losses in

[6] It is not enough just to highlight distinctions between the two torts. In order to adequately address the question, you should consider the impact that these distinctions may have in order to provide a sound justification for the argument that you are trying to make.

[7] The conclusion on the merits of retaining the rule in the previous paragraph on their own were not particularly strong. Therefore, it is important to indicate that you are about to make a more forceful argument in this paragraph, in order to support the proposition that you advanced in your introduction.

[8] What you should be trying to do here is illustrate that you understand that the law has developed in respect of this requirement, without getting too bogged down in the case law and losing the thrust of your argument.

[9] Closer alignment between the torts as a consequence of the decision in *Cambridge Water* would appear to weaken the argument that *Rylands* should be retained as a distinct tort. However, illustrating that reasonable foreseeability has its origins within the rule itself, helps to circumvent this argument.

nuisance tend to take the form of material damage to the property or, more commonly, loss of amenity. These differences in approach between the original formulation of the rule in **Rylands v Fletcher** and nuisance indicate that the rule may have greater ambit than the more restrictive approach to liability found in nuisance which would merit its retention.[6] However, given that in more modern times the courts perceive **Rylands** as a subspecies of nuisance, this argument is legally speaking difficult to support and **Rylands** must be interpreted in light of the more restrictive approach adopted in **Cambridge, Hunter** and **Transco.** These cases have arguably blurred the line between the two torts.

With that said, there are other notable distinctions identified by Murphy (2004) that arguably have more persuasive force.[7] For liability under the rule, the defendant must bring a 'thing' onto their land. This thing need not be inherently dangerous but as a consequence of the House of Lords decision in **Ryland,** must constitute a non-natural use. This has subsequently been interpreted as a use that is not merely an ordinary use of land (**Rickards v Lothian** [1913] AC 263). Although doubted in **Cambridge Water,** the requirement was retained in **Transco** albeit in a slightly amended form.[8] The court will have regard to the particular circumstances of the case in order to assess whether the use of the land is 'non-natural' and although comparisons can be drawn with an assessment of the 'reasonable user' in nuisance, the focus of the two tests is quite different. It can readily be envisaged that a use of land may be 'non-natural' for the purposes of the rule, and yet reasonable for the purposes of nuisance. Abolishing the rule in favour of the tort of nuisance would leave a claimant in these circumstances unable to avail themselves of a remedy in circumstances that the rule was intended to address.

A further requirement that needs to be considered in respect of the two torts is that of reasonable foreseeability of harm. While the addition of this requirement to the rule in **Rylands v Fletcher** in **Cambridge Water** arguably brings the rule into closer alignment with nuisance, thus undermining the merit of retaining it as a standalone tort, the foundations for such a requirement is evident in the original rule itself due to the fact that the 'thing' must be 'likely' to do mischief.[9]

While the judiciary have in more recent years made efforts to subsume the rule in *Rylands* within nuisance, Australia have opted to completely abolish the rule and utilise negligence instead.[10] In *Burnie Port Authority* v *General Jones Pty Ltd* (1994) 120 ALR 42, it was held by a majority of five to two that liability under the rule in *Rylands* v *Fletcher* no longer existed as an independent head of liability and instead that it should be regarded as absorbed by the principles of ordinary negligence. This was on the basis of a non-delegable duty owed to the claimant. The majority regarded negligence as preferable to the rule 'with all its difficulties, qualifications and exceptions'. Claimants who had previously been able to rely on the strict liability regime under the rule, are now required to grapple with the arguably more difficult task of establishing fault on the part of the defendant under the tort of negligence. Murphy (2004) argues that relying on negligence would put claimants at a disadvantage, given the hurdle of establishing a breach of duty and this is exacerbated, given the potential inequity in the respective positions of the claimants and defendants. This perspective is supported by Lord Walker in *Transco* who emphasised the potential disadvantages that the abolition of the rule could have for claimants bringing actions against well-resourced, corporate defendants. He concluded that the case for abolition of the rule had not been made out, although clarification of conditions needed for liability was needed, which could be argued is due to the muddying of waters between the rule and nuisance.[11]

[10] Up until this point you have only really engaged with the first aspect of the quotation in the question. By considering Australia's approach to the rule, you are able to transition effectively into consideration of the latter part of the quotation and the alternative option of abolishing the rule in favour of negligence.

[11] This statement links back to some of the arguments that you made earlier in your answer.

While efforts can be made to justify the retention of the rule as a standalone tort, the efficacy of such arguments are often reliant upon retaining the rule in its original form prior to the efforts made by the judiciary to establish it as merely a subspecies of nuisance. Despite this, there does appear to be merit in arguments centred upon the non-natural use of land/reasonable user distinction that could warrant retention of the rule as a standalone tort. Even if these arguments are not considered sufficiently persuasive, subsuming the rule within nuisance appears to be a preferable approach to abolition of the rule altogether in favour of negligence, for the reasons outlined above.

Make your answer stand out

■ To give your answer more academic depth, specifically read the following articles which deal with this very issue: Nolan, D. (2005) The distinctiveness of *Rylands* v *Fletcher*. *Law Quarterly Review*, 121: 421–51; and the article in the question: Murphy, J. (2004) The merits of *Rylands* v *Fletcher*. *Oxford Journal of Legal Studies*, 24: 643.

■ Evaluate the future role of the rule outlined by Lord Bingham in *Transco plc* v *Stockport MBC* [2004] 2 AC 1 and whether the tort is needed to fulfil those.

■ Discuss the justification of strict liability and whether commercial enterprises should internalise the risks inherent in their activity; should fault be necessary for liability. Look at the opinions of their Lordships in *Transco plc* v *Stockport MBC* [2004] 2 AC 1, particularly Lords Hoffmann and Hobhouse, with regards to this.

■ Write a fuller comparative evaluation of the rule and negligence in order to assess whether the Australian position may be advantageous. To enhance this discussion draw on Paterson, J.M. (1994) *Rylands* v *Fletcher* into negligence: *Burnie Port Authority* v *General Jones Pty Ltd. Monash University Law Review*, 20(2): 317.

 Don't be tempted to . . .

■ Provide an in-depth descriptive narrative of the origin and history of the rule.

■ Go into detail on the torts of nuisance and negligence and their elements. The question allows you to judge whether the function of the rule could be performed by these but it is primarily a question on *Rylands* v *Fletcher* (1866) LR 1 Ex 265.

@ Try it yourself

Now take a look at the question below and attempt to answer it. You can check your response against the answer guidance available on the companion website (**www.pearsoned.co.uk/ lawexpressqa**).

'The rule in *Rylands* v *Fletcher* is a subspecies of nuisance. . . ' *Per* Lord Bingham in *Transco* v *Stockport MBC* [2004] 2 AC 1 at 9.

To what extent has this judicial perception shaped the development of the requirements for bringing an action under the rule in *Rylands* v *Fletcher*?

www.pearsoned.co.uk/lawexpressqa

Go online to access more revision support including additional essay and problem questions with diagram plans, you be the marker questions, and download all diagrams from the book.

Trespass
to the person

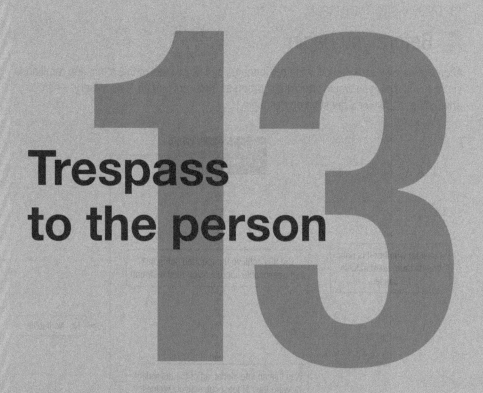

How this topic may come up in exams

Trespass to the person consists of assault, battery and false imprisonment, but each is relatively small in size and straightforward to apply to the facts, so it is common for all of them to appear in the same problem question. You need to take the time to check the scope of how you are taught this tort to determine whether you can expect other torts alongside it, such as the rule from *Wilkinson* v *Downton* or other forms of trespass. Essays will be rarer, but when they do arise will look at the purpose, effectiveness and justification of the tort.

Before you begin

Acquaint yourself with the following components and key issues of this topic; and familiarise yourself with how you would structurally progress through them all, if necessary, when attempting to answer a question on this topic.

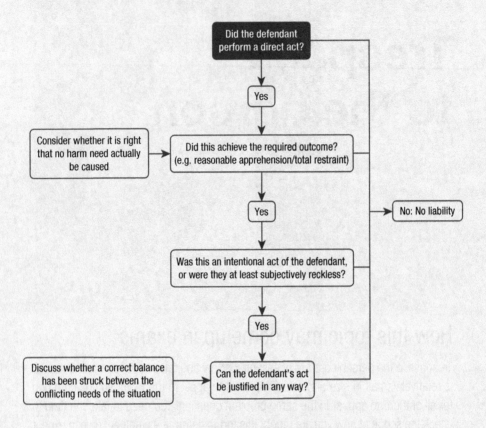

A printable version of this diagram is available from **www.pearsoned.co.uk/lawexpressqa**

❓ Question 1

Adriana and Aadya, who are sisters, were attending the Lighthouse music festival. The music festival is held outdoors and is very popular. Adriana and Aadya were standing very close to the main stage. The festival goers bumped into one another as they sang and danced along to the music.

Adriana was getting frustrated with a girl, Lexi, who was stood behind her and kept shoving her elbow into her back. Adriana turned around and shouted at Lexi 'If I weren't here with my little sister, I would make you stop doing that', while pointing at Aadya. Lexi's friend Madison, annoyed at Adriana, shoved into Adriana hard causing her to stumble into Aadya. Aadya fell to the floor, hurting her knee and ankle. Adriana was not physically hurt.

Adriana helped Aadya up from the floor and escorted her away from the main stage towards a quieter area where the food stalls and portaloos were. Noticing Maddison enter one of the portaloos, Adriana decided to get her own back by locking the door on the toilet from the outside. When Maddison realised that she couldn't get out, she rang Lexi to come and help. Not wanting to get caught, Adriana opened the lock and ran off. Maddison did not realise that she was able to get out until Lexi turned up and opened the door for her.

Advise the parties in respect of any actions they may take as a result of these instances.

Diagram plan

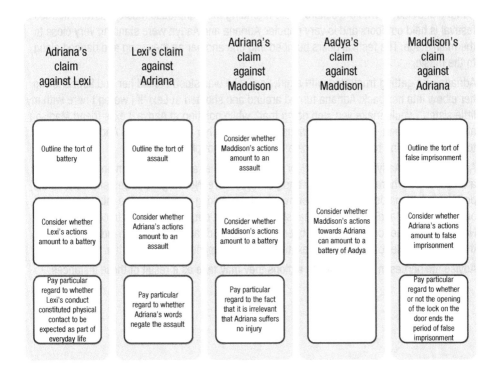

Adriana's claim against Lexi	Lexi's claim against Adriana	Adriana's claim against Maddison	Aadya's claim against Maddison	Maddison's claim against Adriana
Outline the tort of battery	Outline the tort of assault	Consider whether Maddison's actions amount to an assault		Outline the tort of false imprisonment
Consider whether Lexi's actions amount to a battery	Consider whether Adriana's actions amount to an assault	Consider whether Maddison's actions amount to a battery	Consider whether Maddison's actions towards Adriana can amount to a battery of Aadya	Consider whether Adriana's actions amount to false imprisonment
Pay particular regard to whether Lexi's conduct constituted physical contact to be expected as part of everyday life	Pay particular regard to whether Adriana's words negate the assault	Pay particular regard to the fact that it is irrelevant that Adriana suffers no injury		Pay particular regard to whether or not the opening of the lock on the door ends the period of false imprisonment

A printable version of this diagram plan is available from **www.pearsoned.co.uk/lawexpressqa**

Answer plan

→ Assess whether the initial contact between Lexi and Adriana could constitute a battery.

→ Determine whether or not the threat made by Adriana to Lexi could be considered an assault.

→ Assess whether or not Maddison's act of shoving Adriana constituted an assault on Adriana and/or Aadya.

→ Consider whether or not Adriana locking Maddison in the toilet constitutes false imprisonment.

Answer

The instances that have occurred at the musical festival potentially give rise to a number of claims under the tort of trespass to the person. This tort comprises assault, battery and false imprisonment, with

[1] Including this here does
make your introduction longer
than usual. While you could
deal with this as a second
paragraph before you move on
to considering each incident,
it can legitimately be outlined
as part of your introduction,
in order to demonstrate that
you understand the nature of
the torts.

[2] Where your question has
lots of different incidents such
as this one, it is important to
indicate to your marker how
you will be dealing with them
so that your marker is able to
better follow your answer. A
number of different options
are available to you here such
as taking each incident in
turn, taking each tort in turn,
or considering each particular
claimant in turn. It is your
choice as to how best to
structure your answer.

[3] Although you may ultimately
make the argument that this
particular incident gives rise
to the tort of battery, you have
not yet identified the relevant
legal principles upon which to
base an affirmative statement.
Consequently, you should
not refer to the incident as a
definitive tort at the beginning
of your paragraph. This
sentence merely identifies the
issue to be considered.

[4] Explain why there is a debate
about hostility. This allows you
to show your knowledge and
analytical skills.

all three requiring discussion on the facts. These torts are actionable *per se*, meaning that they are actionable without proof of harm by the claimants. The torts aim to protect a person's interests in bodily integrity and liberty, and these interests are considered to warrant heightened protection so that even the slightest interference may give rise to liability.[1] Each incident will be taken in turn,[2] with advice being given to those who are the alleged victims of the torts. It will be argued that Adriana will have a claim against Lexi in battery and Maddison in, potentially, assault and battery. Lexi will be unlikely to be successful in any claim, whereas Aadya will have an action in battery against Maddison. Maddison may also have an action against Adriana for false imprisonment.

Turning to the first incident, where Lexi made contact with Adriana by shoving her elbow into her back, Adriana should be advised that this potentially constitutes a battery.[3] A battery is the intentional, immediate and direct imposition of any unwanted physical contact towards the claimant. Direct physical contact has clearly been made between Lexi's elbow and Adriana's back in this instance. Lexi may argue that she did not intend to make any physical contact with Adriana; however, subjective recklessness will suffice for the purposes of this tort (***Bici v Ministry of Defence*** [2004] EWHC 786). One of the earliest definitions of battery was the 'least touching of another in anger' as *per* Lord Holt CJ in **Cole v Turner** (1704) 6 Mod 149. The word 'anger' has been construed in such a way as to impute a 'hostility' requirement into the tort in order to make the touching unjustifiable[4] (see ***Wilson v Pringle*** [1987] QB 237). However, Lord Goff in ***F v West Berkshire Health Authority*** [1990] 2 AC 1 doubted the usefulness of the term 'hostile' in defining the state of mind required in battery. The term was incompatible with the basic principle that any touching of another's body without lawful excuse, was capable of constituting a battery and did not take into account situations such as non-consensual surgery, which can amount to a battery but lacks any hostility. Although there does not appear to be any requirement of hostility that could undermine her claim, Adriana should be made aware that Lexi is likely to suggest that her actions were within the bounds of the generally accepted standards of everyday life. Given that both Lexi and Adriana were stood in a crowd of people at the musical festival, a certain degree of physical contact is to be expected and, as such, Lexi's conduct

[5] Use the facts of the question to support your evaluation. It demonstrates that you are able to contextualise the arguments within a practical situation.

[6] Where there is more than one potential interpretation of the facts, you should consider the alternatives and their effect on liability.

[7] As you have fully explored the tort and evaluated its applicability, you can convincingly assert that no assault has arisen.

[8] You do not need to outline the requirements of the tort in detail again as you have already done so above. You should focus your efforts on applying the law to the question.

[9] Although this is a criminal law case, there is considerable overlap between the torts of assault and battery and their criminal law counterparts. It is therefore possible to utilise criminal case law in the context of trespass to the person question.

may fall outside the remit of the tort of battery.[5] If Lexi's touching of Adriana exceeded that which would be considered acceptable, i.e. it was more than the jostling expected at a concert, then an action in battery would lie.[6]

Turning now to the words spoken by Adriana to Lexi, this may constitute an assault. An assault is an act which causes another person to apprehend the infliction of immediate and unlawful force on his or her person (***Collins v Wilcock*** [1984] 1 WLR 1172). Although commonly arising together, it is possible to commit an assault in the absence of any battery. Words alone can constitute an assault (***R v Ireland*** [1998] AC 147) and the words 'make you stop it' imply a willingness on Adriana's part to use force on Lexi. However, Lexi may encounter difficulty in establishing that she reasonably apprehended the application of such force, due to the fact that Adriana said that she would only do so if her sister weren't present. Adriana's words, as in ***Tuberville v Savage*** (1669) 86 ER 684, may negate any assault, if Lexi had reasonable grounds to believe that Adriana's sister was present at the concert. As Aadya was stood next to Adriana and Adriana gestured towards her, no assault has occurred.[7]

Considering Maddison's act of shoving into Adriana, this may constitute an assault and/or battery in respect of Adriana and Aadya. Turning to Adriana first, if she saw the shove from Maddison coming, it is likely that she reasonably apprehended the immediate and unlawful infliction of force upon her person as a consequence of Maddison's intentional act and thus an assault would arise.[8] If, however, she was standing with her back to Maddison and she did not see her coming, then there would be no assault. As force was then intentionally applied to Adriana by virtue of the shove, this would amount to a battery as it exceeds physical contact considered as an inevitable part of everyday life. As highlighted above, it is irrelevant that Adriana was not hurt as a consequence of Maddison's actions.

Maddison's actions may also amount to a battery in respect of Aadya. Although the tort of battery requires the direct application of force, this has been construed relatively widely, causing Mullis and Oliphant (2012) to doubt the usefulness of this requirement. In ***Haystead v Chief Constable of Derbyshire*** [2002] 2 Crim App

R 339[9] the defendant struck a woman in the face, with the result that the baby she was holding fell to the floor. The defendant was charged with an offence of assault, which in this context includes battery, on the baby due to the fact that the injury to the baby was entirely and immediately the result of the defendant's actions. Aadya can be likened to the baby in **Haystead,** in the sense that the application of force to her was entirely and immediately a result of Maddison's actions towards Adriana. Consequently, Aadya is likely to be able to bring an action against Maddison in battery for the injuries that she has sustained.

Turning lastly to the locking of Maddison inside the portaloo by Adriana, this may constitute false imprisonment. False imprisonment requires the defendant to have intentionally and directly caused the total restraint of the claimant within an area set by him or her, without lawful authority for doing so (**Bird v Jones** (1845) 7 QB 742). When Adriana intentionally locks the door to the portaloo from the outside, this will constitute false imprisonment as this amounts to a total restraint on Maddison's freedom without lawful authority. The fact that Maddison did not realise that she was so imprisoned until she attempted to exit the portaloo, will not preclude a successful action for this tort (**Murray v Ministry of Defence** [1988] 1 WLR 692). When Adriana unlocks the door she provides Maddison with a reasonable means of escape, which arguably ends the period of false imprisonment. However, Peel and Goudkamp (2014)[10] assert that even if a reasonable means of escape is provided but the claimant is not aware of it, the detention will amount to false imprisonment unless a reasonable person would have realised that he or she had an available escape route. It is clear that Maddison was falsely imprisoned up until the point that the door was unlocked and, as such, she will have a claim in this regard. Whether or not the false imprisonment extends beyond this point, is likely to turn on whether Maddison's actions of not attempting to open the door subsequent to her initial attempt are considered reasonable.

To conclude, Adriana may have claims in assault and battery following the incidents; however; she is likely to find herself sued for false imprisonment by Maddison. Aadya will have a claim against Maddison in battery. It is unlikely that Lexi will be able to claim in respect of trespass to the person from the incidents at the music festival.

[10] Where the law is silent on a matter, it is possible to defer to academic opinion in order to support an assertion as to a likely outcome. You should, however, ensure that the academic opinion that you defer to is credible.

✓ **Make your answer stand out**

■ Where there is a deficit in the case law in terms of answering the question, consider some of the wider academic commentary on the area in order to substantiate the arguments that you intend to make. Consider reading texts such as Peel, E. and Goudkamp, J. (eds.) (2014) *Winfield and Jolowicz on Tort* London: Sweet and Maxwell.

■ From your general academic reading include some material to explain in a bit more depth some of the theoretical basis which underpins trespass and why it has strict liability and is actionable *per se*. You can also draw further on the views of Lord Goff in cases such as *Collins* v *Wilcock* [1984] 1 WLR 1172 and *F* v *West Berkshire Health Authority* [1990] 2 AC 1 for this purpose.

! **Don't be tempted to . . .**

■ View the question as quite straightforward and just race through an application of the law to the facts. Make sure you still try to evaluate the law, such as with regard to the need for hostility in battery, and use this to develop your argument. Otherwise you will miss out on marks for the depth of your analysis and evaluation.

■ Go into aspects of the torts that are not relevant to the scenario as these will only waste time.

■ Repeatedly redefine each tort and state what is required. Repetition of this nature wastes time that could be better spent developing your application and evaluation.

❓ Question 2

Francesco and Edoardo were walking home from university one day, taking the path which runs alongside a very wide, deep and fast-flowing river. As they were walking they saw Bubba and Dustin approaching on the other side of the river on their way to the local golf course. The four had recently had an argument after Edoardo had reported Bubba and Dustin for cheating in an exam, which saw Bubba being expelled while Dustin was found innocent.

When Bubba saw Edoardo he yelled, 'You are dead for reporting me; I am going to put you in hospital for that!' Edoardo, feeling scared, decided to run so he could get home quickly. Feeling aggrieved by being reported when he was innocent, Dustin decided to chip a golf ball across the river at Edoardo as he ran off. However, he misjudged the shot and instead struck Francesco – who had decided to carry on walking home – in the back of the head.

When Edoardo got home, he decided to get his own back by ringing Bubba's house and playing a prank on Bubba's elderly grandfather, Zach, with whom Bubba lived, by informing him that Bubba had been run over and killed on his way to the golf course and that the police would probably be with Zach shortly. Upon hearing this, Zach went into shock.

Advise Bubba, Dustin and Edoardo about any liability they may face.

Diagram plan

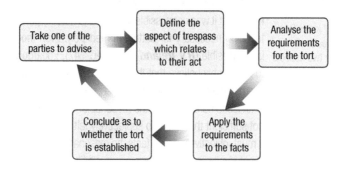

A printable version of this diagram plan is available from **www.pearsoned.co.uk/lawexpressqa**

Answer plan

→ Define assault and consider whether there is sufficient reasonableness and immediacy to Bubba's threat.

→ Outline the requirements for battery and consider the issue of transferred intent in relation to Dustin's act.

→ Advise Edoardo as to the rule in *Wilkinson* v *Downton* and apply it to his call to Zach.

[1] By briefly demonstrating here your understanding of the tort, you can get into the main premise of the question quickly so that you have enough time to fully evaluate the issues arising from the facts. You can then refer back to the tort's nature as required.

[2] Keep this brief as it is only the introduction. Set out in depth what the tort is about when you come to discuss Edoardo's liability. Simply show that you have appreciated that the rule is distinct and requires discussion.

Answer

Bubba and Dustin will need to be advised respectively on the torts of assault and battery, actions which overall constitute the tort of trespass to the person. These protect a person's bodily integrity and are actionable without proof of actual harm. This reflects the importance that tort places on this interest.[1] Advice to Edoardo differs slightly in that he faces liability under the rule in **Wilkinson v Downton** [1897] 2 QB 57 which, while related to trespass owing to it having an element of intention, is a separate tort.[2] Each will be advised in turn.

The tort which Bubba may be liable for is assault. This is intentionally causing a person to reasonably apprehend the immediate infliction of a battery. The fact that Edoardo ran off scared after hearing Bubba's

[3] The reason for only including the name of the case here is that you are seeking to draw a parallel with the facts of the case, in order to use this as the authority for the argument which you will go on to advance. There will be no need to then state the facts as the marker will know from how you have structured the sentence that the two aspects of the definition which you are discussing were at issue in *Thomas* v *NUM*.

[4] This is why, although 'reasonable' comes first in the definition, you should address it second in your answer.

threat would suggest that he felt he was going to attack him. However, Bubba should be advised that this is not sufficient to establish liability and, as in **Thomas v NUM** [1986] Ch 20, there are two aspects of the definition which should mean that Bubba will escape liability.[3] The first is that carrying out the threat, the infliction of the battery, must be immediate. We are told that they were on different sides of a river which, from the description given, would appear impassable. This would mean that it was not possible for Bubba to actually perform the unlawful touching necessary for battery immediately. Even though some delay is permissible (**R v Ireland** [1998] AC 147), Edoardo would still need to reasonably believe that the battery is imminent, which, on the facts, seems unlikely. This leads into the second aspect of the definition which is an issue here,[4] namely the reasonableness of the apprehension. It is not sufficient that Edoardo subjectively felt that he was about to be hit; it must, objectively on the facts, be reasonable for him to apprehend this event. As it seems there was no possibility of Bubba crossing the river, and therefore no immediate danger, any apprehension he felt was not reasonable as Bubba was not going to be able to carry out the threat.

Dustin faces liability under the tort of battery. This is defined as an intentional, immediate and direct act which causes unjustifiable physical contact with the claimant. From the facts, there is clearly no issue around the requirement for an immediate act. Additionally, although it is a golf ball which makes contact rather than Dustin physically touching Francesco, this will also not matter; it is clear from case law that direct does not mean instantaneous and an intervening object can be used (e.g. in **Hopper v Reeve** (1817) 129 ER 278, where throwing water over someone was a battery). Dustin should be advised that even though his intention was to hit Edoardo rather than Francesco, this will not enable him to avoid liability. What must be intended is the act and not the result (**Bici v Ministry of Defence** [2004] EWHC 786), so Dustin's intention to hit Edoardo will simply be transferred to hitting Franceso. The application of the concept of transferred malice was first acknowledged in English law in **Bici** and one of the reasons for its application is by analogy with

[5] You will not need to write the full article title and citation, but provide your marker with enough information to indicate which work you are referring to.

the criminal law. However, its application has been firmly rejected by Beever's (2009) article in the *Legal Studies* journal.[5] He argues that, unlike criminal law, in tort the identity of the claimant has significant importance and is essential to the cause of action and therefore the analogy does not work and the doctrine should not

[6] This is why it is worth commenting on the academic discussion around this issue, as it could form the basis of Dustin avoiding liability, which is what your task is essentially. More importantly, this also allows you to add to the analytical depth of your answer.

[7] Although the question is not on negligence, show your wider knowledge of tort by highlighting that you have seen further potential liability from Dustin's actions.

[8] By highlighting why Edoardo could not be sued in trespass, you not only show more depth to your understanding of that tort, you also create a platform from which to introduce the rule in *Wilkinson* v *Downton*.

[9] Your aim is to pass comment on the rule, not to argue whether there is negligence. As the rule has been subjected to significant criticism, you should reproduce this and assess whether it is a suitable basis of liability for Edoardo.

apply. If this were the case, then Dustin, by not intending to strike Francesco, would not be liable to him for battery.[6] Therefore as **Bici** is only a High Court judgment, it is open for Dustin to defend any claim by Francesco on the basis that the doctrine should not apply in tort, but he should be advised that as the law currently stands he will be liable for battery. However, Dustin should be advised that even if successful on this point, it may instead lead to him being liable in negligence.[7]

In relation to Edoardo, the harm which his actions have led to did not flow directly from what he did: it was more indirect harm. As such, he could not face any claim under trespass.[8] However, where someone intentionally conducts themselves in a way which causes indirect harm, the rule in **Wilkinson** may be used to impose liability. In **Wilkinson,** a prank call caused the recipient to suffer psychiatric injury, which was not recoverable at the time in negligence. The judge found the defendant liable on the basis that he had willfully done an unjustified act calculated to cause harm; therefore, the intention to cause the harm which occurred was imputed by the judge. This appears very similar to what has happened with Edoardo. The rule was subjected, though, to extensive analysis in **Wainwright v Home Office** [2004] 2 AC 406 where it was held that imputed intention should not be used and that there must be an actual intention to cause harm, or the defendant would need to have acted without caring whether he caused harm. We are not told that Edoardo had an intention to cause harm, but it would seem that he was at the very least not caring whether he caused harm. The question is what sort of harm Edoardo's phone call has caused. We are told that Zach went into shock but no more. If this is a fully recognised psychiatric injury, then Edoardo is very likely to face liability either under the rule or in negligence. In **Wainwright,** Lord Hoffmann felt negligence was the better cause of action, but subsequently the rule was used for this type of injury in **C v D** [2006] EWHC 166.[9] However, if the 'shock' was in fact merely a case of distress, then it would appear that Edoardo will not face any liability. Lord Hoffmann stated the rule does not provide a remedy in such instances and, while he was cautious about creating a tort of intentionally causing distress to deal with such a scenario, Lord Scott was strongly opposed to the idea, a view adopted in **Mbasogo v Logo Ltd** [2007] QB 846.

In conclusion, Bubba is unlikely to face any liability for assault, but Dustin is likely to be liable for battery, even if Dustin can avoid this, he may instead be liable in negligence. Determining the position of Edoardo requires more evidence about the nature of Zach's injury. If it was simply distress that was suffered, he will not be liable, but if he suffered a medically recognised psychiatric injury, then Edoardo will face liability under the rule in **Wilkinson** or alternatively in negligence.

✔ Make your answer stand out

- Read Beever, A. (2009) Tranferred malice in tort law? *Legal Studies,* 29(3): 400–20 in full, to be able to add further points to your argument regarding Dustin and whether he should be liable for battery.
- Discuss in more depth the future role of the rule in *Wilkinson* v *Downton* [1897] 2 QB 57 and whether there should be a tort covering the intentional infliction of distress.
- Expand your comment about Dustin being alternatively potentially liable in negligence to illustrate just how this may be the case.
- When dealing with being unable to sue Edoardo in trespass, consider the issue of negligent trespass arising out of the decision in *Letang* v *Cooper* [1965] QB 232.

! Don't be tempted to . . .

- Get too sidetracked regarding the merits of applying transferred malice in tort. Make sure you stay focused structurally on applying the law to the issue.
- Go through and apply all of the requirements of negligence, if you do discuss it. This could lead to your marker thinking that you have misidentified the main essence of the question, which is trespass, and you will also risk running out of time. By highlighting it, you will have shown an appreciation of that tort by way of the fact that you have seen its potential application.

❓ Question 3

Yvette (22) and Ed (21), two university students, had been sitting at a table on the patio of a coffee shop owned by Chuka, a small, elderly man in his sixties. A sign states that the patio area is only to be used by paying customers. As the pair had not purchased anything for about two hours and the shop was getting busy, Chuka approached them and asked if they were finished could they leave so that other customers could use the table. After a further

30 minutes, with the pair still there, Chuka return and shouted, 'If you lazy spongers don't clear off now, I will have to throw you off my property myself, you know!' Chuka then went to shoo them away with a wet tea towel. Yvette was hit, however, and in trying to avoid it she rocked back on her chair. This was done too fast and she fell backwards, falling on a metal railing which pierced her body. Chuka rushed forward to help, but, fearing that Chuka was about to attack him next, Ed picked up a glass ashtray and struck Chuka in the face with it, causing a broken jaw.

Yvette was taken to hospital where she was seen by Dr Burnham, who rushed her into emergency surgery. Due to the level of blood loss, Dr Burnham conducted a blood transfusion. Naturally, Yvette was unconscious at the time and gave no consent for the procedure. Due to her religious beliefs, Yvette would not have consented even if she was conscious. Dr Burnham insisted that she would have died without it.

Advise the parties as to their liability.

Diagram plan

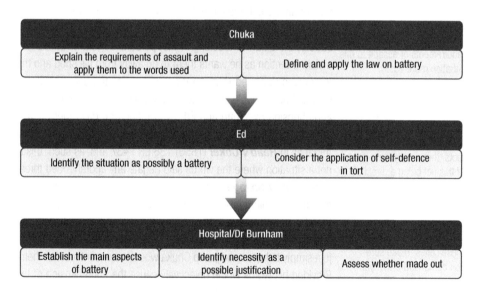

A printable version of this diagram plan is available from **www.pearsoned.co.uk/lawexpressqa**

Answer plan

→ Explain what assault is and discuss the relevance of the condition which Chuka had attached to his words.

→ Outline the requirements for battery in full and apply them to Chuka hitting Yvette with the tea towel.

➡ Consider whether Ed can argue he was acting in self-defence when he struck Chuka with the ashtray.

➡ Advise Dr Burnham as to battery, explaining whether he could claim that he was justified due to the necessity for carrying out the procedure.

Answer

The potential liabilities of the parties all relate to trespass to the person and specifically the torts of assault and battery. While these torts are actionable without proof of damage, clearly some damage has occurred here. However, the issue, particularly for the latter two acts, is whether the actions were justifiable in the circumstances due to self-defence and necessity.[1]

[1] By highlighting these factors here, you show that you have identified all the topics in the question and where the complications may lie.

The first issue is whether Chuka is liable for assaulting Yvette and Ed. For an assault, there must be an intentional and direct act which causes another to reasonably apprehend the immediate infliction of a battery, the unlawful touching of that person.[2] Arguably, Chuka had a clear intention as he wants them to go away from his shop and the threat was designed to make them leave, and the act is obviously direct.[3] Chuka should be advised that this is likely to be a reasonable apprehension by Yvette and Ed, even though he gave them a way of avoiding any battery. His words simply amounted to a conditional threat as in *Read v Coker* (1853) 138 ER 1437 and, as such, this is not a situation where the words said negate any apprehended threat (*Tuberville v Savage* [1669] 86 ER 684). Chuka made clear that if they did not voluntarily leave, he would physically remove them and thereby sought to exert control over their movement and personal autonomy.[4] Yvette and Ed do not have to have been placed in fear, just simply to have anticipated Chuka would make contact with them. Provided his words would objectively cause the apprehension of the battery, which is supported by the movement towards them having previously hit Yvette with the tea towel, Chuka will be liable for the assault.

[2] Obviously, you have not defined battery yet, so provide a brief explanation here. This will enable you to apply the requirements of assault to this situation more easily.

[3] Do not forget to apply this aspect. Generally, you would need to substantiate this statement but here, on the facts, there really is no issue of this not being a direct act. Therefore, this would suffice.

[4] Rather than just show your knowledge of both of these cases, make sure you demonstrate that you understand the difference between them by explaining why one is considered unacceptable.

Chuka faces a more clear-cut case of liability for battery against Yvette. Battery is the intentional, direct touching of another without lawful justification. Intention must relate to intending to make contact with the person, and contact may be direct even if an intervening object has been used to achieve it (**Hopper v Reeve** [1817] 7 Taunt 698). We are told that Chuka simply intended to shoo them away, which is not enough information to determine the matter;[5] however, under **Bici v Ministry of Defence** [2004] EWHC 786 (QB) subjective recklessness will suffice. Therefore, this is likely to amount to battery.

Ed also faces liability for battery. It is clear that by striking Chuka with the ashtray, Ed has satisfied all of the elements of the tort.[6] Ed could avoid liability by proving he acted in self-defence and, therefore, the touching was, in fact, justified and so not a battery. Ed's issue is that while he felt Chuka was going to attack him imminently, he was mistaken. Under the criminal law, acting under an honest, but mistaken, belief is sufficient for self-defence irrespective of how unreasonable the mistaken belief was (**R v Williams (Gladstone)** [1987] 3 All ER 411).[7] However, self-defence is different in tort, and the mistaken belief must have been reasonable to hold (**Ashley v Chief Constable of Sussex** [2008] UKHL 25). Lord Scott[8] noted the different purposes of tort and crime. Therefore, if tort adopted the same approach to self-defence, the wrong balance would be struck between a person's right not to be subjected to physical harm and another's right to prevent an imminent attack with reasonable force. As a person's liberty would be at stake, not imposing a criminal sanction on a person in such circumstances is justifiable. However, setting aside one's right to physical integrity based on an unreasonably held belief would not be justifiable. Therefore, Ed's liability rests on the reasonableness of his belief that he was going to be imminently attacked. Arguably, Chuka's demeanour could suggest an imminent physical attack. However, much depends on how the words were said and his demeanour. Further, the proximity of Ed to Yvette would be a factor. If there was distance between them it is hard to maintain a belief that Ed reasonably thought Chuka was coming for him. Overall, while perhaps honest, the reasonableness of the belief is questionable which might, in turn, raise questions over whether there was an assault by Chuka.[9]

However, even if Ed satisfies the reasonableness requirement, he must also have acted proportionately to the threat posed by Chuka (**Lane v Holloway** [1968] 1 QB 379). Here Chuka was, at the time in

[6] Again this is self-evident so you should simply state this fact and move on to the main discussion point of whether the touching was justified as an act of self-defence. As you have defined battery above, there is no need to do so again.

[7] Although a tort answer, you are still making an assertion of legal principle to set out your argument, so you should cite the criminal law authority for it. Your aim is to compare the two approaches and show that you have a real grasp of the basis of tort law and the principles underpinning it.

[8] All of the judges stated an opinion on this so remember to be specific about who you are referring to, as this shows that you have a greater level of knowledge of the case.

[9] Raise this as a prospect in order to show that you appreciate the connection between the two torts.

question, unarmed and significantly older that Ed, yet Ed struck him in the face with a glass ashtray. This could be said to be disproportionate and so Ed would be liable for the battery.

The remaining issue is whether Dr Burnham is liable in battery for operating on Yvette without her consent. By performing the transfusion, the initial elements of a battery are clearly present. The issue is whether this was a justifiable intrusion of Yvette's physical integrity due to the situation. Liability will, therefore, rest on whether the intrusion was justified on the grounds of necessity. If so justified, the fundamental essence of the tort, unlawfulness, is missing.[10] This issue is governed by *F v **West Berkshire HA*** [1990] 2 AC 1 and the touching must be shown to be necessary in the circumstances, and that it was not practicable to communicate with Yvette. As she was unconscious, it was clearly not possible to ask for her consent. Therefore, it must be considered whether it was practicable to wait until she regained consciousness. We are told that Dr Burnham felt it was an emergency and Yvette would have died from the blood loss without the transfusion.[11] While this needs to be proven, on that basis[12] it was not practicable to wait to seek Yvette's consent.

The action taken must also have been reasonable in the circumstances in which it occurred. This requires evidence from a reasonable body of medical opinion demonstrating support for Dr Burnham's action. We are not told whether this is the case, but if it was a life and death matter it would be likely. If it was reasonable, there would be no liability under *F.* However, in any event, Dr Burnham should be advised that any claim would probably be brought against the hospital under the doctrine of vicarious liability. Therefore, even if the transfusion was an unjustified intrusion, and thus there was a battery, he should avoid personal liability for his performance of the operation[13] (***Cassidy v Ministry of Health*** [1951] 2 KB 343).

In conclusion, Chuka is likely to be found liable for assault and battery; Ed is also likely to be liable for battery as, even if deemed reasonable, it was potentially disproportionate. Dr Burnham and/ or the hospital will, however, not be liable due to his acting out of necessity.

[10] The point of writing your answer in this way rather than talking about the 'defence' of necessity is that it indicates you have a deeper understanding of the tort by recognising that, if the touching is not unlawful, there is no tort from the start – not that there was a tort but a defence applies to negate liability.

[11] It is important on this point to make sure to draw on the specific factual wording of the question to support the conclusion you are forming.

[12] You have just created some doubt, so make sure you clearly explain that you are proceeding with your advice on the basis that it will be proven. Otherwise your answer could lack coherence.

[13] In terms of advising Dr Burnham of his liability, this would be an important piece of information for him and impacts ultimately on whether he would be held liable or not. Although no specific mention is made of advising the hospital, or of vicarious liability, by mentioning this you will gain marks for having recognised that the doctrine will operate here.

Make your answer stand out

- Consider including a short discussion on trespass to land. The question does not limit you to trespass to the person, and the facts would support the view that Yvette and Ed had become trespassers. This would demonstrate the breadth of your knowledge.

- Include a discussion of the need for hostility in relation to battery.

- Ensure that you explain why the hospital is vicariously liable for Dr Burnham. It is something which should be considered, but it can easily be forgotten in the exam room, especially when the question is not specifically on vicarious liability.

- Discuss the merits of adopting the solution proposed by Lord Scott in *Ashley* v *Chief Constable of Sussex* [2008] UKHL 25. This would require you to think of the consequences of such a change and its merits. To aid this, you may want to look at the Court of Appeal judgment from the case and particularly paragraphs 63 to 78 where Lord Clarke MR discusses this.

- Read *Re A, (Children) (Conjoined Twins: Surgical Separation)* [2001] Fam 147 for a detailed overview of the law on necessity, which you could then draw on in your answer.

! Don't be tempted to . . .

- Repeatedly define each tort and state what is required. Structure your answer in a way which avoids this.

- Avoid the debate over self-defence, or deal with it too briefly, as this is arguably the key point in the question where you can gain extra marks for the level of evaluation within your answer.

- Turn your answer into an essay on the nature of self-defence. It may seem tricky, but you have to strike an appropriate balance between demonstrating a deeper level of knowledge and understanding and adding analytical depth with the fundamental need to employ a good structure and answer the question that has been set.

- Discuss other defences which have no application on the facts just to show that you know them. This will just show that you have not understood the question properly and is indicative of a descriptive, narrative-type answer.

 # Question 4

'At the level of enforcement, rights do not permit trade-offs between the interests of the right-holder and of the right-infringer. Such trade-offs take place at the earlier stage of right-definition. This is mirrored in the distinction between defences and justifications: justifications are part of the definition of the right whereas defences are trade-offs at the level of enforcement.'

P. Cane (1999) Fault and strict liability for harm in tort law, in *The Search for Principle: Essays in Honour of Lord Goff of Chieveley,* ed. W. Swaddling and G. Jones, Oxford: OUP.

In light of this statement, evaluate the purpose of trespass to the person and what must be proven to succeed in a claim.

Diagram plan

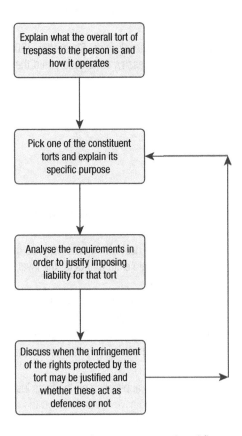

A printable version of this diagram plan is available from **www.pearsoned.co.uk/lawexpressqa**

Answer plan

➡ Discuss the overall function of the tort, explaining the justification for it.

➡ Evaluate battery, illustrating its aim and showing how its requirements aid the overall purpose of the tort.

➡ Consider assault in the same manner.

➡ Assess false imprisonment in similar fashion.

Answer

[1] Structurally it makes more sense if you deal with the generic theoretical aspects of the tort first before going into depth on each component tort. This passage should be written as an extended introduction and then it can act as your foundation for the answer from which the rest of your arguments build.

[2] This may just read like a restatement of the quote, but it is important that you include a passage such as this in your answer, in your own words. This shows firstly that you understand what the quote means and allows you to tie it in to the overall theory and purpose of the tort.

Trespass is one of the oldest torts protecting individuals from unjustified, intentional harm. Consisting of battery, assault and false imprisonment, it seeks to provide meaning to one's right to physical integrity and liberty by imposing liability without the need to prove any damage was suffered due to the intentional infringement of the right.[1] Protection is strong as vindication of an infringed right is not prevented through the pleading of a defence; however, this raises issues in respect of personal autonomy and criminal justice. Therefore, certain actions are justified in order to balance the competing rights of others. Where the defendant's actions are justified there is no tort in the first instance as the key characteristic of unjustness is missing, whereas a defence to an action implies that a tort has been made out initially.[2]

Battery is the direct and intentional unlawful touching of another, although subjective recklessness will suffice (***Bici v Ministry of Defence*** [2004] EWHC 786). It aims to protect physical integrity by prohibiting any form of unjustified molestation, not just touching, which causes injury (***F v West Berkshire HA*** [1990] 2 AC 1). This reflects the sacrosanct nature of physical integrity meaning the smallest infringement, even an unwanted kiss, is prohibited.

The defendant's intention to make contact justifies such a strong approach. If actual harm is necessary, the protection afforded is greatly reduced, the system for vindicating one's rights is far simpler by merely requiring that there should be no unjustified touching rather than assessing the degree of touching. Liability will arise even if an object is used to make contact with the claimant (***Pursell v Horn*** 112 (1838) ER 966) or if the intentional act was originally directed at a third party (***Bici***). In this latter scenario, the intention is transferred to the person who was actually touched.

Clearly, this could greatly restrict one's right to freedom of action; greater harm to the claimant could even be caused if all touching required consent to be justified. For example, doctors could not perform emergency operations on unconscious patients. Therefore, the law has sought to reasonably restrict the tort's application by creating categories of lawful touching. It is for this reason why Cane (1999) highlights the distinction between defences and justifications in trespass.[3] These situations go to the heart of what battery is and thus negate its existence. The key categories are necessity (**F**), self-defence (**Ashley v Chief Constable of Sussex** [2008] UKHL 25) and all touching within the bounds of what is acceptable as part of everyday life (**F**).

[4] The question does not expressly ask for details of these, but at this stage of your answer, check how you are doing for time and perhaps add some detail here. The important point is to at least get across that the categories of justifications are needed to provide the balance which tort strives to achieve.

The first of these is clearly a justified intrusion to prevent a greater harm such as death or serious injury and covers the medical scenario above. The second is also needed as it allows one to prevent their physical integrity from being infringed themselves. The third category covers 'the exigencies of everyday life' such as jostling in the street (*per* Lord Goff in **F**). However, reflecting tort's overall approach to balancing conflicting rights and interests none of these automatically make the touching lawful; there are set requirements outlined in the cases which must be satisfied in order to justify the touching.[4]

[5] As battery is in the definition of assault, it is best to discuss it first as then you will have already defined this term, allowing you to now get straight into assault.

[6] Offer some reasoning as to why the operation of assault is justified; this stops your answer becoming a descriptive piece on each tort. Instead you are showing analytical skills, which will help you get more marks.

Physical integrity can also be infringed without actual touching, hence the tort of assault. Assault consists of an intentional, direct act which causes the claimant to reasonably apprehend the immediate infliction of a battery.[5] The fact that a battery is unlawful means it is equally right to impose liability when someone intentionally causes another to apprehend that one will occur. Power and control can be exerted simply by threat of violence and one's quality of life should not be hindered by the constant apprehension of a battery. One's right to physical integrity would be hollowed as liability is avoided simply by not carrying out the threat, yet the consequence may be the same.[6] Causing such a state of mind cannot be justified on any public policy basis. It should also be noted that, as with battery, a subjectively reckless act will suffice (**Bici**). Perhaps the most significant word in the definition of 'assault' is 'reasonable'. It is too great an infringement into another's freedom of action if the claimant could succeed by simply perceiving a threat in non-existent circumstances, particularly when great emphasis is now placed on freedom of expression. Requiring reasonableness ensures that any restriction on freedom of expression is justified. A good illustration is ***Thomas v NUM*** where the striking miners had no way of actually reaching the non-strikers to commit battery[7] and so any apprehension was unreasonable. Therefore, the full context must be considered. An assault can be carried out by simple gestures, words are not needed (***R v Ireland*** [1998] AC 147); however, if words are present alongside an action, they must be considered in order to assess whether they reinforce the reasonableness of the apprehension or, in fact, negate it (***Tuberville v Savage*** (1669) 86 ER 684).

[7] All you need here is to state enough of the basic facts to illustrate the point you are making. So do not feel the need to go into more factual depth here than is stated.

Finally, false imprisonment is the total restraint of someone without lawful authority (***Bird v Jones*** (1845) 7 QB 742). Therefore, the fundamental right to liberty is protected. Reflecting the importance of this right, liability arises from a restraint lasting the smallest amount of time and the claimant may not even need to realise they were restrained (***Murray v Ministry of Defence*** [1988] UKHL 13). However, there is some doubt about the validity of this view. ***Murray*** approved ***Meering v Graham-White Aviation*** (1919) 122 LT 44 on this point, but the issue was only *obiter*. Subsequently, in ***R v Bournewood Mental Health Trust (ex parte L)*** [1999] 1 AC 458), the patient did not know that if he left his actual ward he would be detained. However, because he could physically leave the ward, there was deemed no total restraint as he could in theory leave that area. This would mean that the claimant must know of the restraint. Significantly, the minority view was favoured in ***HL v UK*** [2004] ECHR 471 regarding a claim under Article 5, thus arguably if the situation arises again the ***Murray*** position will be adopted.[8] This would better reflect the purpose of the tort, otherwise a person drugged then taken, but released before gaining consciousness, would have no claim.

[8] Although this is not an English law authority, it is worth mentioning as it involved the same claimant and therefore you show that you know this and also that you understand the implications of the case.

Clearly, it would not be possible to have a criminal justice system or policing without some restraint being justifiable. Therefore, the Prisons Act 1952 permits imprisonment upon sentence or pending trial and PACE 1984 provides the power to make arrests. However, in order to allow the police to perform their function while also ensuring that function is not abused and due process is observed, certain procedures must be followed. This is crucial in any democracy to prevent the devaluing of the tort's protection.

[9] The key to your conclusion in this answer is to offer a personal view as to whether a good balance has been struck between the rights that the tort protects and the conflicting interests of society. This should be a restatement of what you have been advancing throughout your answer.

Therefore, the three torts play a vital role in protecting one's key right to personal integrity. The fact that they have existed for so long without any fundamental restructuring of principle suggests that they are doing this job effectively, while not causing problems for day-to-day society by justifying actions which would otherwise infringe one's physical integrity.[9]

✓ Make your answer stand out

- Try and read the chapter on Trespass in Fifoot's *History and Sources of the Common Law: Tort and Contract* (1970), Eversham: Greenwood Press, as well as the essay from which the quote is taken. The first will provide you with material on the historical purpose of the tort which you can use in your answer. Reading the essay from the question will also help you to understand the distinction that Cane is making between defences and justifications, which will allow you to discuss this more confidently in your answer.
- Expand the discussion of the distinction when it comes to defences or justifications in trespass; the idea being that justified actions remove the key element of the definition of each tort and so prevent it from ever coming into being. This is contrasted to defences which acknowledge the presence of the tort but prevent liability.
- Provide some more details of specific requirements for the conduct in question to be justifiable and thus negate the existence of each tort.

! Don't be tempted to . . .

- Talk independently about the justifications too much as the question does tell you to focus on the requirements of the tort. You will, therefore, limit your scope to explore these in depth and show your analysis and evaluation of the torts.
- Give excessive factual detail of cases in order to explain your points. The question is more concerned with the theory of the tort and the underlying principles and so you just need to discuss the facts to the extent that they help to illustrate these. Simply give enough to help substantiate the point and act as the basis for the issue which you are dealing with at that time.

@ Try it yourself

Now take a look at the question below and attempt to answer it. You can check your response against the answer guidance available on the companion website (**www.pearsoned.co.uk/lawexpressqa**).

Tiago runs a coffee shop that also doubles up as a reading centre and so Tiago tries to maintain as low level of noise as is possible. One day Leo came in to the shop carrying a laptop, which Tiago did not mind as he thought Leo was probably going to do some work. However, when Leo sat down he started playing an online game that made a lot of noise and Leo would shout out a commentary as he was playing. Concerned that the noise was going to disturb his customers, Tiago shouted at Leo, 'if you don't shut up and get out of my shop that thing is not the only thing that is going to get broken'. Tiago then stormed back to his counter and bent down to pick something up. Fearing that Tiago was about to come back and hurt him, Leo threw his glass latte cup and hit Tiago in the face, cutting his cheek.

When Tiago had stopped the bleeding he decided he would play a prank on Leo's elderly aunt that he lived with, Alix. Tiago rang up and said that he had seen Leo get run over earlier that day and he was ringing to pay his condolences. Immediately thinking Leo had been killed, Alix collapsed with shock and broke her hip in the fall.

Advise Tiago as to all of the above incidents.

www.pearsoned.co.uk/lawexpressqa

Go online to access more revision support including additional essay and problem questions with diagram plans, you be the marker questions, and download all diagrams from the book.

Interests in reputation and private information

14

How this topic may come up in exams

The scope and media prominence of these issues make them a popular exam area. You should check your module to see the extent you cover the misuse of private information in conjunction with defamation as, while separate torts, they are linked. The structure of defamation and its defences lends itself well to problem questions. Whereas the wide-ranging arguments as to whether there should be a general tort protecting privacy and the development of a tort of misuse of private information means that this lends itself extremely well to essay questions; the opposite in relation to both is also common. Overall, it is important to know the influence of human rights on both torts as both consist of a balance between Articles 8 and 10.

■ Before you begin

Acquaint yourself with the following components and key issues of this topic; and familiarise yourself with how you would structurally progress through them all, if necessary, when attempting to answer a question on this topic.

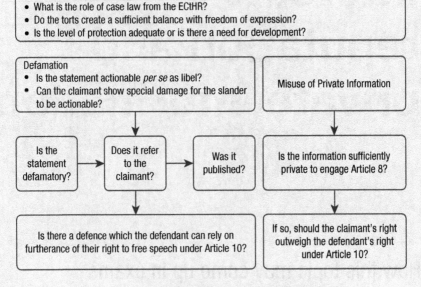

A printable version of this diagram is available from **www.pearsoned.co.uk/lawexpressqa**

❓ Question 1

Michael Paxman is an investigative reporter for *The Westminster Echo*, a weekly political news magazine with a sales circulation of 20,000, but whose stories are always picked up by larger news outlets. He has been looking into Peter Seldon, MP, who is also currently the housing minister with responsibility for planning applications, and before entering Parliament was a director of a national house-building company. Michael's investigations have uncovered that Peter's previous company has received preferential treatment in planning decisions. Additionally, he has established that Seldon had retained shares in the company, which he has just sold for a sizeable profit after the company had obtained planning permission for a new town development. Michael has now published his investigation in the latest edition of *The Westminster Echo;* an extract on the front page reads:

> Today we reveal how housing minister, Peter Seldon, joins the list of corrupt MPs who shame Parliament. Evidence indicates he is favouring former business associates in deciding planning applications. Not content with doing favours for those associates, he has also pocketed thousands of pounds from a shareholding in the company.

Inside the magazine, however, the story states that Peter had registered the shares in the Register of Members' Interests, and stresses that there is no evidence of him receiving financial payments from the company for the decision.

During a televised debate in the House of Commons on housing policy, Peter responds:

> 'Michael Paxman, a two-bob journalist with a history of fabricating and plagiarising stories: it is he who brings shame on his profession.'

Advise both parties as to whether they have a claim for the respective comments in defamation.

Diagram plan

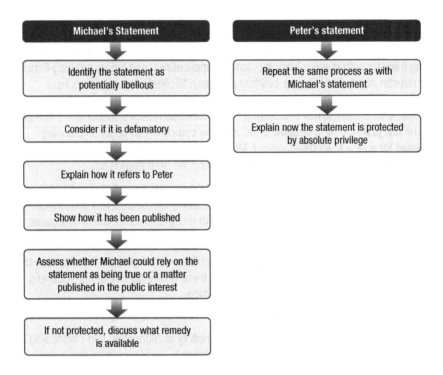

A printable version of this diagram plan is available from **www.pearsoned.co.uk/lawexpressqa**

Answer plan

→ Define what defamation is and establish that we are concerned with libel.

→ Apply the three requirements of defamation, in turn, to the newspaper story and ensure that you identify the key allegation against Peter.

→ Consider the possible defences which could apply to the paper, namely truth and publication on a matter of public interest. If not applicable, advise of the remedy available.

→ Repeat the application of the requirements of defamation to the comments by Peter.

→ Discuss the defence of absolute privilege for Peter.

Answer

The issue to consider is the validity of claims by both parties for defamation. Such claims bring into focus the tension between protecting one's reputation, while recognising free speech and the need for a free press. This is significant here as the matter involves investigative journalism into parliamentary corruption. It will be argued that while both statements appear defamatory, the defence of privilege will protect Peter, but his own claim may be defeated due to the statement being in the public interest.

Advising Peter first, it should be noted that while the comment was made by Michael any action should be brought against *The Westminster Echo*[1] as ultimately being responsible for the story. Defamation is the publication of a statement about a person, which lowers their reputation in the eyes of society, and Peter should be advised that has two forms: libel and slander. The former is where the comment is made in a permanent format and is traditionally viewed[2] as being actionable *per se,* meaning proof of damage is not needed. As the comment has been printed, it would be libel. Under section 1 of the Defamation Act 2013, the statement must cause, or be likely to cause, serious harm to Peter's reputation, and, as interpreted in *Lachaux* v *Independent Print Ltd* [2016] QB 402, this needs to be proven, although it can be inferred from a wide publication. This would all appear to be satisfied in light of the allegation, his position and the size of the publication. As such, three elements need satisfying.

The first requirement is whether the statement is defamatory, meaning Peter's reputation is lowered in the estimation of right-thinking members of society (*Sim* v *Stretch* [1936] 2 All ER 1237). This is determined with reference to the fair-minded and not unduly suspicious reasonable person (*Lewis* v *Daily Telegraph* [1964] AC 234). There appears to be no issue here: looking at the front page extract, the allegation is that Peter is corrupt, making ministerial decisions for profit. However, under *Charleston* v *News Group Newspapers* [1995] 2 All ER 313, a passage cannot be taken in isolation where other parts negate the effect of the libel. From the overall story, it is clear that no financial wrongdoing is alleged. Therefore, Peter could not base a claim on such suggestions, but the story does not negate

[1] In a defamation action it is important to note who the claim is against as it is an expensive process. A media organisation is well equipped to fight such claims, as opposed to an individual journalist, and this may have a bearing on whether Peter will want to bring a claim, especially if you advise him that the claim may not succeed.

[2] As you will need to go on to explain, *Lachaux* has suggested the position under the Act is now different. By using this wording you can highlight your knowledge of the previous position and thus the significance of the change.

[3] Not only is it important that you clarify for the purposes of this element which statement may be actionable, but it is also important when you discuss defences, so make sure you spell out what exactly it is that was said which was defamatory.

[4] As there are no contentious issues in the facts on these points, keep them brief to save you time to discuss the more relevant aspects.

[5] Although the old law referred to the 'sting' and you may still see it used, this is the word in the section so demonstrate your knowledge by using it.

[6] This is why you should discuss this defence second. It comes into play if the statement cannot be shown to be true so you can show your knowledge of both, whereas it would not make sense to talk about trying to show the statement is true if you have satisfied the other defence.

[7] Set out some background to the new defence to provide context and show your wider knowledge, but don't get too diverted into a tangential discussion.

the allegation of corruption by favouring associates,[3] which would lower the reputation of a politician in the public's eyes. The second and third elements, that the statement refers to the claimant and is then published to a third party, respectively, are clearly satisfied as the article is about the housing minister, Peter Seldon, and has been printed in a national magazine.[4]

While Peter may have a claim for defamation, reflecting the need to create a balance with freedom of expression, several defences are recognised which may assist *The Westminster Echo*. These have recently been placed on a statutory footing by the Defamation Act 2013. The first defence is whether the story is true (s. 2). The key imputation[5] is that Peter is corrupt by favouring former associates in determining planning decisions and *The Westminster Echo* will need to show it is substantially true (s. 2(1)). The extract suggests Michael has evidence that Peter's former company has received preferential treatment so this may be the case.

In the event of not being able to prove it is substantially true *The Westminster Echo* could rely on the section 4 defence[6] of publication on a matter of public interest, which has replaced the old defence from **Reynolds v Times Newspapers Ltd** [2001] 2 AC 127. Although it will apply in similar circumstances to the **Reynolds** defence, it aims to be clearer and simpler in its application, particularly by breaking the link with privilege. It is broader in that it applies to the statements of fact and opinions.[7] The defence has two limbs: first the statement must be one of a matter of public interest (s. 4(1) (a)) and must be determined in light of all of the circumstances of the case (s. 4(2)). In light of the nature of the allegation, this would clearly seem to be satisfied as it relates to a government minister abusing his position. Further, the public would want to know all aspects of the story as it involves how the government is operating and making important decisions, notwithstanding any suggestions of corruption.

The second aspect of the defence is that *The Westminster Echo* reasonably believed that publishing the statement was in the public interest (s. 4(1)(b)). Peter must be advised that this is again determined in light of all of the circumstances of the case, and allowance must be given for editorial judgement (s. 4(4)). Under the old law, focus was given to how responsible the journalist had been in gathering the story and the statement could not be motivated out of malice. However, while these concepts are not expressly covered by the new defence, similar considerations do apply.[8] If *The Westminster Echo* has acted irresponsibly or maliciously, it would affect the reasonableness of their belief in the story being in the public interest. Indeed, it would also raise questions about whether it was even in the public interest to publish the statement in the first place. Ultimately, the statement in issue – preferential treatment – is sufficiently integral to the overall story to warrant inclusion: it is the story itself, so the exercise of such editorial judgement can be justified. As we are informed that *The Westminster Echo* has evidence to support its claims, on the basis that it is credible and sourced responsibly, it would be reasonable to believe the public should know the allegation, especially as there is no apparent countervailing public interest in not publishing the story.[9] Therefore, *The Westminster Echo* would most likely have a defence to a claim by Peter. In switching to advise Michael now, the matter would again be libel as, although it involved spoken words, the debate was televised (Broadcasting Act 1996, s. 166). The words spoken are therefore published and by naming Michael directly it would be considered as referring to him.

Even though it is a common name, the context clearly refers to Michael (*Jameel v Wall Street Journal Europe* [2006] UKHL 44). There is also no apparent issue with the statement being defamatory, as it clearly suggests that Michael makes up his stories and copies the work of others.[10] However, Peter will have the defence of absolute privilege. MPs, under Article 9 of the Bill of Rights 1689, cannot be questioned in court on statements from parliamentary proceedings. As the statement was made during a parliamentary debate, the defence will apply unless Peter waives his right to the defence under the Defamation Act 1996, s. 13. Otherwise, Michael cannot seek redress. In conclusion, it appears that *The Westminster Echo* may well have a defence to any claim by Peter; however, Michael would certainly be unsuccessful in any claim against Peter.[11]

[8] This allows you to show your knowledge of how the new and old defences relate to each other. Further, as the defence is still new it has not been developed through case law as yet; therefore, some of the old law will still be relevant for now to help explain some aspects.

[9] Include something like this to indicate that you have picked up on the subtlety and nuance of the section in that something may be a matter of public interest, but would not be reasonable to publish in the public interest, e.g. claims of police incompetence not being reasonable to publish due to the impact on national security.

[10] As before, you need to simply apply the elements to the statement and show how they are made out.

[11] Although you have effectively concluded each party's claim and this may seem like repetition, you should round off the answer with a summary of the position.

✓ Make your answer stand out

■ Consider the position for the parties of any re-publications which may occur.

■ Highlight the human rights considerations regarding freedom of expression which are inherent in the tort.

■ Read Mullis, A. and Scott, A. (2014) Tilting at windmills: the Defamation Act 2013. *Modern Law Review*, 77(1): 87–109 to supplement your discussion regarding the application of the new defence with academic opinion and commentary.

! Don't be tempted to . . .

■ Discuss aspects of the tort, such as whether the statement was published, which are not issues in dispute; similarly don't consider defences just to show you are up to date with the changes brought about by the new Act.

■ Go into great detail about the *Reynolds* v *Times Newspapers Ltd* [2001] 2 AC 127 defence and the factors to consider to determine whether something is responsible journalism.

■ Make definitive statements about the liability of the parties, as the facts do not support such findings.

■ Give detail on slander, as it is not the form of defamation within the question.

❓ Question 2

Bevis Langton is a social media influencer and vegan activist. He advocates for living a vegan lifestyle through his social media accounts and through appearances that he makes on television and at vegan festivals. His strong views have gained him a great amount of support in the vegan and wider community. He has developed a range of vegan cookbooks and an all-vegan clothing range, both of which have generated a significant income for him.

Rex Armstrong, an investigative reporter and prolific meat eater has organised a meeting with Bevis to discuss his new cookbook and get a short interview for *Delicious*, the magazine that he works for. The meeting is due to take place at Bevis's home. As Rex approaches Bevis's front door he notices through the kitchen window to the left of the front door that Bevis is eating a huge beef burger. Rather than ring the bell, Rex pulls out his camera and takes a number of photos of Bevis eating the burger and licking meat juices from his fingers.

Instead of running the story in *Delicious* magazine, he sells the photographs and story to a popular daytime television show, *Good Morning Today* that Bevis had previously appeared on. They ran the story with the tagline, 'Langton's lies: vegan activist exposed as a fraud.' The photos were shown on the television show and on the companion website for the programme.

Bevis now seeks your advice over the matter.

Diagram plan

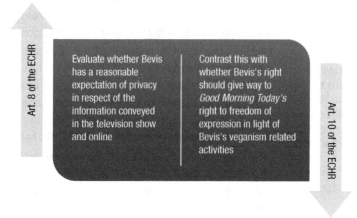

A printable version of this diagram plan is available from **www.pearsoned.co.uk/lawexpressqa**

Answer plan

→ Outline what the cause of action would be.

→ Explain why there is no general tort regarding the invasion of privacy.

→ Set out the requirements for the tort of misuse of private information.

→ Balance Bevis's right to privacy against *Good Morning Today's* right to freedom of expression.

→ Consider whether the details of the story and the inclusion of the photos were a necessary and proportionate response to any public interest in publishing.

Answer

The matter that Bevis requires advice in respect of is whether or not he may have an action in tort for the publication of the news story and accompanying photographs regarding his eating the beef burger. In order to do so, the extent to which the law recognises rights to privacy and protects them under the tort of misuse of private information will need to examined.[1] It will be argued that although Bevis may have a reasonable expectation of privacy in respect of the information published, the *Good Morning Today* may, nevertheless, be justified in publishing the information.

[1] As privacy is a broad issue that interacts with a number of different areas, you should identify the basis of any claim in tort from the outset in order to focus your answer.

Lord Hoffman in **Wainwright v Home Office** [2003] UKHL 53 confirmed that in English law there is not, nor does there need to be, a specific privacy tort. Notwithstanding the incorporation of Article 8 of the ECHR, by virtue of the Human Rights Act 1998, the legislature and judiciary have been averse to the creation of a tort for the protection of privacy. The reasoning for such reluctance has included a lack of precedent, lack of suitable definition of privacy, concerns regarding frivolous claims, and concerns regarding placing constraints on freedom of expression.[2] With this said, the HRA has clearly influenced more recent developments in the equitable doctrine of breach of confidence, which have in turn opened the doorway for recognition of a tort of misuse of private information. The landmark case of **Campbell v MGN Ltd** [2004] UKHL 22 established that where private information is concerned, the modern approach of the courts is to reflect the privacy issues that may be raised, in line with Art. 8 of the ECHR. The House of Lords acknowledged that Art. 8 of the ECHR had reshaped the action for breach of confidence so that it now included protection against the misuse of private information.[3]

[2] Although each of these rationales could be explored in considerably more detail, this is not what the question requires. Mentioning them briefly indicates that you have relevant knowledge; however, to elaborate on them further would be likely to detract from your answer.

[3] Demonstrate your knowledge of the background to the action and how it arose to make the existing laws compatible with the Convention.

The existence of a *tort* of misuse of private information was later confirmed in **Vidal-Hal and Others v Google Inc** [2015] EWCA Civ 311. In order to bring an action under this tort, Bevis will need to demonstrate that the information in question was private, in the sense that it is protected by Art.8 of the ECHR. He must then demonstrate that his interest in keeping the information private outweighs *Good Morning Today's* right to freedom of expression under Art. 10 of the ECHR (**McKennit v Ash** [2008] QB 73).[4]

[4] Although you will inevitably address each of these requirements in your subsequent paragraphs, in order to provide a clear indication of the issues that you will be addressing, a short paragraph of this nature is useful.

In determining whether the information, namely the story and photographs of him eating meat, is private, the courts will apply the 'reasonable expectation of privacy' test (**Campbell**). This is ultimately a question of fact to be determined by the courts (**Murray v Express Newspapers Plc** [2008] EWCA Civ 446) and will be assessed on an objective basis (**Napier v Pressdram Ltd** [2009] EWCA Civ 443).

5 The circumstances that the court can consider are more numerous than those identified in the answer. However, you want to avoid simply providing a list with every possible consideration. This wastes time/words as some of the considerations will not be relevant to the question asked of you. You should identify the relevant considerations and then apply them to the question that has been set.

While some information is obviously private in nature, for example information regarding health, personal relationships and finances, in respect of information that does not fall within these categories, the court will ask what a person of 'ordinary sensibilities' would feel if placed in the same position as the defendant and faced with the same publicity. In **Murray v Express Newspaper Plc** [2008] EWCA Civ 446, Sir Anthony Clark MR confirmed that all of the circumstances of the case need to be considered, including but not limited to,[5] the nature of the activity in which the claimant was engaged, the place at which it happened, the absence of consent, the effect on the claimant and the circumstances in which the information came into the hands of the publisher. It would appear as though people would have a reasonable expectation of privacy in respect of what they legally do in their own home, particularly as it is possible for such an expectation to attach itself to mundane tasks (**Murray**). The photographs were taken surreptitiously of Bevis and there is no evidence of actual or implied consent to such photographs being taken. Despite the fact that Bevis is a well-known public figure, he is still entitled to a private life[6] (See **X v Persons Unknown** [2006] EWHC 2783 (QB)). As such, a reasonable expectation of privacy potentially[7] arises in these circumstances. In the event that it does not, Bevis will be unable to claim.

6 Although Bevis is a well-known public figure, this may not work in his favour when assessing whether or not the interference is justified.

7 In situations such as this, where each case will depend on its individual facts, and in the absence of any directly analogous authority, it is often difficult to say with certainty whether the law will or will not be applied in Bevis's favour. Using words such as 'potentially' highlights this uncertainty. You should explore the different possibilities and the effect that these may have on any claim.

Bevis should be aware that just because he may have a reasonable expectation of privacy, it does not necessarily mean that he has a right to keep that information private. Once Art. 8 of the ECHR has been engaged, the courts must decide whether or not the interference is justified. Where the defendant's right to freedom of expression is involved, the courts must weigh the competing rights in the balance, in order to assess whether any interference is proportionate and justified (**Campbell**). The protection of one right must be weighed against the harmful impact on the other. Bevis will need to demonstrate that his interest in keeping the story and photographs private, outweigh the public interest in the story. Disclosure of the details of a public-figure's private life is only justifiable when it adds to the political or public debate (***Von Hannover v Germany*** (2005) 40 EHRR 1). While the story in isolation may not satisfy this requirement, Bevis is likely to encounter difficulty as the information in the story exposes him as a meat eater, despite the fact that he has portrayed himself as a vegan and made a career out of this portrayal. The dissemination of the information 'sets the record straight' and exposes the false image that he has represented. The same issue was the basis for the claim in ***Campbell;*** however, the case concerned drug-taking. In ***Campbell*** it was accepted that there was a public interest in publicising her drug-taking in light of her previous denials.[8] It should, however, be noted that in ***Campbell*** the hypocrisy concerned an illegal activity, whereas in Bevis's case there has been no illegal conduct. However, the fact that Bevis has obtained substantial sums of money by endorsing a vegan lifestyle and developing his line of cookbooks and clothing, it is likely that his actions do carry a sufficient public interest and therefore it is justifiable for *Good Morning Today* to run the story.

Despite the apparent public interest in the story, Bevis should be advised that any publication should be proportionate to the legitimate aim that is being pursued by *Good Morning Today* as an exercise of their freedom of expression. If the publication is disproportionate, Bevis's claim will succeed. In ***Campbell*** the publication of the claimant's condition and the fact that treatment was being sought was a proportionate response; however, details of Campbell's treatment and the publication of photographs of her leaving a treatment centre were deemed to exceed that which was considered proportionate and, as a consequence, her claim succeeded. While on the face of it the photographs surreptitiously taken by Rex Armstrong could be likened to the photographs in ***Campbell,*** the courts may consider these as merely providing evidential credibility to the claims in the story that the public had an interest in knowing.

In conclusion, Bevis should be advised that even if he were able to establish that he had a reasonable expectation of privacy in respect of the story and photographs of him eating meat, he is unlikely to have a successful claim due to the legitimate public interest in the publication of the story. Despite the similarities between ***Campbell*** and Bevis's case, *Good Morning Today*'s publication of the story appears to be proportionate to the legitimate aim that is being pursued.

[8] Drawing an analogy between Bevis's case and *Campbell* helps to support the argument that is being made. However, you should be conscious of any distinguishing factual features of the cases, which could warrant a different approach being taken in respect of Bevis. Examining any distinguishing features and their potential effect demonstrates to the marker that you have a good understanding of the relevant legal authorities and can apply them effectively to the question.

✓ Make your answer stand out

- Make sure you fully understand the case of *Campbell* v *MGN Ltd* [2004] UKHL 22 and use your knowledge to substantiate your answer by drawing parallels and/or distinctions.
- Further your understanding by reading the following articles:
  - Hunt, M. (1998) The 'horizontal effect' of the Human Rights Act 1998. *Public Law*, Autumn, 423–43.
  - Aplin, Tanya (2007) The development of the action for breach of confidence in the post-HRA era, *IPQ*, 19.
- Highlight the seemingly different approach that the courts take between claims based around misuse of private information and those based on defamation.

! Don't be tempted to . . .

- Spend too long discussing why there is no general tort and whether this is justified. Remember there is a recognised action which he could use, and it is your knowledge and understanding of that action which the question is seeking to assess you on.
- Give a long factual account of *Campbell* v *MGN Ltd* [2004] UKHL 22; while you need to compare the two situations, this does not necessarily mean you have to provide a detailed factual account of *Campbell*. Concentrate on applying the legal principles to Bevis and using *Campbell* to simply support your reasoning.
- Include numerous references to other cases in your application just to show you know them. If citing them adds substance to your argument, then do so; if not then leave them out.

❓ Question 3

Dermott is an ageing but still famous singer who has just released a new album containing a series of love songs, which is a radical departure from his usual rock tracks. This followed his recent secret wedding to a young fan, Tulisa, and was recorded as a sign of his everlasting love for her, although only a handful of people in the record industry knew this. The album was exclusively reviewed in the influential music magazine, *Top Hits!* However, the review was quite negative, with the writer Louis Barlow ending by saying:

'While it may seem out of place on the album musically in light of the reason for this change of music direction, it is surprising not to see a cover version of *Money, Money, Money* by Abba on there.'

Additionally, the online version of the review had a comment section where readers could leave their views. One blogger, 'Singing Simon' posted the following:

'This album is so cheesy it should come with a sideboard of crackers and grapes. It may not be that bad if he could sing, but the way he tries to hit the high notes on track 6 is laughable! This is the voice of an angel . . . being throttled! I feel so let down.'

To leave a comment, people must register their personal details with the magazine. To gauge the response to the album, Dermott went online to read the comments. Dermott was furious, claiming Louis Barlow's comment was a clear criticism of Tulisa. He was also furious with the comment by 'Singing Simon' and, as it was one of the first, thought it may put people off the album and complained. However, several days later the comment was still there, and *Top Hits!* have refused to reveal the identity of 'Singing Simon'.

Advise Dermott as to his options in relation to the makers of each statement.

Diagram plan

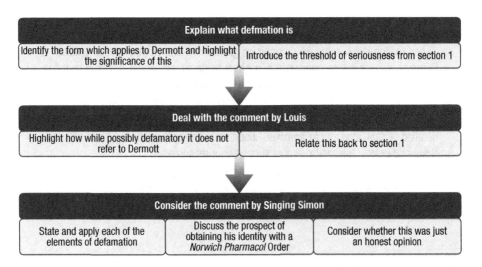

A printable version of this diagram plan is available from **www.pearsoned.co.uk/lawexpressqa**

Answer plan

➜ Define defamation and identify what form we are dealing with.

➜ Apply the criteria for the tort in turn to the blogger's comments.

➜ Explain the steps that Dermott will need to undertake in order to obtain the registration details of the blogger from *Top Hits!*

➜ Touch on any defences 'Singing Simon' may have if he is identified.

Answer

Dermott requires advice on the tort of defamation and its application to the Internet. This is an important issue as it involves balancing the competing interests of protecting one's reputation with free speech and press freedom. The issue is further complicated by the Internet itself, which emboldens people through perceived anonymity to express their views with reduced inhibition.[1] It will be argued that Louis's comment will not be actionable by Dermott personally[2] and Dermott may struggle to mount a claim against 'Singing Simon', who may have a defence. The possibility of a claim against the magazine is considered if the claim can be established.

Dermott should be advised that there are two forms of defamation: libel and slander. Although blogging can be seen to be analogous to slander in that it is similar to an oral conversation, it has been held to be libel (***Nigel Smith v ADFN plc*** [2008] EWHC 1797). Importantly, this means that no proof of actual damage is needed.[3] However, under section 1 of the Defamation Act 2013, to block trivial claims, the statement must cause, or be likely to cause, serious harm to Dermott's reputation. As will be discussed below,[4] it is questionable whether either statement will overcome this requirement.

[5] While it is more common to deal first with the requirement that the statement is defamatory, taking this element first allows you to draw a line under the comment by Louis, as Dermott clearly does not satisfy this requirement in relation to that comment. This leaves you to then concentrate on the action in which he has more chance of succeeding.

[6] Include this here, even though it relates to a different requirement, as it allows you to show the marker that you picked up on the innuendo and allude to your knowledge of the law in relation to that. Then simply dismiss the comment as being actionable by Dermott for not referring to him.

[7] Do not just assume that this element is satisfied as the comment does not use his name.

[8] As in relation to the comment with Tulisa, it is important to expressly emphasise that you have dealt with this point now so that the marker knows that you have covered it.

[9] Where you have two contrasting positions, make sure that you take a view on which is best, and use the facts to show why. Otherwise, your answer will not make total sense as to why you are proceeding with your advice.

Clearly, any statement must refer to Dermott otherwise he has no basis to make a claim.[5] However, the facts suggest that Louis's comment is an innuendo inferring that Tulisa is a gold-digger.[6] This is potentially actionable, but only by Tulisa as it refers to her. As such, it is also unlikely to overcome the threshold requirement in section 1 on this basis. While the second comment does not directly refer to Dermott,[7] as it is a comment on a review about his album, then it is reasonable that people would believe Dermott is being referred to (***Morgan v Odhams Press Ltd*** [1971] 2 All ER 1156).

The next requirement is that the statement is defamatory. The statement must lower the regard in which right-thinking members of society hold the claimant (***Sim v Stretch*** [1936] 2 All ER 1237). Applying this to 'Singing Simon's' comment, the natural meaning which Dermott will seek to apply is that he cannot sing, especially high notes. It is unlikely that people will shun Dermott personally, but they may avoid his album. Similarly, it could cause people to lower the regard that they have for his singing. However, Dermott should be advised that the comment could instead be viewed as simple abuse, which is why it may struggle to satisfy the section 1 threshold.[8] Abuse can amount to defamation in libel (***Berkoff v Burchill*** [1996] 4 All ER 1008), but following the ***Nigel Smith*** case it would need to be shown that the comment was intended to be taken seriously by casual readers, which was held to not often be the case. However, this is a comment on an album review by someone who may be a fan. Looking at the words 'I feel so let down', a casual reader may well take this to be a reflection of Dermott's singing and its impact on his fans, particularly in light of any negative tone in the review.[9]

Finally, the statement must be published to a third party. This was satisfied once the comment was posted on the website (***Godfrey v Demon Internet Ltd*** [2001] QB 201). Every download of the page will be another publication, although only one action will result, and Dermott will have one year from the date the comment was uploaded

[10] Refer to this so that you show that you are aware of the practicalities of bringing a claim and issues such as the limitation period. This enables you to demonstrate that you have a full range of knowledge about the subsidiary issues of the tort as well as the fundamental requirements.

[11] It would be important to phrase this along these lines if you have indicated some doubt about the defamatory nature of the comment previously in your answer.

[12] While this is relevant to the answer, it also shows that you are aware of the context in which decisions are taken, and so it shows that you have a broader understanding of the area.

[13] Although the question says to advise Dermott regarding a claim against the blogger, the facts allude to a possible claim against the magazine, so do not dismiss it, especially as the claim against the blogger may fail.

[14] Until case law builds up on the new defences, make sure you draw on what Parliament said in relation to what the sections mean and require.

to bring a claim (s. 8).[10] The amount of any damages will be reflected by the overall scale of publication (*John v MGN Ltd* [1997] QB 586).

However, even if all the elements are satisfied, the tortfeasor needs identifying as only a pseudonym is provided. As 'Singing Simon's' identify has not been revealed by *Top Hits!* Dermott will need a Norwich Pharmacal order, which would require the magazine to reveal the blogger's identity from their registration details. The requirements for this were outlined in *Mitsui Ltd v Nexen Petroleum UK Ltd* [2005] EWHC 625. First, Dermott needs to show that he has suffered a wrong; this will be satisfied if the elements of defamation are met.[11] Secondly, the order must be needed to bring an action against the wrongdoer, which is also satisfied, as Dermott only knows the tortfeasor as 'Singing Simon'. Lastly, the magazine will need to be shown to be involved in the wrongdoing so as to have facilitated the wrong, while also being able to provide the information needed to bring an action. This latter part is satisfied as the statement appeared on their website and all users register their personal details. On similar facts, *Sheffield Wednesday FC v Hargreaves* [2007] EWHC 2375 acknowledged the privacy concerns of bloggers/posters[12] stating that courts have discretion not to grant the order where the statement, while strictly defamatory, is more trivial in nature. This is an issue for Dermott because, as noted previously, the post could be said to simply be abusive and not serious. If the court does not grant the order though, or upon learning of his identity it appears futile to sue him, Dermott would have the possibility of suing the magazine instead in relation to this statement (Defamation Act 2013, s. 5(3)).[13]

If granted, the next issue is whether the blogger has any possible defence. As the post is a reply to the album review, which invited comments, the defence of honest opinion arises. This requires the statement to be one of opinion, which also includes the basis for the opinion (s. 3(2), (3)). The opinion here is that Dermott cannot sing and the performance on track 6, in particular, is cited as the basis. The opinion then needs to be capable of being held by an honest person on the basis of any fact existing at the time it was expressed and is assessed objectively. The explanatory notes to the section explain[14] that provided the fact relied on is capable of supporting the belief, it can be honestly held; we would need to hear the album to say this definitively. However, in theory the fact could support the belief, but if the blogger, subjectively, did not honestly hold the belief, the defence would fail (s. 3(5)).

[15] There is not much that can be argued here by way of application of the facts, so instead demonstrate that you understand the theory behind the defence by highlighting what it is for and how it compares to that which it replaced.

This continues the trend of the old common law version of the defence whereby the spite of the statement maker is irrelevant so as to not be inconsistent with the aim of the defence: to protect hard-hitting views.[15]

In conclusion, Dermott may succeed in a claim against 'Singing Simon' provided that he can show the statement was likely to cause serious harm to his reputation. Naturally, Dermott would have to obtain 'Singing Simon's' identity first. However, owing to the nature of the comment and where it was published, it is likely that the claim could be successfully defended as honest opinion. If the identity of 'Singing Simon' was not obtained, Dermott could instead successfully claim against the magazine as a website operator that, when notified of the content of the post, took no action (s. 5(3)).

✓ Make your answer stand out

- Make sure you have read and understood cases such as *Nigel Smith* v *ADFN plc* [2008] EWHC 1797, which are to do with blogging and the Internet rather than applying old, albeit more well-known, cases to a new situation. This will show that you are up to date with developments and the new context within which the law is operating. The application of the tort to the Internet is very important and topical so this knowledge will help you.
- Explore the merits of the analogy of blog posts and comments to slander and consider the consequences for Dermott.
- Familiarise yourself with the Explanatory Notes to the 2013 Act, and academic opinions on it, to help develop your discussion on how the new defences will operate. Similarly, make sure you keep looking for new cases dealing with the provisions and providing insight into how they should operate.
- Explain more fully the basis for bringing a claim against the magazine for not removing the comment. Read the Ministry of Justice's (2014) *Guidance on section 5 of the Defamation Act 2013 and Regulations: Complaints about defamatory material posted on websites* to help with this.

! Don't be tempted to . . .

- Simply conclude that the comment will not be defamatory due to failing to overcome section 1(1) and not consider any further matters.
- Also conclude at the end of your discussion of the elements of the tort that it has not been made out, and ignore discussing the consequences of it being found to be defamatory.

- Get sidetracked by the comment made by Louis as it is clear on the facts that the innuendo is not referring to Dermott, but do not completely ignore it as you can briefly show your knowledge of innuendo before applying the requirement of reference to the claimant to finish the discussion.

- Dwell on the elements for establishing defamation which are not really in issue, as you may well not get on to the other issues which are more relevant for discussion.

- Overlook the need to discuss the procedural issue of how Dermott could bring a claim, and how he will need to obtain a Norwich Pharmacal order.

 # Question 4

'The task of designing any libel regime must involve reaching an appropriate accommodation between individual rights and social interests in both freedom of expression and reputation.' (Mullis, A. and Scott, A. (2012) The swing of the pendulum: reputation, expression and the re-centring of English libel law, in D. Capper (ed.), *Modern Defamation Law: Balancing Reputation and Free Expression.* Belfast: Queens University Belfast Press)

In light of this statement critically evaluate the justifications of the new main defences under the Defamation Act 2013 and whether they have helped to reach an appropriate accommodation between the competing interests which lie at the heart of the tort.

Diagram plan

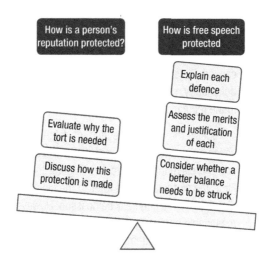

A printable version of this diagram plan is available from **www.pearsoned.co.uk/lawexpressqa**

Answer plan

→ Overview the two types of defamation, their differences and why the tort is needed.

→ Explain the elements of defamation.

→ Balance the need for the tort with an evaluation of the defences, assessing whether they tip the balance too far back in favour of the defendant or do not go far enough.

→ Consider the need for reform if the balance is still not right.

Answer

Defamation seeks to balance the seemingly irreconcilable issues of protecting one's reputation with the right of others to say what they want. A satisfactory balance is vital so that unfounded claims do not ruin lives, while giving effect to the notion of a free society through the promotion of freedom of expression. In assessing the reformed long-standing defences,[1] it is argued that while the recent reforms provide a balance, it is the potential cost of litigation which causes the main hurdle to adequately accommodating both interests.

[1] The point here is just to give your marker an indication of what defences you will be covering, as in an exam it will be impossible to adequately cover all of them.

Defamation is where a person is lowered in the estimation of society. As Lord Hoffmann observed in **Jameel v Wall Street Journal Europe** [2006] UKHL 44, it protects the immortal part of oneself, one's soul. Defamation has two forms: libel and slander. Slander is transient statements and generally requires proof of financial loss, or loss which is capable of financial assessment. However, libel, which is a permanent publication, was traditionally actionable *per se* as the permanence meant more people could see it and greater damage caused. Regardless of which form it takes, now, for a statement to be defamatory, serious harm must be caused or be likely to be caused to the reputation (s. 1).

[2] Rather than just explain the elements of the tort, explain the purpose of the elements. You should consider whether insisting on these counters the harshness of not needing to show damage.

To receive the tort's protection, certain requirements must be met which ensure that a sufficient nexus exists between the statement and the claimant to warrant restricting the maker's free speech.[2] First, the statement must refer to the claimant. Where reference is direct, there will generally be no issue. However, it is sufficient if the reasonable person, having knowledge of the circumstances, would understand the statement as referring to the claimant (**Morgan v Odhams Press Ltd** [1971] 1 WLR 1239). The statement must then be published, which requires communication to a third party, otherwise there is no damage to their reputation. Finally, the statement must be defamatory. Fair-minded people within society, as a whole, must think less of the claimant (**Lewis v Daily Telegraph** [1964] AC 234). Protection extends also to situations where the ordinary words themselves are not defamatory but they contain an innuendo which is damaging. If seemingly weighted in favour of the claimant, some balance has been restored by section 1 which seeks to eliminate trivial actions. This rebalancing is particularly the case in light of **Lachaux v Independent Print Ltd** [2016] QB 402, which held that this can no longer be presumed and must be proven. This could certainly be said to tip the balance away from protecting reputations.[3]

[3] While the question focuses on the defences, offering a comment on the judicial interpretation of this part of the Act allows you to assess the merits of the defences, and the balance struck, in light of this significant change.

The primary defence is that the statement is true (s. 2), as damages should not be awarded for injuring a false reputation (**M'Pherson v Daniels** (1829) 10 B & C 263).[4] Statements are presumed to be untrue and the defendant must prove otherwise. This is compliant with Article 10 (**Jameel v Wall Street Journal Europe** [2006] UKHL 44) and justified as one should have to substantiate one's claims.[5] However, allegations can be difficult to prove, particularly when they are specific, but provided the statement is proven to be substantially true, the defence will hold. Where a statement has distinct imputations, provided those which cannot be proven are not shown to seriously harm the claimant's reputation, the defence can still be relied upon (s. 2(3)). This is important as the lack of concrete evidence combined with the cost of defending an action may deter people from making statements which are in fact true.[6]

[4] Although the defence is not based in the statute, its rationale still lies in the judicial reasoning of old cases, so show your understanding by drawing on those to explain why the defence exists.

[5] The fact that the law presumes that one is lying requires you, in light of the statement in the question, to explain the justification for such a position, as it would seem to tilt the balance in favour of the claimant.

[6] After stating why the law adopts the position it does, it is important to evaluate the consequences of that position and where it leaves the balance between the parties.

The next substantial defence is honest opinion (s. 3), which embodies the whole idea of free speech as it protects one's right to criticise another.[7] It is a vital defence as the free expression of opinions is essential for good debate, which enhances a democratic society, and allows the truth to come to light. The new defence has sought to retain the essence of the old defence while simplifying and clarifying certain elements. However, so that reputations are protected certain requirements must be met. The statement must be an opinion and the statement containing the opinion must indicate, generally or specifically, what the basis for it is (s. 3(2), (3)). The latter is important in further justifying the defence as readers can make up their own

[7] As with truth, as these are exceptions to when you can injure a reputation, you ought to start with the reason for the defence and then assess its merits against the importance of protecting reputations.

[8] Make sure that you go further in your analysis of the defence by assessing whether the justification of each requirement has merit. If not, it could be argued that the defence is undermined and thus the necessary balance is lost. Alternatively, if the requirements are not rigorous enough, the balance is tilted too far from protecting reputations.

[9] While developed under the *Reynolds* principles, reportage was arguably a distinct defence with its own operation, so it is important you show that you are aware that it has survived and thus understand the full scope of the new defence.

[10] Although no longer the law, it is useful to show your understanding of the old law as you are essentially undertaking a comparison of the two defences.

[11] Allude to your knowledge of the background to the drafting of the Act by referring to how it could have looked. You can then use this knowledge to build up your argument as to the merit of the section's final wording.

[12] While the question refers to the main defences, there are clearly more and you will not be able to cover them all. It is worth at some stage just making your marker aware that you do appreciate more exist.

minds about the validity of the opinion if they can see what it is based on.[8] It supports the idea that misguided opinions do less harm than assertions of facts. The opinion must be capable of being held by an honest person based on a fact existing at the time the opinion was expressed, or anything asserted to be a fact in a privileged statement before the opinion was expressed (s. 3(4)). The defence will fail where the maker, subjectively, does not honestly hold the opinion. This replaces the old bar of malice and is better as it reflects the purpose of the defence while recognising that the benefits the defence brings do not materialise if the opinion is not genuine; debate is not legitimately being fuelled.

The next substantial defence is that in section 4, publication on a matter of public interest. The defence replaces the old form of qualified privilege known as the *Reynolds* defence, while retaining the reportage defence (s. 4(3)),[9] and has sought to be simpler by breaking the link with privilege altogether in order to give it a stronger jurisprudential foundation. Whereas the old defence was based on the concept of responsible journalism (even though it applied beyond newspapers)[10] this does not feature in the new defence. The defence requires the statement to, first, be on a matter that is in the public interest and, secondly, the publisher reasonably believed that publication was in the public interest. The interesting thing about the wording of the requirements is that it suggests that some matters may be in the public interest generally, but it is not reasonable to believe it is in the public interest to publish them, perhaps due to how the story was gathered. When determining the requirements, all of the circumstances of the case should be considered and allowance should be made for editorial judgement. This should mean that the old factors highlighted by Lord Nicholls in **Reynolds v Times Newspapers Ltd** [2001] 2 AC 127 have a role to play still. While denying the defence some certainty as to what is required, it does provide the essential flexibility needed to ensure the defence can apply to a wide array of publications, which is why certain factors to consider were expressly left out of the final version of the section.[11]

However, while these defences, and the others within the Act,[12] afford suitable theoretical protection of free speech, particularly in their reformed state, the relative ease in satisfying the requirements for

[13] Relate this back to your initial discussion on the elements; if they are meant to act as a hurdle for claims but then are too easy to overcome, does this mean the balance is in the claimant's favour?

[14] You need to bring home to your marker why you think this is the bigger problem and explain how the balance sought by the law could be undermined by this state of affairs.

defamation still means that the threat of litigation restricts speech.[13] Indeed, the cost means that the prospect of financial ruin is detrimental to both parties; damaged reputations may go unchallenged and damning information of public importance left unpublished. In light of the importance of both competing interests, such a state of affairs in unacceptable. Therefore, the cost of the litigation process must now be the focus of further reform.[14]

 Make your answer stand out

- Refer back to the quote in your answer when assessing the importance and justification for each defence.
- Include aspects of the Act's Explanatory Notes as well as the parliamentary debates leading to its enactment in order to assess what the defences are trying to do and whether a better version was rejected.
- Draw on some of the wider causes of concern regarding the tort, such as cost and libel tourism.
- Look out for recent high-profile cases from the news which you can use to show that you are aware of recent developments; notably the libel claim of politician Andrew Mitchell and the 'Plebgate' affair, which is reported to have a costs bill of £3 million.

! Don't be tempted to . . .

- Dwell too long on the requirements for a claim. The question is focused on the role of the defences, so you will not leave yourself enough time to address these otherwise.
- Discuss every defence as you will not have the time to do so in the required depth and provide any worthwhile evaluation. Stick to the substantive defences which provide a full defence to an action.
- Simply describe the elements of the defences; always aim to consider the justification of each as their existence allows infringements of a fundamental right to go without redress.

Question 5

'Misuse of private information is a civil wrong without any equitable characteristics. We do not need to attempt to define a tort here. But if one puts aside the circumstances of its "birth", there is nothing in the nature of the claim itself to suggest that the more natural classification of it as a tort is wrong.' *Per* Lord Dyson MR and Sharp LJ in *Google Inc. and Vidal-Hall & Others* [2015] EWCA Civ 311; [2015] 3 WLR 409, [43]

Evaluate the need to create an action for misuse of private information and, in doing so, assess whether it is correct to regard the action as a tort.

Diagram plan

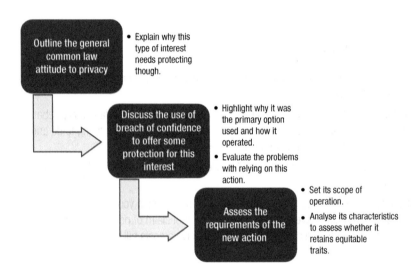

A printable version of this diagram plan is available from **www.pearsoned.co.uk/lawexpressqa**

Answer plan

➜ State the general position regarding protecting privacy at common law.

➜ Explain why an action is needed to protect this type of interest.

➜ Outline the historical method of protecting this interest.

➜ Evaluate the difficulties with that method and how a tort came into being.

➜ Assess the requirements of the tort so as to set its scope of operation and the extent it has equitable characteristics.

Answer

An evolutionary process has seen the creation of an action offering protection for misuses of private information derive from the equitable action of breach of confidence. This has proven controversial, as it was not initiated by Parliament and has implications for the media and free speech. As such, there must have been a clear need for such a development and any resultant action must be clear in character and scope to validate its existence and chart the path of future development. It is argued that the creation of this action was a proportionate response to the need to give effect to one's right to control the dissemination of information about oneself and is now appropriately settled as a tortious action.

The incorporation of the right to respect for private and family life, within Article 8 of the ECHR,[1] into English law only means that a citizen has protection from state intrusion. It does not correlate to equivalent common law rights actionable against private citizens; the Human Rights Act 1998 (HRA) has no direct horizontal effect.[2] Therefore, without the assistance of the common law, an individual would have no redress against another private person, such as a media outlet, who seeks to publicise personal information about them against their wishes. The opportunity to provide assistance arose in **Wainwright v Home Office** [2003] UKHL 53; however, it was held that no tort protecting general invasions of privacy existed and nor was one needed. Lord Hoffmann observed that compliance with Article 8 did not require a specific action, merely an adequate remedy for infringements. His Lordship felt that the common law had the means of doing this and where gaps existed, the HRA could fill them.

While a diverse range of torts, e.g. trespass, defamation and malicious falsehood, offered adequate remedies in particular circumstances, they do not specifically seek to protect privacy and private information and, as such, they had limitations (as illustrated in **Kaye v Robertson** [1991] FSR 62).[3] However, as the HRA operates vertically it cannot fill these gaps.

The equitable action for breach of confidence was a more adequate means of protection as it was at least concerned with keeping

[1] The right is often shortened to the right for privacy, but that it not what it is officially called. Demonstrate your more precise knowledge of the area by spelling it out in full. It is also important to make sure that you do not get confused between referring to sections under the Act and Articles under the European Convention on Human Rights and so use the appropriate label.

[2] This is something which is often misunderstood, so it is vital that you show you do know how it operates. Remember that it is because of this fact that there is a need to develop a form of horizontal protection.

[3] You would not need to get into *Kaye* here; your aim is to reinforce what you stated above regarding the need for an effective action that would protect a person's privacy against interference by another citizen.

confidential information secret through the imposition of a duty not to disclose it.[4] While primarily focused on commercial and governmental information, it could cover the situation that occurs in modern privacy cases: a third party (the media) receives information from a person under a duty of confidence and knowing that disclosure is a breach. However, the action was based on the idea of a confidential relationship between the person whose information it is and the person receiving it. In **Campbell v MGN Ltd** [2004] UKHL 22 Lord Nicholls acknowledged, in the types of case coming before the courts, such as 'kiss and tell' stories, talk of duties of confidence and classifying information about one's private life as confidential was not a comfortable fit. The idea of a confidential relationship was also being strained by how it was being adapted to these situations. If the action was applied in situations which were not a natural fit and further away from its origins, it risked distortion and falling into disrepute.

Baroness Hale argued in **Campbell** that although the HRA does not mean that new rights can be created to give effect to Convention rights, under section 6, as a public authority the court must interpret and develop existing rights in a Convention-compatible manner.[5] This also reflects Lord Hoffmann's opinion in **Wainwright** where he acknowledged that privacy, while not a principle of law, was an underlying value which could point the way for developing existing legal principles. As such, in **Campbell,** breach of confidence was developed so that the requirement of a prior confidential relationship was removed for these types of cases. Reflecting this, Lord Nicholls rechristened the action as the tort of misuse of private information to maintain a distinction with breach of confidence, which he would later hold dealt with a different interest altogether (**Douglas v Hello! Limited** [2008] 1 AC 1) and needed to be kept distinct.

The new terminology was used in **McKennit v Ash** [2008] QB 73,[6] which reviewed the opinions in **Campbell** to set out the requirements. First, the information in question must be private, thus protected by Article 8. This involves assessing whether the claimant had a reasonable expectation of privacy over the information. In **Campbell,** Lord Hope suggested that this exists where the information is obviously private or easily identifiable as such. However, where there was doubt, recourse should be had to the 'highly offensive test' from **Australian**

[7] Naturally, you have to evaluate the differing views in *Campbell,* but this then gives the impression of a law in a state of confusion. By referring to what later cases have said to round off the point, you show your detailed knowledge of the leading case, while showing how it has subsequently been dealt with by the courts. It allows you to argue the new tort is coherent and understood, and thus effective. Without it you raise questions as to what is covered by the action and how it operates, which your marker would expect you to then explore.

[8] Outline how the balancing exercise works, then give an opinion about what this means and how the results flowing from the exercise arise. Someone's right will have been interfered with and so you need to decide whether this has been done fairly, as this goes to the heart of whether the tort is good or not.

Broadcasting Corporation* v *Lenah Game Meats Pty Ltd (2001) 1 ALR 185. This requires asking what a reasonable person of ordinary sensibilities would feel in the claimant's position. While doubts over using this test were expressed by Lord Nicholls, who felt it blurred the differing questions of what is private and what interference is proportionate, their views are compatible in that it is what the claimant objectively thinks which matters – a view shared in ***Murray* v *Big Pictures (UK) Ltd*** [2008] EMLR 12[7] – and leads to more effective protection.

If the information is sufficiently private, the second question is whether it should remain private or yield to the defendant's freedom of expression. While the latter right is essential for a free press operating in a democracy, it must be balanced with ensuring responsible behaviour and respecting Article 8. As both Articles in question state that each right may be restricted where necessary in a democratic society so as to give effect to the other, neither takes precedence.

When performing this balancing exercise, Baroness Hale in ***Campbell*** stated three factors to consider to ensure that interference with either Article is proportionate and necessary. First, there must be a pressing social need, which protecting the opposing right provides. Secondly, any interference must be proportionate to simply meeting that social need. Finally, the reasons advanced for the interference must be logical and sufficient to justify it. The party which satisfies these most effectively will succeed in the aim of preventing or obtaining publication. This will be warranted as they have demonstrated that their interference with the other's right is necessary to give effect to the social need while not being too overbearing.[8]

That some form of action was needed to protect personal information was unarguable, as the then law was insufficient. However, due to its origins in equity, some cases used equitable terminology even after ***Douglas.*** While this may not have hampered the courts defining the scope of the new action, it was at odds with it being a new action, with new requirements, not rooted in equity, and it would have consequences in terms of procedure as seen in ***Google Inc. and Vidal-Hall & Others*** [2015] EWCA Civ 311; [2015] 3 WLR 409. In light of the different interests being protected and how, it is clear the action has thrown off its equitable past and is appropriately classified as a tort.

✓ Make your answer stand out

- Make sure you have read the passages of *Google Inc. and Vidal-Hall & Others* [2015] EWCA Civ 311; [2015] 3 WLR 409; and *Douglas* v *Hello! Limited* [2008] 1 AC 1 that deal with the nature of the action and why it is a tort, drawing on the judicial quotes to supplement your arguments, and contrast it with cases which have drawn on the terminology of breach of confidence to see if it really is a distinct action.
- Consider whether the case has settled the issue or whether it is in fact a narrowly focused decision.
- Read McLean, A. and Mackey, C. (2007) Is there a law of privacy in the UK? A consideration of recent legal developments. *European Intellectual Property Review*, 29(9): 389–95 and their case commentary to *Mosley* v *Newsgroup Newspapers Ltd* [2008] EMLR 20 from (2010) *European Intellectual Property Review*, 32(2): 77–89 to get a good understanding of the development of the tort and academic opinion that you can draw on.
- Draw on articles such as Alpin, T. (2007) Commercial confidences after the Human Rights Act. *European Intellectual Property Review*, 29(10): 411–19 for more of a breach of confidence perspective. Looking at specific equity texts such as *Snell's Equity*, McGhee QC, J. (ed.) (2016). London: Sweet & Maxwell will also give you more depth to the nature of the original action so you can then make a fuller comparison with the new tort.

❗ Don't be tempted to . . .

- Cover the specific issue from *Google Inc. and Vidal-Hall & Others* [2015] EWCA Civ 311; [2015] 3 WLR 409 of service of claims forms out of jurisdiction from the case, nor get sidetracked by the data protection issues. The question itself focuses on the general nature of the tort of misuse of private information.
- Describe the development in narrative form; make sure you evaluate it at each stage.
- Embark on a wider, more general consideration of the theory of privacy and human rights.

Question 6

'First, the good name of a company, as that of an individual, is a thing of value. A damaging libel may lower its standing in the eyes of the public and even its own staff, make people less ready to deal with it, less willing or less proud to work for it. If this were not so, corporations would not go to the lengths they do to protect and burnish their corporate images. I find nothing repugnant in the notion that this is a value which the law should protect.' (*Per* Lord Bingham in *Jameel* v *Wall Street Journal Europe Sprl* [2006] UKHL 44 at [26])

Exploring the judicial reasoning in the case, critically assess whether Parliament was right to effectively overturn the decision of the majority with the passing of section 1(2) of the Defamation Act 2013.

Diagram plan

The minority

- Companies can be just as powerful as government institutions
- Reflects the importance of freedom of expression
- The rule helps to protect the soul of an individual which companies do not have
- Injury to commercial assets in other torts requires proof of damage

The majority

- Company reputations are of monetary value
- Their profits flow from the amount of custom, which in turn is dependent on the public's perception
- Impacts on the quality of staff they can attract
- Creates different rules for different corporations or hits non-trading corporations

A printable version of this diagram plan is available from **www.pearsoned.co.uk/lawexpressqa**

Answer plan

➡ Set out what defamation is and what it seeks to protect and, in doing so, briefly distinguish between libel and slander.

➡ Discuss the justifications for not requiring proof of damage in libel and why this is not contested for individuals.

➡ Comment briefly on the challenge to the rule in relation to governmental bodies.

➡ Consider what the reason was for incorporating the change and making the position different for trading corporations.

➡ Evaluate which reasoning best suits the modern trading corporation.

Answer

The issue here is whether corporations should be treated differently from individuals when it comes to libel and have to prove financial damage. This is important as corporations place great value on their reputation and they have always been treated equally by the courts. However, section 1(2) requires them to now show more harm than individuals. It is submitted that it was justifiable to alter the rule for trading corporations in order to protect the public interest.

Defamation's purpose is to protect one's reputation from harm where a statement is published which refers to them and would tend to lower their reputation in the minds of right-thinking people. Defamation takes two forms: slander, which is a transitory statement, or libel, which is a statement in permanent form. Reflecting the fact that this permanence means the statement is more easily disseminated and any reputational damage is more durable over time, traditionally there has been no requirement in libel to prove the damage did occur. This is further justified on the basis of the difficulties of an individual establishing that the loss was due to the statement.[1]

[1] This is the most important part of this paragraph as it explains why we have the rule. Therefore, focus more on this than what defamation is, as this will provide the foundation upon which the actual arguments take place.

Traditionally, this rule applied to all claimants (**South Hetton Coal Co. Ltd v North-Eastern News Association** [1894] 1 QB 133). However, the first successful challenge was in **Derbyshire County Council v Times Newspapers Ltd** [1993] AC 534. It was held that government institutions could not sue to protect their governing reputations as otherwise it was contrary to the public interest. Defamation claims could be used to censor criticism. In a democracy, governmental bodies should be subject to criticism: otherwise, party political systems could not function[2] as they are based on trying to undermine confidence in your opponent's competence.

[2] While this may seem slightly off at a tangent, you should briefly cover this case and the principle that it determined as you can use this later in support of Baroness Hale's view when you look at the minority view in *Jameel*.

[3] Using this wording here gives you the scope to proceed seamlessly to discussing the majority or the minority, depending on your viewpoint. Remember to lay out the view that you ultimately favour the second, as this will mean your answer will end on a stronger note and flow into your conclusion.

That companies should be able to bring an action has always been acknowledged; what has long been disputed is whether they should benefit from the same rules as individuals.[3] However, with the passing of section 1(2) of the Defamation Act 2013, companies that trade for profit must show, as individuals must, that the statement complained of has caused, or is likely to cause, serious harm, but for them this now means serious financial loss. In doing so, this has effectively overturned the decision in **Jameel v Wall Street Journal Europe**

Sprl [2006] UKHL 44 at [26], which only recently held that both types of claimant should be treated alike.

In ***Jameel,*** Lord Scott opined that a corporation's reputation is an asset of monetary value; this is why many advertise on TV shows and sponsor events. Companies try to enhance their reputation by association for commercial advantage. However, if their reputation suffers, these opportunities are reduced, leading to lost custom and ultimately profits. Weir (1972) suggested that as this is financial injury it can be proved evidentially, unlike with individuals, and thus should be proved.[4] At first glance this seems a strong point. Lord Scott, though, felt that it was not so simple for companies to prove this loss and attribute it to the statement. Trade variations happen for a variety of reasons and so it is difficult to show that loss resulted from the published statement. Lord Bingham agreed with these sentiments, highlighting that a corporation's reputation also impacts on those wanting to work for it. Therefore, reputations should be protected by a favourable judicial verdict, as this carries more weight than a denial by press release. Significantly, Lord Scott also noted that such a change would exclude corporations from obtaining interim injunctions.

[4] By including this here, you make the arguments in favour of the rule stronger as you are fully testing them at the same time. You will also have a greater degree of cohesion to your answer than if you include this later on with the specific arguments of the minority.

Lord Hope's opinion was that the arguments for change could not be soundly based in principle as they singled out trading corporations for differential treatment from non-trading corporations. The distinction was because, as Lord Hope noted, bodies such as charities would find it even harder to put a value on their loss, let alone prove it. However, this distinction has now been entrenched by the Act and is arguably unfair in light of the similar evidential difficulties both types of corporation may face and the equal asset value of each's reputation.

[5] This links your answer to the discussion of *Derbyshire CC* and why you discussed the issue of public authorities.

Notwithstanding the ***Derbyshire CC*** case holding that there were distinctions between public authorities and corporations, Baroness Hale felt that, today, the boundary is blurred with multinational corporations wielding enormous power.[5] As such, she felt it may well be of democratic interest to similarly open such corporations to 'uninhibited criticism'. It is important to reiterate that Baroness Hale was not suggesting removing standing from trading corporations. Indeed, she did not even advocate that loss must be caused: simply that they must prove that the statement was likely to cause them financial loss.

[6] By highlighting these you show some wider knowledge, and strengthen the assertion that this was a modest development of the law with wider support.

[7] Include some practical examples of how the majority's arguments can be rebutted, as these will carry more force than a purely jurisprudential argument.

[8] Obviously, as the House was split, it is worth showing your knowledge of each judge and explaining what side they were coming from.

[9] As you have just ended the previous paragraph with why there is no practical reason for the rule, it is beneficial to highlight that you are now addressing the remaining arguments advanced by the majority. As the answer is about supporting the legislation by arguing against the majority, it is important to include Lord Hoffmann's brief views on the issues as this allows you to counter the theoretical reasons of the majority.

[10] This allows you to end on a strong note with high-level judicial endorsement for your concluding argument.

Reflecting the view of the Faulks Committee on Defamation, this was a slight modification of the position advanced in **Derbyshire CC,** and is the position adopted by the Act.[6]

This obviously raises the majority's contention that proving such loss may be difficult. However, this is not necessarily the case. Companies, particularly large corporations, will have year-on-year sales figures and so can contrast the period following the publication to previous years.[7] As companies do now, an assessment of external factors could be made in order to determine whether any loss was caused by those factors such as bad weather or the holding of national events. Furthermore, under section 1(2) concrete evidential proof is not required, so causative uncertainties will not be detrimental. The loss must simply be shown to have been 'likely' to be caused by the statement. This is easier to do when looking at the size of the claimed loss and the nature of the statement in light of other external factors. Therefore, on a practical basis there was no need to maintain the rule.

Lord Hoffmann, supporting Baroness Hale,[8] somewhat countered Lord Hope's theoretical issues regarding creating distinctions.[9] He noted and agreed that a company's reputation is a commercial asset, but felt not requiring proof of damage would mean that defamation is at odds with other torts such as malicious falsehood. This could be justifiable in that defamation serves a different purpose. However, Lord Hoffmann felt that the justification for not requiring proof by individuals is that their reputation is part of their 'immortal' self – it is their soul. Therefore, it warrants greater protection. However, as a company has no soul there was no reason to treat it more favourably in defamation than in other torts dealing with harm to commercial assets.

Therefore, while there are strong practical and theoretical difficulties in treating trading corporations differently, they are not insurmountable. Further, reflecting the new landscape identified by Lord Steyn in **Reynolds v Times Newspapers Ltd** [2001] 2 AC 127 that the starting point should be free speech, they should be overcome.[10] To favour the protection of a company's reputation without proof of damage is, in Weir's view, a 'grim perversion of values' and therefore it is right that Parliament stepped in and legislated on the basis of the minority decision.

✓ Make your answer stand out

■ Read *Jameel* v *Wall Street Journal Europe Sprl* [2006] UKHL 44 in full so that you can draw on all of the judicial opinions in support of your arguments, as each judge says something different. You can then show deep and wide-ranging knowledge of the issue.

■ Consider the earlier versions of the Act, including Lord Lester's draft Bill, and the parliamentary debates over this issue. The provision was not always going to be included in the government's legislation, and you can get the full range of arguments for and against its inclusion by reading these. You can then build them into your answer.

■ Also read the Report of the Faulks Committee on Defamation (1975), Cmnd 5909, to which their Lordships referred and which made a recommendation on this point. It would also be beneficial to look more closely at the views of Weir, T. (1972) Local authority *v* critical ratepayer: a suit in defamation. *Cambridge Law Journal,* 30: 238, which is his case commentary of *Bognor Regis Urban District Council* v *Campion* [1972] 2 QB 169.

■ Undertake a comparative evaluation with other jurisdictions which do require a company to prove actual damage.

❗ Don't be tempted to . . .

■ Spend too long on what defamation is; you can take it almost as a given in the question that it is known. The question is assessing your understanding of what its purpose is and thus why the damage rule is, or is not, needed.

■ Avoid stating which position from the case you prefer, as this is ultimately what you have been asked to argue.

@ Try it yourself

Now take a look at the question below and attempt to answer it. You can check your response against the answer guidance available on the companion website (**www.pearsoned.co.uk/lawexpressqa**).

'On any reading, the emergence of the Defamation Act 2013 is the culmination of a phenomenally successful political campaign. The changes in the law of defamation that it has introduced will be significant, although it is as yet not clear precisely how profound they will be.' Mullis, A. and Scott, A. (2014) Tilting at windmills: the Defamation Act 2013. *Modern Law Review*, 77(1) 87–109, at p. 108.

Evaluate the impact of the Defamation Act 2013 and assess whether the reforms leave the law on defamation in a better state that before it came into force.

www.pearsoned.co.uk/lawexpressqa

Go online to access more revision support including additional essay and problem questions with diagram plans, you be the marker questions, and download all diagrams from the book.

Bibliography

Aplin, T. (2007) Commercial confidences after the Human Rights Act. *European Intellectual Property Review,* 29(10): 411–19.

Aplin, Tanya (2007) The development of the action for breach of confidence in the post-HRA era, *IPQ,* 19.

American Psychiatric Association (2013) *Diagnostic and Statistical Manual of Mental Disorders,* 5th edition, American Psychiatric Publishing.

Arden, M. (2010) Human rights and civil wrongs: tort law under the spotlight. *Public Law,* January: 140–59.

Bailey, S. (2010) What is a material contribution? *Legal Studies,* 30: 167.

Barker, K. (1993) Unreliable assumptions in the modern law of negligence. *Law Quarterly Review,* 109: 461–84.

Beever, A. (2009) Transferred malice in tort law? *Legal Studies,* 29(3): 400–20.

Bell, J. (2013) The basis of vicarious liability. *Cambridge Law Journal,* 17.

Brazier, M. and Miola, J. (2000) Bye-bye *Bolam*: a medical litigation revolution? *Medical Law Review* 8(1): 85–114.

Buckland, W.W. (1935) The duty to take care. *Law Quarterly Review,* 51: 637.

Buckley, R.A. (1984) Liability in tort for breach of statutory duty. *Law Quarterly Review,* 100: 204.

Cane, P. (ed.) (1999) Fault and strict liability for harm in tort law, in *The Search for Principle: Essays in Honour of Lord Goff of Chieveley.* W. Swaddling & G. Jones, Oxford: Oxford University Press.

Cotter, B. and Bennett, D. (2013) *Munkman on Employer's Liability,* 16th edition. London: LexisNexus.

Davies, M. (1982) The road from Morocco: *Polemis* through *Donohue* to no-fault. *Modern Law Review,* 45(5): 535–55.

Farrell, A and Brazier, M. (2016) Not so new directions in the law of consent? Examining *Montgomery* v *Lanarkshire Health Board. Journal of Medical Ethics* 42(2): 85.

Faulks Committee (1975) Report of the Committee on Defamation. Cmnd 5909.

Fifoot, C.H.S. (1970) *History and Sources of the Common Law: Tort and Contract,* Eversham: Greenwood Press.

Fleming, J. (1998) *The Law of Torts,* 9th Edition, Sydney: LBC Information Services.
Foster, S and Gladwin-Geoghegan, R. (2018) Police liability in negligence: immunity or incremental liability? *Coventry Law Journal,* 23(1): 38–47.

Geach, N. (2012) The nuisance of the proprietary interest: Lord Cooke's dissent in *Hunter* v *Canary Wharf Ltd* [1997] AC 655, in N. Geach and C. Monaghan (eds.), *Dissenting Judgments in the Law.* London: Wildy, Simmonds & Hill Publishing.
Geach, N. (2012) Re-establishing the search for principle: the dissent of Lord Goff in *White* v *Chief Constable of South Yorkshire Police* [1999] 2 AC 455, in N. Geach and C. Monaghan (eds), *Dissenting Judgments in the Law.* London: Wildy, Simmonds & Hill Publishing.
General Medical Council (2008) *Consent: Doctors and patients making decisions together.* https://www.gmc-uk.org/-/media/documents/consent---english-0617_pdf-48903482.pdf.
Giliker, P. (2006) The ongoing march of vicarious liability. *Cambridge Law Journal,* 489: 492.
Giliker, P. (2010) *Lister* revisited: vicarious liability, distributive justice and the course of employment. *Law Quarterly Review,* 126: 521–24.
Gore, R. (2012) Loss of chance, Lord Hope's dissent in *Gregg* v *Scott* [2005] UKHL 2, in N. Geach and C. Monaghan (eds.), *Dissenting Judgments in the Law.* London: Wildy, Simmonds & Hill Publishing.
Goudkamp, J. (2017) *Tort Law Defences.* Hart Publishing: Oxford.

Hedley, S. (1995) Negligence: pure economic loss: goodbye privity, hello contorts. *Cambridge Law Journal,* 54(1): 27.
Hodges, C. (2001) Compensating patients: case comment on *A* v *National Blood Authority* [2001] 2 All ER 289. *Law Quarterly Review,* 117: 528.
Hoffmann, Lord (2005) Causation. *Law Quarterly Review,* 121: 592–603.
Hope, Lord (2013) Tailoring the law on vicarious liability. *Law Quarterly Review,* 129: 514.
Howarth, D. (2003) The House of Lords and the Animals Act: closing the stable door. *Cambridge Law Journal,* 62(3): 548–51.
Howarth, D. (2006) Many duties of care: or a duty of care? Notes from the underground. *Oxford Journal of Legal Studies,* 26: 449.
Howells, G. and Mildred, M. (2002) Infected blood: defect and discoverability: a first exposition of the EC Product Liability Directive. *Modern Law Review,* 65: 95.
Hudson, A.H. (1960) Nuisance or trespass. *Modern Law Review,* 23: 188.
Hunt, M. (1998) The 'horizontal effect' of the Human Rights Act 1998. *Public Law,* Autumn: 423–43.

Jones, M., Dugdale, A. and Simpson, M. (eds.) (2014) *Clerk & Lindsell on Torts,* 21st edition. London: Sweet & Maxwell.

Law Commission (1967) Report, *Civil Liability for Animals,* No. 13 www.bailii.org/ew/other/EWLC/1967/13.html.
Law Commission (1969) Report, *The Interpretation of Statutes,* No. 21 www.bailii.org/ew/other/EWLC/1969/21.html.

Law Commission (1973) Report, *Liability for Damage or Injury to Trespassers and Related Questions of Occupiers' Liability,* No. 52. London: HMSO and www.bailii.org/ew/other/EWLC/1973/c52.pdf.

Law Commission (1998) Report *Liability for Psychiatric Illness,* No 249. http://www.bailii.org/ew/other/EWLC/1998/249.html.

Law Reform Committee (1954) *Third Report: Occupiers' Liability to Invitees, Licensees and Trespassers.* London: HMSO.

Lee, J. (2008) Causation in negligence: another fine mess. *Professional Negligence,* 24: 194.

McDonald, B. (2005) Blameless? *Public Interest Law Journal,* 34: 15–17.

McGhee QC, J. (ed.) (2016) *Snell's Equity.* London: Sweet & Maxwell.

McIvor, C. (2010) Getting defensive about police negligence: the Hill Principles, the Human Rights Act 1998 and the House of Lords. *Cambridge Law Journal,* 69:133.

McLean, A. and Mackey, C. (2007) Is there a law of privacy in the UK? A consideration of recent legal developments. *European Intellectual Property Review,* 29(9): 389–95.

McLean, A. and Mackey, C. (2010) *Mosley* v *News Group Newspapers Ltd*: how sadomasochism changed the face of privacy law: a consideration of the Max Mosley case and other recent developments in privacy law in England and Wales [2008] EMLR 20, from (2010) *European Intellectual Property Review,* 32(2): 77–89.

Ministry of Justice (2014) *Guidance on section 5 of the Defamation Act 2013 and Regulations: Complaints about defamatory material posted on websites.* www.gov.uk/government/uploads/system/uploads/attachment_data/file/269138/defamation-guidance.pdf.

Morgan, P. (2013) Vicarious liability on the move. *Law Quarterly Review,* 129: 139.

Mullis, A. and Scott, A. (2012) The swing of the pendulum: reputation, expression and the re-centring of English libel law, in D. Capper (ed.), *Modern Defamation Law: Balancing Reputation and Free Expression.* Belfast: Queens University Belfast Press.

Mullis, A. and Scott, A. (2014), Tilting at windmills: the Defamation Act 2013. *Modern Law Review,* 77(1): 87–109.

Mullis, A. and Oliphant, K. (2012) *Torts.* Palgrave MacMillan.

Murphy, J. (1996) Expectation, losses, negligent omissions and the tortuous duty of care. *Cambridge Law Journal,* 55(1): 43–55.

Murphy, J. (2004) The merits of *Rylands* v *Fletcher. Oxford Journal of Legal Studies,* 24: 643.

Murphy, J. (2007) The juridical foundations of common law non-delegable duties, in J. Neyers, S. Pitel and E. Chamberlain (eds.), *Emerging Issues in Tort Law.* Oxford: Hart Publishing.

Murphy, J. (2010) *The Law of Nuisance.* Oxford: Oxford University Press.

Murphy, J. and Witting, C. (2012) *Street on Torts.* Oxford: Oxford University Press.

Newark, F.H. (1949) The boundaries of nuisance. *Law Quarterly Review,* 65: 480.

Nolan, D. (2005) The distinctiveness of *Rylands* v *Fletcher. Law Quarterly Review,* 121: 421–51.

Nolan, D. (2018) Strict Product Liability for Design Defects. *Law Quarterly Review,* 134:176.

Ogus, A.I. (1969) Vagaries in liability for the escape of fire. *Cambridge Law Journal,* 27(1): 104.

O'Sullivan, J. (2007) Suing in tort where no contract claim will lie: a bird's eye view. *Professional Negligence,* 23(3): 165–92.

Paterson, J.M. (1994) *Rylands* v *Fletcher* into negligence: *Burnie Port Authority* v *General Jones Pty Ltd. Monash University Law Review,* 20(2): 317.

Peel, W. and Goudkamp J. (ed.) (2014) *Winfield and Jolowicz on Tort.* London: Sweet & Maxwell.

Reece, H. (1996) Losses of chances in the law. *Modern Law Review,* 59: 188.

Sokol, D. (2015) Update on the UK law on consent. *BMJ,* 350:h1481.

Stanton, K. (2006) Professional negligence; duty of care methodology in the twenty-first century. *Professional Negligence,* 22(3): 134.

Stapleton, J. (1991) Duty of care and economic loss: a wider agenda. *Law Quarterly Review,* 107: 249.

Stapleton, J. (1994a) In restraint of tort, in P. Birks (ed.), *The Frontiers of Liability.* Oxford: Oxford University Press.

Stapleton, J. (1994b) *Product Liability.* London: Butterworths.

Teff, H. (1998) Liability for negligently inflicted psychiatric harm: justifications and boundaries. *Cambridge Law Journal,* 57: 91–122.

Tofaris, S. and Steel, S. (2016) Negligence liability for omissions and the police. *Cambridge Law Journal,* 75:128.

Walton, C. HHJ *et al.* (eds.) (2016) *Charlesworth & Percy on Negligence,* 13th edition. London: Sweet & Maxwell.

Weir, T. (1972) Local authority v critical ratepayer: a suit in defamation. *Cambridge Law Journal,* 30: 238.

Weir, T. (1992) *A Casebook on Tort.* London: Sweet & Maxwell.

Weir, T. (2006) *An Introduction to Tort Law.* Oxford: Oxford University Press.

Williams, G. (1956) Tort of the master or tort of the servant. *Law Quarterly Review,* 72: 522.

Williams, G. (1960) The effect of penal legislation in the law of tort. *Modern Law Review,* 23: 233.

Winfield, P.H. (1934) Duty in tortious negligence. *Columbia Law Review,* 34(1): 41–66.

Witting, C. (2012) *Street on Torts.* Oxford: Oxford University Press, 27.

Index